VSE COBOL II
Power Programmer's
Desk Reference

Books and Training Products From QED

Database

Migrating to DB2
DB2: The Complete Guide to Implementation and Use
DB2 Design Review Guidelines
DB2: Maximizing Performance of Online Production Systems
Embedded SQL for DB2: Application Design and Programming
SQL for DB2 and SQL/DS Application Developers
Using DB2 to Build Decision Support Systems
The Data Dictionary: Concepts and Uses
Logical Data Base Design
Entity-Relationship Approach to Logical Data Base Design
Database Management Systems: Understanding and Applying Database Technology
Database Machines and Decision Support Systems: Third Wave Processing
IMS Design and Implementation Techniques
Repository Manager/MVS: Concepts, Facilities and Capabilities
How to Use ORACLE SQL*PLUS
ORACLE: Building High Performance Online Systems
ORACLE Design Review Guidelines
Using ORACLE to Build Decision Support Systems

Systems Engineering

Effective Methods of EDP Quality Assurance
Handbook of Screen Format Design
Managing Software Projects: Selecting and Using PC-Based Project Management Systems
The Complete Guide to Software Testing
A User's Guide for Defining Software Requirements
A Structured Approach to Systems Testing
Storyboard Prototyping: A New Approach to User Requirements Analysis
The Software Factory: Managing Software Development and Maintenance
Data Architecture: The Information Paradigm
Advanced Topics in Information Engineering
Software Engineering with Formal Software Metrics

Management

Introduction to Data Security and Control
CASE: The Potential and the Pitfalls

Management (cont'd)

Strategic and Operational Planning for Information Services
Information Systems Planning for Competitive Advantage
How to Automate Your Computer Center: Achieving Unattended Operations
Ethical Conflicts in Information and Computer Science, Technology, and Business
Mind Your Business: Managing the Impact of End-User Computing
Controlling the Future: Managing Technology-Driven Change

Data Communications

Data Communications: Concepts and Solutions
Designing and Implementing Ethernet Networks
Network Concepts and Architectures
Open Systems: The Guide to OSI and its Implementation

IBM Mainframe Series

QMF: How to Use Query Management Facility with DB2 and SQL/DS
DOS/VSE: Introduction to the Operating System
DOS/VSE: CICS Systems Programming
DOS/VSE/SP Guide for Systems Programming: Concepts, Programs, Macros, Subroutines
Advanced VSE System Programming Techniques
Systems Programmer's Problem Solver
VSAM: Guide to Optimization and Design
MVS/JCL: Mastering Job Control Language
MVS/TSO: Mastering CLISTS
MVS/TSO: Mastering Native Mode and ISPF
REXX in the TSO Environment

Video

DB2: Building Online Production Systems for Maximum Performance
Data Architecture: An Information Systems Strategy (Video)
Building Online Production Systems with ORACLE 6.0
Practical Data Modeling

Programming

C Language for Programmers
VAX/VMS: Mastering DCL Commands and Utilities

This is Only a Partial Listing. For Additional Information or a Free Catalog contact

QED Information Sciences, Inc. • P. O. Box 82-181 • Wellesley, MA 02181
Telephone: 800-343-4848 or 617-237-5656 or fax 617-235-0826

VSE COBOL II
Power Programmer's
Desk Reference

David Shelby Kirk

QED Technical Publishing Group
Boston • Toronto • London

Library of Congress Catalog Number: 91-18239
International Standard Book Number: 0-89435-344-6

Printed in the United States of America
91 92 93 10 9 8 7 6 5 4 3 2 1

Library of Congress Cataloging-In-Publication Data

Kirk, David Shelby.
VSE COBOL II : power programmer's desk reference / David S. Kirk
    p.   cm.
  Includes index.
  ISBN 0-89435-344-6
    1. COBOL II (Computer program language)   2. DOS/VSE
(Computer operating system)   I. Title.
QA76. 73.C252K574   1991
650'.0285'5133—dc20
                                                            91-18239
                                                            CIP

DEDICATION

This book is dedicated to those professional programmers who write code to be read and understood by others. Theirs is too often a thankless task. It was only by constantly reading the code of such programmers that I learned what quality and productivity are all about. I am indebted to them.

This book is also dedicated to the many other people who helped me throughout my career and especially to those who assisted me in preparing this book. The people who make life more pleasant are fortunately too numerous to mention or to even remember. Those who particularly helped me with this book include Carol Longo (IBM), who helped me get the material I needed for research; Beth Roberts (QED), who guided my writing efforts; and Ed Kerr (QED), who listened to my ideas. They helped make this book happen.

Contents

List of Figures

Preface

What This Book Is

Writing quality, high-performance code is what this book is about. The idea for the book grew from a course I developed: "COBOL II Power Programming." This book was written for the professional COBOL programmer who wants to always write the best, most efficient, and cleanest code possible and who needs a ready reference for day-to-day use of COBOL II in a VSE/ESA environment. With this as the focus, the book is not organized for the novice. Knowing the demands for maintenance and compatibility that the professional programmer faces, I have devoted the majority of this book to explaining differences and demonstrating techniques. While COBOL II is the foundation of the book, other techniques are also given. The book will also be useful to managers and others who are planning to convert to COBOL II and want to understand more about its features. Topics may appear in several places because I felt you might look for them in several places. The ideas for this book were formed over many years of teaching and managing programmers, watching and observing what skills were useful and what skills were not needed. From these observations, I attempted to structure the book—and the topics—for their appropriateness in the world of application development and maintenance.

While most of the book focuses on COBOL II, the book attempts also to assist you with other challenges you face in the programming process. Additional topics include interfacing with programs written in DOS/VS COBOL, using the Linkage Editor, and using SORT/MERGE II within your COBOL II programs. There are also reference aids on other topics, ranging from hexadecimal tables to the EBCDIC collating sequence and even to JCL. These references are not complete, but they include the information most likely needed by a COBOL programmer working with VSE/ESA.

In addition to providing reference material, this book includes suggested design and coding guidelines for programs. While your shop may already have guidelines, those in this book focus on simplicity, compatibility with earlier versions of COBOL, and on avoidance of unfamiliar terms. Emphasis is on clarity, structure, and style using minimum syntax.

What This Book Is Not

This is a desk reference, not an encyclopedia. This book does not contain every facet of information available about COBOL II or VSE/ESA nor does it attempt to tutor you in programming fundamentals or elementary COBOL syntax (for example, you won't find the definition of a COBOL paragraph or the purpose of a SELECT statement in this book). This book also does not attempt to explain the ANSI standards and its many levels because these topics typically do not interest the professional programmer who has little or no say on such issues anyway. There are references to specific environments, such as CICS, but again there is no tutorial information on the basics of programming for those environments.

How This Book Is Organized

Chapter 1: Introduction. Read this chapter thoroughly for an overview of COBOL II features. If your shop hasn't yet converted to COBOL II, this chapter will highlight some of the benefits to be gained from doing so.

Chapter 2: Coding Differences. This chapter is designed to help you learn a new version of COBOL by answering the question "What's different or new?" This is the instruction chapter. You will want to read this chapter more than once.

Chapter 3: Programming with COBOL II. This chapter is not designed to be read sequentially, but rather to be used to address specific COBOL design and coding issues. The chapter is organized by topic, not by feature, so some COBOL features may appear more than once or be cross-referenced. Included in the chapter are information on JCL, the Linkage Editor, and SORT/MERGE II. Any topic related to coding, compiling, linking, or executing COBOL II programs will be found here. While Chapter 2 explains the new features of COBOL II, this chapter demonstrates how to use these new features (and some old features) most effectively. Nearly all of the techniques of *Power Programming* are in this chapter.

Chapter 4: Debugging Techniques. No, this chapter does not teach dump reading, although it does have a brief tutorial on debugging concepts for the less experienced reader. Instead this chapter gives tips and information on debugging facilities new with COBOL II and most likely to be used. This includes several tips and techniques for your "testing toolkit." The emphasis here is on developing a proactive approach to problem control.

Chapter 5: Design Guidelines. This chapter is designed to assist professionals who do not have well-defined standards for program design at their shop or who have difficulty developing "GO TO-less" programs. Techniques to design SORT applications are also included.

Chapter 6: Coding Guidelines. Several topics in this chapter are also in Chapter 3. The difference is that while Chapter 3 focuses on using COBOL II effectively, this chapter focuses on the mechanics of coding, with a suggested coding format for each COBOL division. Even if your shop already has COBOL coding standards, you may find this chapter provides new ideas.

Chapter 7: Summaries, Tables, and References. If it isn't here, you probably don't need it. This summary includes charts and information on much besides COBOL. Information on JCL, acronyms, comparisons to DOS/VS COBOL, and hexadecimal/decimal conversion are among the topics available here for instant reference.

Chapter 8: Sample Programs. These sample programs demonstrate some COBOL II features, in addition to examples of DOS/VS COBOL compatibility. All examples demonstrate the design and coding guidelines from Chapters 5 and 6.

Chapter 9: Related Publications. This book doesn't contain everything there is to know about COBOL II or VSE/ESA. No book could contain it all. This chapter serves to help you quickly locate related texts from QED and IBM. As a professional programmer, I know one of your personal goals is to build and maintain a library of useful reference materials. This chapter can help you make those choices.

Who This Book Is For

If you have difficulty with some topics in this book, the reason may be that the topics 1) add depth to subjects you thought you already knew, or 2) uncover areas of VSE/ESA about which you were unaware. As the saying goes, "Just do it." As you explore the various topics, you may find yourself learning about more than the topic at issue.

Programmers who see their jobs as just a way of earning a paycheck will benefit little, if at all, from this book. They know all the COBOL they need to make a program function. The readers who will benefit from this book are those who continually seek a better way. Making a program function correctly is part of the job; making the program work better and more efficiently is a higher goal. They know, as I do, that being a professional programmer is one of the most interesting and challenging jobs of the technology professions. By having this book in your hands, I assume you are one of us. Welcome. I hope you find the book useful.

To any grammarians among you, I confess that I knowingly used "programmerese" in many places. I did so because this is how most programmers discuss programming. For example, you will find that the word *ABEND* has been used as a noun, as an intransitive verb, as a transitive verb, and as an adjective. While this may not be proper use of the language, I doubt that any programmer misunderstands expressions such as "the program ABENDed," or "locate the ABENDing instruction."

This book was written for you, the professional programmer. If I've omitted some useful topic, made a technical error, or included information you haven't found to be useful, please let me know. There is a response form in the back of the book, and I would enjoy hearing from you.

David Shelby Kirk
Cicero, New York

Acknowledgments

No book that attempts to move COBOL to a higher level can do so without acknowledging that much has been done by others through the years to bring COBOL to its current level. It was not only improvements in COBOL, but improvements in many other technologies as well, that have made it possible to write this book. I have attempted to list here specific acknowledgment of those efforts.

Extract from Government Printing Office Form Number 1965-0795689:

Any organization interested in reproducing the COBOL report and specifications in whole or in part, using ideas taken from this report as the basis for an instruction manual or for any other purpose is free to do so. However, all such organizations are requested to reproduce this section as part of the introduction to the document. Those using a short passage, as in a book review, are requested to mention COBOL in acknowledgment of the source, but need not quote this entire section.

COBOL is an industry language and is not the property of any company or group of companies, or of any organization or group of organizations.

No warranty, expressed or implied, is made by any contributor or by the COBOL Committee as to the accuracy and functioning of the programming system and language. Moreover, no responsibility is assumed by any contributor, or by the committee, in connection therewith.

Procedures have been established for the maintenance of COBOL. Inquiries concerning the procedures for proposing changes should be directed to the Executive Committee of the Conference on Data Systems Languages.

The authors and copyright holders of copyrighted material:

FLOW-MATIC (Trademark of Sperry Rand Corporation), Programming for the UNIVAC (R), I and II, Data Automation Systems copyrighted 1958, 1959, by Sperry Rand Corporation; IBM Commercial Translator, Form No. F28-8013, copyrighted 1959 by IBM; FACT, DSI 27A5260-2760, copyrighted 1960 by Minne-apolis-Honeywell,

have specifically authorized the use of this material in whole or in part, in the COBOL specifications. Such authorization extends to the reproduction and use of COBOL specifications in programming manuals or similar publications.

References in this book to the ANSI Standard or to ANSI 85, are to the American National Standard Programming Language COBOL, X.3.23-1985.

Use of the following terms in this book are references to these specific IBM products:

Term used	IBM product
MVS	MVS/SP, MVS/XA, and MVS/ESA unless noted
VSE	VSE/Enterprise Systems Architecture
COBOL II	VS COBOL II Compiler and Library and Debug
DOS/VS COBOL	DOS/VS COBOL Compiler and Library
SORT/MERGE II	DOS/VS SORT/MERGE II
CICS	Customer Information Control System/VSE
DL/1	Data Language/1 DOS/VS
SQL/DS	Structured Query Language/Data System

The following terms used in this book are trademarks of International Business Machines Corporation:

VSE/ESA, MVS/XA, MVS/ESA, IBM, SAA, CICS/VSE, SQL/DS,
Systems Application Architecture,
System/360, System/370

Introduction to COBOL II

This first chapter of this book is different from those that follow. Instead of dealing with the day-to-day issues you face as a programmer, it addresses concepts and features of COBOL II that are appropriate for a wider audience than just programmers (maybe your boss would enjoy reading it on a cold winter's night). Oh, reading the other chapters will also help your boss, but those other chapters are designed explicitly for you. They are intended for desktop reference for specific questions or for design and coding issues.

This chapter addresses the programmer who is new to COBOL II and wants to know the differences between COBOL II and earlier versions and who also wants to know what some of the advantages of using COBOL II are. As a professional programmer, you take pride in your skills and the need to learn a new version of COBOL may seem threatening. It won't be. While there are many differences, you will find that much of what you've always done in COBOL programs will still work. In many ways, COBOL II frees you to do tasks more simply, more efficiently, and with better structure.

1.1. WHAT IS COBOL II?

As a reader of this book, you already know the fundamentals of COBOL, so you may be wondering, "Why is COBOL II considered a different animal?" Let's hold that question for a moment and cover some COBOL history. COBOL II (the proper name is VS COBOL II) is only the latest in a long line of COBOL compilers developed by IBM.

Until the early 1970s, COBOL was bundled with the equipment (that is, if you bought or rented IBM's hardware, COBOL was available at no extra charge). For reasons beyond this book, IBM began pricing hardware and software separately, and while customers considered it a disadvantage at the time, it proved to benefit everyone. With a fee charged for software, IBM and other vendors began to develop a software industry, providing superior software designed to run on IBM or compatible hardware.

IBM's first COBOL compilers complied with the standard of the day, the one provided by the U.S. Department of Defense. Those compilers were identified by a letter of the alphabet (for example, COBOL E). The first ANSI COBOL standard was published in 1965 and revised in 1968. IBM released an ANSI 68 COBOL Compiler in the early 1970s. Later in the mid-1970s, IBM developed similar compilers for the VSE and MVS worlds, each supporting the ANSI 68 and the ANSI 74 standards. Those two compilers were DOS/VS COBOL and OS/VS COBOL. This move by IBM—developing compilers to support two standards—was undoubtedly a smart move since the industry had seen too many standards over too short a period. Unfortunately, it was probably this compatibility that put many COBOL shops in poor condition to migrate to COBOL II. Why? Because most of what was dropped from COBOL II dates back to the ANSI 68 standard. Some of those techniques (for example, MOVE CURRENT-DATE TO data-name) are still taught to new programmers, causing the problem to continue to expand. If you've been programming in a VSE environment, you've been using that compiler, DOS/VS COBOL. Throughout this book, key differences between the two will be identified.

Compiler	Approximate year	Standard level
COBOL E and F	1968	DOD (Department of Defense)
ANS COBOL Ver 2	1971	ANS 1968
ANS COBOL Ver 3	1974	ANS 1968
DOS/VS COBOL	1976	ANS 1968 and ANS 1974

Figure 1.1. COBOL compilers for VSE prior to COBOL II.

Now, back to your question, "Why is COBOL II considered a different animal?" There are two primary reasons, and I'll try to give you some information as well as background on each.

First, COBOL II supports the American National Standards Institute (ANSI) 1985 standards, which are the first major upgrade to the COBOL language since its inception, embodying structured programming components and removing obsolete features. Since IBM introduced COBOL II prior to approval of the 1985 standards, the earlier versions of COBOL II (versions 1 and 2) did *not* meet ANSI 1985 standards and are not covered in this book. Fortunately for VSE users, those earlier versions were not available for VSE. I say fortunately because VSE users will avoid the conversion headache from COBOL II versions 1 and 2 to the new Version 3. IBM's support for COBOL II with VSE began with release 3.2.

Second, IBM developed COBOL II to be a part of the operational environment. What does that mean? It means that COBOL II is not just a compiler but an active part of the resident software environment on your mainframe and the compiler-generated code expects to run within some degree of control by the COBOL II run-time facilities. It also means that COBOL II can take advantage of IBM's strategic operating software, such as VSE/ESA, MVS/XA, and MVS/ESA. It means that COBOL II is an environment in itself, not just a compiler, and that it recognizes other environments such as CICS.

The importance of those two reasons isn't obvious until you assess the history of COBOL. When COBOL first became available in the early 1960s, many people felt it would eliminate the need for programmers, allowing business analysts to write application logic in English. COBOL's terminology supported that belief, using terms such as *verb*, *sentence*, *statement*, and *paragraph*. While the dream of eliminating programmers proved untrue, COBOL remained a language that had no proper structure, as did other procedural languages because it attempted to appear as English prose.

PL/1, for example, has DO and END structural components to contain procedural substructures, allowing procedural control of any grouping of statements. For COBOL, the only structural components available in earlier versions of COBOL were paragraphs, sections, statements, and sentences. For structured programs, sections are too big to control effectively (and open to misuse of GO TOs), sentences are uncontrollable, and statements are controllable only within the confines of a sentence. That left only the paragraph as an element that could be controlled, normally with the PERFORM statement. The restrictions imposed by the other structures, combined with the limited conditional logic of IF, ELSE, and NEXT SENTENCE, left the professional programmer with few structural tools. With ANSI 85, COBOL now qualifies as a professional's language. With COBOL II, true structured code is now possible. The opportunities for structured code will be addressed in other parts of the book, including Chapter 3 (Programming with COBOL II), Chapter 5 (Program Design guidelines) and Chapter 6 (COBOL Coding Guidelines).

Also true in earlier versions of COBOL was a total dependence on a shop's technical staff or trial and error to determine what compile and link-edit options should be used with COBOL. COBOL object code was insensitive or unaware of the presence of CICS or DL/1 and reference manuals for the earlier versions of COBOL rarely, if ever, acknowledged the existence or programming considerations necessary for VSE/ESA, CICS, or SQL/DS. Today's IBM manuals are a far cry from those earlier versions, with extensive information and guidance on using COBOL II with other environments.

COBOL II then is no longer just a language. As such, it is more complex, more flexible, and more sensitive to an environment. Therefore, the need arises for this book. As you read through this book, the importance of these issues will become more apparent.

1.2.   IMPORTANCE OF UPGRADING TO COBOL II

Converting your applications to COBOL II has many benefits, some for the application (user) and some for you, the professional programmer. Since conversion is a one-time process, it isn't a special topic within this book. If your shop has COBOL II, your technical support area may have installed some conversion assistance software, either from IBM or other vendors. If such conversion software is available, your efforts to change your programs from DOS/VS COBOL to COBOL II will be less—not eliminated, but less. For more information that may assist you in such a conversion from DOS/VS COBOL to COBOL II, see Chapter 2 ("Coding Differences") and Chapter 3 (Section 3.2, Module Structures).

1.2.1.   Newer IBM Features Supported

One of IBM's major points when COBOL II was announced was that this language would be kept current with IBM's plans. IBM has kept its word on this; COBOL II has had major upgrades and enhancements since its announcement. As new announcements continue, DOS/VS COBOL will be left further and further behind. Keeping your applications, and you, current on technology is important. You will stay aware of new technology and continue to grow in your profession, and your application takes advantage of new operating opportunities. What follows is an overview of some of the enhanced capabilities of COBOL II. Where a technique requires a conscious effort on your part, it will be covered in detail in later chapters.

VSCR (Virtual Storage Constraint Relief).

With COBOL II, your application can use features of your shop's operating environment, either consciously or automatically. For example with VSE/ESA, COBOL II applications can use the Shared Virtual Area (SVA) to relieve memory constraints, yet DOS/VS COBOL programs are unable to be loaded there. COBOL II can generate object code that is sensitive to the environment, allowing COBOL II programs to be loaded into any memory space. The address space in the SVA can be compared to the sunshine above the clouds during a storm. Down below, most programs and systems software are thrashing and competing for restricted memory space. Up above, the memory is virtually (pardon the pun) empty. This is a significant part of COBOL II's ability to improve application performance.

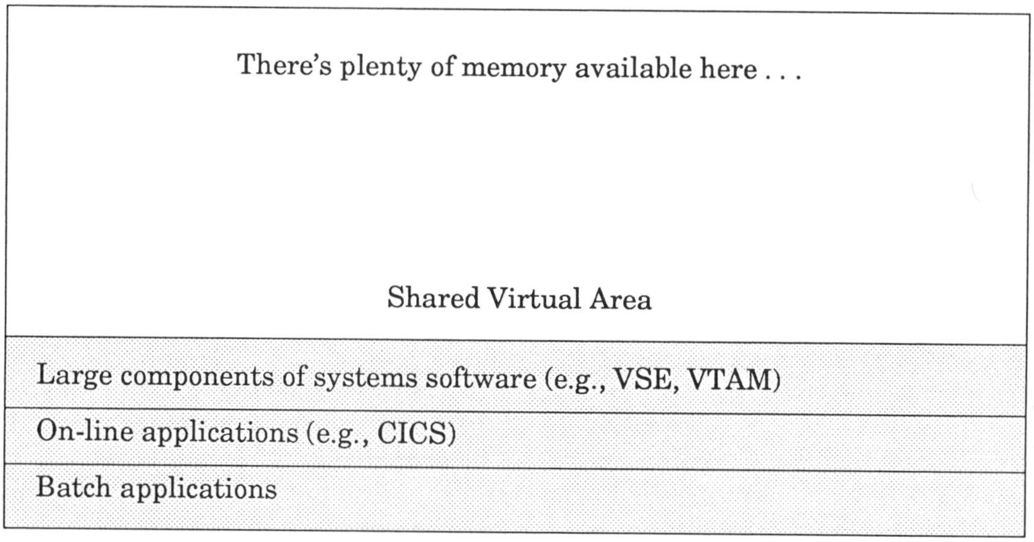

There's plenty of memory available here . . .

Shared Virtual Area

Large components of systems software (e.g., VSE, VTAM)

On-line applications (e.g., CICS)

Batch applications

Figure 1.2. Symbolic representation of SVA opportunity.

You may be wondering why other programs can't run in the SVA. The reason is that application programs written with DOS/VS COBOL do not have the addressing support necessary for VSE to appropriately manage a systemwide shared area. COBOL II object code is more compatible with the operating environment and takes advantage of newer features.

Reentrant code.

Your applications can be reentrant, making the applications available to multiple users without being reloaded into memory. This applies especially to a CICS environment, where an application may be used concurrently by many terminal users. Before COBOL II, reentrant code was available only from skilled assembler programmers. Also, only reentrant COBOL II programs can use the SVA mentioned above. The RENT option will be covered more thoroughly in Chapter 3.

Faster sorting.

Although there are restrictions, most SORTs will run more efficiently in COBOL II. In addition to this enhancement, you will find throughout this book much about using SORT within COBOL programs .

VSAM enhancements.

If you use VSAM files, COBOL II now provides the opportunity for your application to get detailed feedback from any VSAM I/O request. This is not a replacement to the FILE STATUS clause; it is an enhancement to it.

Higher compiler limits.

If you're like I am, you never think about compiler limits. The size of an 01-level, the number of data items possible, and other such limits seldom interfere with designing an application. By increasing the limits significantly (due to COBOL II's expanded use of the GETVIS area), COBOL II provides the opportunity to rethink how WORKING STORAGE should be used in a program. With COBOL II, WORKING STORAGE can be allocated in the GETVIS area (depending on compiler options), where it doesn't compete with partition limits. Imagine what you could do if you could define an 01-level to be several million bytes. That is larger than many databases. What if you loaded that data file into a table in memory to improve response time for that critical application of yours? Hmm . . .

XA-mode portability.

Whether your shop shares VSE and MVS machines, or only anticipates the possibility of migrating to MVS at some future date, XA-Mode Portability is a benefit. The object code generated by the COBOL II compiler will execute on VSE/ESA, MVS/XA, and MVS/ESA machines without recompiling. This feature can be a real plus for any migration project or when multiple environments coexist. The migrated executable code will execute in 24-bit or 31-bit mode in the MVS environment, depending on compiler options selected.

LIOCS support.

LIOCS (Logical Input/Output System) is a VSE feature in which the device type for sequential access method datasets can be defined outside the program. This is similar to the "device independence" provided by the much larger MVS operating system. By changing the JCL, a programmer can test a program with one device type for datasets (e.g., tape) and later use the program with a different device type (e.g., DASD). This device independence simplifies the programming process and minimizes the need to change the program for device types. This feature will simplify the coding of SELECT statements, allowing the SELECT/ASSIGN statements for VSAM and SAM datasets to be coded alike. You will need to check with your technical staff to assess how this is implemented at your shop.

1.2.2. ANSI 85 Support

Being at the latest ANSI level may not seem important to you, but this issue has a wide ripple effect in the industry. New features implemented from the latest ANSI level represent the evolving sophistication of COBOL. As COBOL continues to evolve, the language gets more power and becomes more consistent across multiple platforms. When COBOL was new (early 1960s), people envisioned that a COBOL program would be able to operate properly on any computer with no need for a conversion. In hindsight those early dreams had little chance of success. Every vendor implemented COBOL a little differently and there was little consistency even within the products of one vendor. The industry now has an opportunity to achieve a level of standardization not possible back then. With your application compatible with the ANSI 1985 standard, you will stand a better chance than ever that much of it will be compatible in a future environment.

Although books could, and have been, written about the many modules and levels of ANSI, you won't find that information in this book. Programmers rarely want to know what modules and subsets of ANSI are available. Instead they want to know what works and what doesn't. This isn't to criticize those other books. Some people need to know that information (I did, to write this book), but the scope of this book is what you probably need on a regular basis. *The major benefit you will see with ANSI 85 features is the ability to do true structured programming.*

1.2.3. Standards Control Opportunities

You'll need to check with your shop to find out whether this feature is implemented. COBOL II can restrict what statements are used (yes, some programmers still use the ALTER statement), provide customized messages for designated statements, and even restrict what compile options are allowed. For an individual programmer, this isn't a benefit, but for a large MIS shop, knowing what options are specified and what statements are or aren't used is important for departmental planning. Good standards can also protect you the programmer from inheriting maintenance responsibility for programs that only work correctly with a nonstandard use of compile options or with unfamiliar COBOL statements.

Actually, COBOL II provides the opportunity to do much more, such as providing shorthand for certain statements or even support for languages other than English. Since this pertains to customizing COBOL II for an entire installation, it isn't part of this book. For more information on how to customize COBOL for an entire installation, see Chapter 9 ("Related Publications").

1.2.4. SAA Opportunity

IBM's strategic plan to integrate a variety of operating platforms is called Systems Application Architecture (SAA). This is a major step for the industry and provides impetus for companies to start standardizing how they use computers. One of the SAA building blocks is COBOL II. If your company has decided to move toward an SAA environment, COBOL II provides a monitoring facility to warn you if incompatible features are used.

SAA is an exciting concept, especially if your company wants to share applications across mainframes, midframes, and PCs. With COBOL II, programs you develop for a mainframe environment can be more easily transported to other environments, freeing you from the requirement to program for different platforms. For more information on how COBOL II and VSE/ESA fit in with SAA, see Chapter 9 ("Related Publications").

1.2.5. Improved Tuning and Cost Control

Although much of this is done by your systems programmers, COBOL II can be configured for specific environments. There are also new compile options that cause different code to be generated depending on how data are defined and used within your application. These options are explained in Chapter 3 ("Programming with COBOL II").

Optimization.

Have you ever placed an "*" in column 7 to comment out procedural code that was to be temporarily bypassed? Most of us have at one time or another. Now, COBOL II locates code that is out of the logic flow and flags it and doesn't generate code for it. So if you have code that is not to be deleted, but is also not to be executed, just move it out of the logic path and you're done. Providing that service is part of the enhanced OPTIMIZE facility, but it does much more. COBOL II will restructure the object code if that is more efficient, and in some situations will even eliminate redundant computations within the application. The OPTIMIZE feature with COBOL II is a significant expansion over that provided with DOS/VS COBOL.

Batched compiles.

Another cost-control feature is the ability to batch several programs together and invoke the compiler once to generate several object programs. COBOL II further builds on this facility by also providing the option to generate appropriate VSE Librarian CATALOG statements preceding each object module to cause object modules to be catalogued separately in one invocation of the VSE Librarian.

1.3. BENEFITS OF COBOL II TO AN APPLICATION

Applications benefit from many of the above features, primarily because they reduce resource usage and allow programs to be created that are less costly to maintain. Some of the features, however, provide the opportunity for applications to expand and to incorporate new services. Until COBOL II provided the opportunity to exploit use of the SVA, many shops had been facing a continual problem: finding virtual storage constraint relief (VSCR) for their mission-critical applications. There wasn't enough memory for the application to run efficiently. This occurred for two reasons. First, the application probably continued to grow in size as new functions were added. Second, IBM and other vendors kept adding new functions to the operating software to meet customer needs. A shop running CICS, DL/1, VTAM, VSE, POWER, and other software in addition to your application eventually found the memory full.

COBOL II's use of the SVA in VSE/ESA provided the opportunity for programs to operate outside the old environment, thereby freeing the programs from the constraints of competing for memory with other applications in a finite space. This ability to free a program from memory constraints is one of the major benefits an application can realize with COBOL II.

Another benefit the application realizes is the opportunity to develop programs that are cleaner and easier (cheaper) to maintain. By consciously applying the new structured components of COBOL II, you will create applications that are easier to read, easier to debug, and less costly to maintain.

1.4. BENEFITS OF COBOL II TO A PROGRAMMER

Much of what COBOL II means to you has already been mentioned, and after you finish this book, you will probably feel this list is too short. COBOL II provides such a large menu of features that it is difficult to sample them all. These are what I believe are the features most impressive to programmers.

Structured programming.

Yes, for the first time, COBOL has the ability to implement a true DO-UNTIL or CASE statement and can contain nested conditional statements within a paragraph. With previous levels of COBOL, a programmer could always justify a situation in which the GO TO statement was necessary. Not so with COBOL II. This gives you the opportunity to create cleaner code than you could with DOS/ VS COBOL.

Documentation.

Okay, so documentation isn't the programmer's favorite word. All the more reason to use COBOL II. With COBOL II, you can control what error messages you get and where they appear. The cross-reference facility even tells you where data fields are modified, not just referenced. There are summaries of statements used, summaries of programs CALLed, and you can even control what portions of the source program are listed. The operative word is *control*. These features weren't in DOS/VS COBOL. You will find more information on these techniques in Chapter 3 ("Programming with COBOL II") and in Chapter 4 ("Debugging Techniques").

Another documentation improvement is more subtle. Finally, you can mix upper- and lower-case text, making the program more readable. No longer must you code

```
IF DS1-INCOME IS NUMERIC
    MOVE WS1-TAX-ID TO PR1-TAX-ID
```

Instead, you may now code

```
If Ds1-income is numeric
    Move Ws1-tax-id to Pr1-tax-id
```

Many people feel that mixed upper- and lower-case text, such as used above, are easier to read than all upper-case text. Which you prefer isn't the issue, however. The point is that you are in control. An extension of this concept is that you may now specify whether you want the COBOL II messages and other information on the source listing to appear in upper-case or in both upper- and lower-case text. Again, your choice. In this book, all COBOL statements will be shown in upper-case text.

Debugging.

What I haven't mentioned yet is that COBOL II includes improved debugging facilities. (See Chapter 4, "Debugging Techniques.") There you will find that COBOL II provides even more debug aids than were available in DOS/VS COBOL, including a new COBTEST debug tool that lets you create and execute batch test plans.

There are two other debugging aids you will find useful and easier to use than COBTEST. One is the new subscript range intercept feature (SSRANGE), which intercepts subscripts that go beyond the range of a table. If you've ever had a 2:00 A.M. phone call because of an 0C4 ABEND of a critical productional program, you will appreciate the benefits of this new feature.

The other debugging aid is the new formatted dump (FDUMP). The new compile option for formatted dumps imbeds the debug code directly within the object code, eliminating the need for additional JCL that was required by DOS/VS COBOL. This formatted dump presents your DATA DIVISION areas in readable format and can save valuable time when you need to determine the content of a number of data fields.

CICS enhancements.

Do you use CICS? If so, the coding becomes simpler, with some coding requirements removed. For example, no longer do you need to maintain base locator pointers (BLLs) for your LINKAGE SECTION. You will need to convert CICS COBOL programs that use the BLL technique because that approach is no longer allowed, but there are software products available to do this. More details for CICS are contained in Chapter 3 ("Programming with COBOL II"). See your technical support staff for availability of any in-house conversion aids.

1.5. DEVELOPING AN APPROACH TO LEARNING COBOL II

When you first learned COBOL, you probably studied many parts of the language before you were able to code a simple application. My recommendation to learning this new version of COBOL is quite different. Rather than reading this entire book before attempting any of the new facilities, just jump in and swim. This is my recommended approach to get you up and running in COBOL II quickly.

Compile a known DOS/VS COBOL program. Assuming that you know the COBOL II JCL to use for your shop (I'll cover JCL in Chapter 3), compile a program with which you're familiar using the COBOL II compiler. This will give you some immediate feedback on some of the errors that might occur. If you've been using the LANGLVL(2) and MIGR options in your DOS/VS COBOL compiler, you might find no errors at all. If so, you are positioned to move quickly toward mastering COBOL II. If there were errors, don't worry. Most are not difficult to correct. Don't attempt to correct the errors yet; I'll get to that shortly.

Read Chapter 2. In Chapter 2 ("Coding Differences"), you will discover the more visible differences between the two compilers. Although COBOL II can't be so easily dissected, I have attempted to organize the chapter into three categories: what was dropped, what was changed, and what is new. In your first reading, focus on what was dropped and what has changed, not on what is new. Your immediate goal is to learn which, if any, of your current programming techniques must be changed. Since changing old techniques is much harder than learning new ones, address this first. Also, Chapter 2 does not cover every nuance of COBOL II. Instead, it covers the most likely features you'll encounter or use.

Compare compile options. There is a summary of compile options in Chapter 7 ("Summaries, Tables, and References"). Don't worry about new ones; just concentrate on the differences. With this information, you can use COBOL II as you used DOS/VS COBOL.

Remove syntax errors from a known program. Now, go back to that listing you compiled and start removing syntax errors. If you've used some coding techniques that aren't in this book, you may need additional assistance. With new compiler releases, there are usually several little known or undocumented features that are changed. Your goal is reaching the level of proficiency where you can use COBOL II to compile programs without using new features. (Note: If you are going to be working in an environment where you must continue to maintain applications in DOS/VS COBOL and also write applications in COBOL II, you will find specific help in Chapter 3 (Section 3.2, Module Structures) and Chapter 8 ("Sample Programs").

Try EVALUATE and remove all occurrences of FILLER. By the time you reach this step, you will be familiar with COBOL II and will have successfully compiled a program with the COBOL II compiler. Now is the time to experiment with some new features, preferably those that are visible and that will let you feel comfortable with new features. I recommend some experimental use of the EVALUATE statement (explained in Chapter 2), since it can replace a variety of nested IF statements or even replace some table searches. If you are using an on-line text editor such as ICCF or ISPF, also try replacing all FILLER by spaces. Although a small item, this makes a DATA DIVISION noticeably more readable.

Reread Chapter 2 and remove unnecessary items. On the second reading of Chapter 2, focus on removing all paragraphs and clauses that aren't needed. Some of the statements you remove will probably be in violation of your shop standards, but your old standards may need to be reviewed and updated if they still reflect DOS/VS COBOL. (Chapter 6 in this book might be a good place to start.) For example, the LABEL RECORDS ARE STANDARD clause and the DATA RECORDS clause are required in FDs at many shops, yet both are obsolete statements in ANSI 85. COBOL II treats them as comments—so why bother coding them? You will also discover that the ENVIRONMENT DIVISION isn't needed at all in several circumstances (for example, an on-line CICS application with no FD statements).

By removing every item that doesn't cause the compile to fail, you will start to discover changes you may want to make in how you develop applications. Clinging to old techniques and continuing to code obsolete statements prevents you from improving your coding productivity—and may cause you to spend extra time at some future date removing those statements because a future release of the compiler might no longer recognize them.

Set a goal to use new features in your next program. This is the hard part. Now that you feel confident with COBOL II, there is a normal tendency to get on with it and to stop learning new features. For example, over the years I've encountered many COBOL programmers who did not know how to use a binary search (SEARCH ALL). It happens. Learning all of the primary features of a compiler takes work. Otherwise, the pressure of the project causes all of us to keep doing things the same old way. Don't let that happen.

SUMMARY

This chapter has touched on differences you will experience in using COBOL II. The following chapters will provide information that clearly demonstrates that COBOL II is, indeed, a different animal. In teaching COBOL II, I am constantly enthused by the excitement of programmers who suddenly see COBOL as a true programming language. I'm sure you will too.

Coding Differences Between COBOL II and DOS/VS COBOL

To learn COBOL II, your first priority is to understand what you must unlearn. This is normal, since new versions of COBOL have traditionally dropped some features and modified others. This chapter is intended to serve as a periodic reference on these features for you, and in addition serve as a first-time tutorial on the differences between COBOL II and its predecessor DOS/VS COBOL.

For readability purposes, the terms *components* or *elements* are used throughout this book when referring to a collection of terms that form the syntax of COBOL programs. This includes, but is not limited to paragraphs, clauses, statements, sections, divisions, and data description entries. The term *feature* will normally be used to describe a capability of COBOL that would also include any components that implement that feature. For example, Report Writer is a feature, but GENERATE is a component of Report Writer.

This chapter is organized in decreasing order of importance from a maintenance or conversion perspective, covering first the elements that are no longer available, followed by the elements that have been modified, followed by elements that are new to the language. Determining whether a feature was dropped, modified, or new wasn't always obvious and was subject to my interpretation. You may feel, after reading the chapter, that some features I listed as modified were, indeed, sufficiently changed to be classified as new.

Overall, most changes reflected here are because COBOL is evolving into a cleaner, simpler language. The trend is to

- Remove elements that belong elsewhere within the software inventory (such as the Communications feature).
- Remove features that were hardware or vendor dependent (such as ISAM or CLOSE WITH DISP).

- Eliminate overlapping elements (e.g., EXAMINE and TRANSFORM).
- Remove requirements that have outlived their intent (such as SEG-MENT-LIMIT and LABEL RECORDS ARE STANDARD).
- Remove requirements for elements where a general default is sufficient (such as SOURCE-COMPUTER).
- Provide a debugging language that is separate from the source language (e.g., READY TRACE is removed).
- Provide new facilities to improve program-to-program communications and to use memory more effectively.
- Provide new facilities to give the programmer more control of processes and more opportunities to use structured techniques.

With practice, you will soon find that your programs use fewer lines of code and are easier to read.

2.1. HOW TO READ THE SYNTAX CHARTS

Throughout this book, and in IBM books as well, you will encounter a new format to represent COBOL syntax. The format is simpler than earlier versions, but let me explain, briefly. Below is the syntax for minimum items for the IDENTIFI-CATION DIVISION. The basic rules are

- Entries appearing on a top line are mandatory.
- Items appearing beneath a line are optional for the above line.
- Entries appearing beneath another entry are alternatives.
- New elements will be shown in **BOLD.**
- The symbol to continue to the next line is shown by "—>".
- The end of a statement is shown by "—><".

In the example on the first line the format is indicating that IDENTIFICA-TION DIVISION is mandatory, but since there is an element beneath it, that element may be used instead.

On the second line, PROGRAM-ID and paragraph-name are mandatory and may be followed, optionally, by either COMMON or INITIAL or both.

```
 ┌ IDENTIFICATION DIVISION.────────────────────────────>
 └─ ID DIVISION. ──────────────────┘

 ── PROGRAM-ID. paragraph-name ┬──────────┬──────────┬─.─><
                               └ COMMON ──┘└ INITIAL ┘
```

Figure 2.1. Example of COBOL syntax chart.

If you compare the charts in this book with those in IBM reference manuals, you will find that IBM's are more complete and identify all options. The charts used in this chapter are subsets intended to highlight new features. The complete (almost) set of syntax charts are in Chapter 7. Those charts are usually all you will need if you are comfortable with the basics of COBOL syntax.

2.2. DOS/VS COBOL FEATURES THAT WERE DROPPED IN COBOL II

This section lists the most visible (most commonly used) elements of DOS/VS COBOL that are not in COBOL II. The dropped elements were either ANSI 1968 components or were early IBM extensions of COBOL. If your shop used ANSI 74 COBOL (the LANGLVL(2) compile option), you should have few problems in a move to COBOL II. If you are unfamiliar with any particular element so much the better because that means you won't need to unlearn that element. Most if not all of the elements in this section may be converted to their COBOL II equivalent (if one exists) by conversion software on the market. Your technical support staff can assist you.

2.2.1. Report Writer

Many shops didn't discover Report Writer until the 1980s, although it has been in use at some shops since the 1960s. Report Writer is still a module in the full ANSI 1985 standard (although an optional module), and IBM chose not to incorporate it into COBOL II.

When COBOL II was introduced, there was no choice: you had to abandon use of Report Writer. Since then, IBM has developed a Report Writer preprocessor that converts Report Writer code into equivalent COBOL II code, allowing a shop to use the preprocessor either on a one-time basis to convert existing applications or on a routine basis, converting programs with Report Writer prior to each compile. The choice here is not easy or simple. Consider:

1. If a shop does a one-time conversion, the shop is free from the Report Writer issue, but it loses the productivity feature that caused the shop to use it initially.
2. If a shop continues using Report Writer, the preprocessor increases the cost of each compile; the generated COBOL code does not match what the programmer wrote and may be more difficult to debug; when report output is incorrect, the problem may be in one of three places: the compiler, the preprocessor, or the program logic, which causes finger-pointing.

Whether Report Writer should be available at your shop is something I can't tell you. It is not part of COBOL II, but you can continue to code Report Writer if your shop uses the optional preprocessor. Neither choice is perfect.

Report Writer

Communications

ISAM & BDAM

Segmentation

Macro-level CICS

EXAMINE & TRANSFORM

READY/RESET TRACE, EXHIBIT, USE FOR DEBUGGING

CURRENT-DATE & TIME-OF-DAY

NOTE & REMARKS

ON (the statement, not the clause within statements)

WRITE AFTER POSITIONING

STATE & FLOW Compile options

OPEN & CLOSE obsolete options

Figure 2.2. Major DOS/VS COBOL components absent in COBOL II.

2.2.2. ISAM and BDAM

If you use ISAM or BDAM, you need to convert such files to an equivalent VSAM format before using COBOL II. While conversion software may address all, or most, of the COBOL changes, the files must be separately converted.

2.2.3. Communications Feature

This feature (which required a CD entry and used SEND, RECEIVE, ENABLE, and DISABLE statements) has been removed, and no equivalent feature exists. This was a feature that allowed COBOL programs to interact with a user-written telecommunications program. The feature was rarely used because most shops use specialized software, such as CICS, for sending and receiving messages.

2.2.4. Segmentation Feature

While this is no longer supported, any such references are treated as comments. With virtual storage, the need for segmenting COBOL programs is considered obsolete.

2.2.5. Macro-level CICS

If you have CICS programs at the macro level, they need to be converted to CICS Command level before using COBOL II. There are some conversion programs on the market that address this conversion issue.

2.2.6. EXAMINE and TRANSFORM

EXAMINE and TRANSFORM have been eliminated in favor of INSPECT. DOS/VS COBOL supported all three verbs.

2.2.7. READY/RESET TRACE, EXHIBIT, and USE FOR DEBUGGING

COBOL II is evolving to a point where no debugging facilities will exist in the code proper. At this writing, READY TRACE and RESET TRACE are obsolete. USE FOR DEBUGGING is still supported, but even it will be removed from the next revision of the ANSI standard, so I don't encourage its use. For debugging assistance, IBM provides the COBOL debugging facility (see Chapter 4, "Debugging Techniques"). If READY TRACE or RESET TRACE appear within a COBOL II program, they are ignored. The EXHIBIT statement will cause a compile error.

2.2.8. CURRENT-DATE and TIME-OF-DAY

Removing CURRENT-DATE and TIME-OF-DAY is part of COBOL's evolution toward using procedural elements to accomplish objectives rather than relying on special registers. DOS/VS COBOL supported both ANSI 68 and ANSI 74 facilities to access date and time. These ANSI 68 statements are not allowed:

```
MOVE CURRENT-DATE TO data-name
MOVE TIME-OF-DAY TO data-name
```

Whereas these ANSI 74 statements work both in DOS/VS COBOL and in COBOL II:

```
ACCEPT data-name FROM DATE (implicit PIC is 9(6))
ACCEPT data-name FROM TIME (implicit PIC is 9(8))
```

The PIC definitions are changed from ANSI 68. In ANSI 68, CURRENT-DATE was X(8), for MM/DD/YY (slashes were included) and TIME-OF-DAY was X(6), for HHMMSS. In COBOL II, DATE is 9(6) for YYMMDD (different order and no slashes), and TIME is 9(8) for HHMMSShh (for hours, minutes, seconds, and hundredths of seconds).

For more information on additional options of ACCEPT, see the next section of this chapter.

2.2.9. NOTE and REMARKS

Neither of these is listed in the IBM DOS/VS COBOL Reference Manual, but both were acceptable. Use the * in column 7, instead.

2.2.10. ON Statement

This is part of the debugging extensions IBM provided with DOS/VS COBOL. You possibly have never used it. This is not a reference to ON clauses, such as ON SIZE ERROR, which continue to be valid.

2.2.11. WRITE AFTER POSITIONING Statement

This statement was a carryover from pre-ANSI compilers. It is replaced by WRITE AFTER ADVANCING.

2.2.12. STATE and FLOW Compile Options

While not COBOL elements, these two debug options were popular in some shops while unknown in others. Their functions are available in the new COBTEST debug facility (Chapter 4).

2.2.13. OPEN and CLOSE Obsolete Options

Those optional clauses that were hardware dependent—the LEAVE, REREAD, and DISP options for the OPEN statement and CLOSE WITH DISP and CLOSE WITH POSITIONING—are no longer valid. In both cases, other options have been available for several years, so I don't anticipate these changes will cause application problems. Also, these OPEN and CLOSE options, as were many of the changes listed in this section, were not specified as being part of DOS/VS COBOL proper; they were documented in the appendix as IBM extensions.

As I mentioned earlier, the best way to evaluate the implication of the dropped features is to compile one or more of your programs. Also, specifying the LANGLVL(2) and MIGR options when compiling with DOS/VS COBOL will help sensitize you to incompatible elements.

2.3.   MODIFIED COBOL COMPONENTS

This section requires a careful reading because the fundamental syntax of these components existed in DOS/VS COBOL. Features identified in the previous section (e.g., Report Writer) will not be repeated here.

All options and syntax will not be presented. This section will review only those portions that are sufficiently different to warrant your interest. The examples shown in this section may also be incomplete, not displaying all options of a particular clause. The purpose of this approach is to focus on what has changed without requiring you to cope with the full syntax of COBOL. (Note: A listing of COBOL II statements and their syntax is contained in Chapter 7, "Summaries, Tables, and References"). I have classified entries in this section as modified COBOL components, rather than as new COBOL components because these features are made available using clauses or statements with which you are probably already familiar.

2.3.1. IDENTIFICATION DIVISION

The major change in the IDENTIFICATION DIVISION is that it now allows you to specify how the program will participate within a run unit. This is accomplished by the PROGRAM-ID clause. No other entries are required, nor should they be used.

Required entries (those that must always be present). IDENTIFICATION DIVISION or ID DIVISION and PROGRAM-ID.

Obsolete, treated as comments. All other entries, including AUTHOR, INSTALLATION, DATE-WRITTEN, DATE-COMPILED, and SECURITY.

Obsolete and not allowed. REMARKS.

Enhanced elements (descriptions follow this list). PROGRAM-ID.

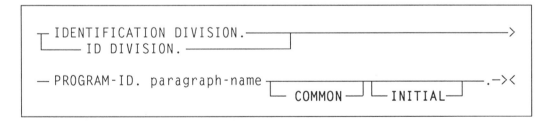

Figure 2.3. IDENTIFICATION DIVISION requirements.

PROGRAM-ID modifications.

The new features of PROGRAM-ID are intended to provide additional features for multi-module structures, where one program is CALLed by another. The optional clause COMMON specifies that the program may be accessed from any other programs sharing a nested run unit. (See Chapter 3, "Programming with COBOL II" for more information on module structures.) Unless your shop starts using nested programs, you won't have use for this feature.

The clause INITIAL specifies that the program is to be in its initial state every time it is CALLed. Even without INITIAL coded, a program is in its initial state the first time it is CALLed and on the first CALL following a CANCEL statement. Use of INITIAL should be reserved for those structures in which a subprogram does not reinitialize variables or maintain any information from one CALL to the next, and where the program logic always assumes that it will be CALLED only once. Your use of INITIAL will be dependent on how your shop writes and mixes subprograms.

Recommendation for using IDENTIFICATION DIVISION features.

Instead of using the obsolete elements, use the COBOL comment facility (an * in column 7) to provide any needed documentation. The date the program was compiled appears on source listings and is imbedded within the object program. Be careful of misinterpreting COBOL II syntax messages (this applies to all divisions, not just the IDENTIFICATION DIVISION entries). For example, consider this error from a compile listing (notice how COBOL II embeds the error message in the source listing—a nice improvement):

```
        PROGRAM-ID.
            DKA101BN.
        AUTHOR.
==> IGYDS1128-W "AUTHOR" PARAGRAPH COMMENTARY WAS FOUND IN AREA "A".
            PROCESSED AS IF FOUND IN AREA "B".
            DAVID S. KIRK.
        REMARKS.
            THIS SUBPROGRAM CALCULATES VACATION DAYS.
            .
            .
```

It appears that AUTHOR is incorrect, yet no error appears for using REMARKS. This appears to contradict my previous statements. In fact, because COBOL II ignores obsolete elements, the compiler saw REMARKS in column 8 and assumed it was part of the AUTHOR paragraph. Errors such as this can be confusing.

2.3.2. ENVIRONMENT DIVISION

The major change of the ENVIRONMENT DIVISION is that you may now get full VSAM status code feedback for your VSAM files. This is provided by the FILE STATUS clause. Other notable changes are a continuing reduction of required and optional clauses. In fact, there are now many situations where this division serves no purpose and need not be coded.

Required entries (those that must always be present). None. (This would be true if all defaults were acceptable and there were no files to SELECT.)

Obsolete, treated as comments. MEMORY SIZE, SEGMENT LIMIT, and MULTIPLE FILE TAPE.

Obsolete and not allowed. ACTUAL KEY, NOMINAL KEY, TRACK-AREA, TRACK-LIMIT, and PROCESSING MODE.

Optional entries (ignored). ORGANIZATION IS in SELECT statement.

Enhanced elements (descriptions follow this list). FILE STATUS.

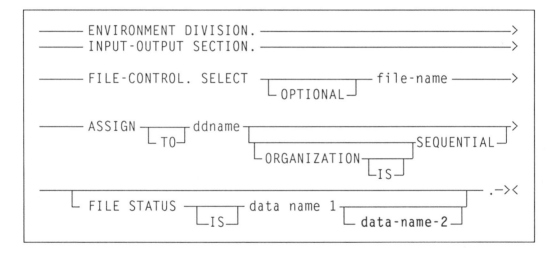

Figure 2.4. Example of FILE STATUS for sequential file (all SELECT options not shown).

Use of expanded FILE STATUS codes for VSAM

From the example in Figure 2.4, the "data-name-1" entry is the normal FILE STATUS field from DOS/VS COBOL. The new entry is "data-name-2," which must be defined in the WORKING-STORAGE SECTION (or the LINKAGE SECTION, if appropriate) as a six-byte group item. The group item must contain three subordinate entries, each a half-word binary entry. For example,

```
01   VSAM-STATUS-CODE.
     05  VSAM-RETURN-CODE      PIC  S99   BINARY.
     05  VSAM-FUNCTION-CODE    PIC  S99   BINARY.
     05  VSAM-FEEDBACK-CODE    PIC  S99   BINARY.
```

This new feature allows a COBOL program to access the status for a variety of VSAM processes. The returned codes are from Access Method Services. For more information on the content and use of these fields, see the *VSE/VSAM Commands and Macros* manual (Chapter 9, "Related Publications"). (Note: Notice the use of the word *BINARY* in the example. COBOL II allows programs to use *BINARY* in place of *COMP*, and *PACKED-DECIMAL* in place of *COMP-3* if desired. *COMP* and *COMP-3* still work fine.)

Recommendation for using ENVIRONMENT DIVISION features. The ENVIRONMENT DIVISION contains many optional entries that are rarely used. If you use VSAM files, you already know what options are necessary and where the new VSAM status codes will help your applications. From programs I've seen or worked on, the example in Figure 2.4 exhibits complete syntax adequate for more than 90 percent of programs. If your application uses the default collating sequence (most do) and has no special names to define (few do), then you need to define the ENVIRONMENT DIVISION only if there are files to process.

2.3.3. DATA DIVISION

Most of the big changes in the DATA DIVISION were identified earlier in section 2.1 (COBOL Features Dropped). Other changes reflect an ongoing process of cleaning up the COBOL language, removing the requirement for clauses that are either irrelevant or are self-evident. For example, labels for a file are handled via VSE and JCL, so the LABEL RECORDS clause is irrelevant. The 01-level that follows an FD is always identified with the FD, so the DATA RECORD clause is also irrelevant. Since FILLER always means a data description with no name, the word FILLER only documented what would be self-evident if FILLER were omitted. Now it can be.

These changes don't require that you modify existing programs, but they do allow you to code less and achieve the same results.

Required entries (those that must always be present). None. (Having no entries would be rare.)

Obsolete, treated as comments. LABEL RECORDS clause in FD (illegal in SD), DATA RECORD clause, and VALUE OF clause (in FD).

Obsolete and not allowed (see section 2.1). Report Writer statements, Communications statements, and ISAM and BDAM statements.

Optional entries. FILLER.

The FILLER entry.

This is an easy and optional change that improves readability of a program. The word FILLER, used to define data descriptions with no name, may be replaced by spaces. For years, it was a meaningless entry in COBOL. Now, it is no longer needed. Consider the example in Figure 2.5. The second entry for the record is easier to read.

```
With FILLER:


01 WS1-RECORD-AREA.
    05   WS1-NAME          PIC X(20).
    05   FILLER            PIC X.
    05   WS1-ADDRESS       PIC X(25).
    05   FILLER            PIC XX.
    05   WS1-JOB-CODE      PIC X.
    05   FILLER            PIC X(30).

Without FILLER:


01 WS1-RECORD-AREA.
    05   WS1-NAME          PIC X(20).
    05                     PIC X.
    05   WS1-ADDRESS       PIC X(25).
    05                     PIC XX.
    05   WS1-JOB-CODE      PIC X.
    05                     PIC X(30).
```

Figure 2.5. Example with and without FILLER.

Enhanced elements. USAGE clause, VALUE clause, OCCURS DEPENDING ON, and COPY statement.

Modifications to the USAGE clause.

One of the changes to USAGE was mentioned earlier: the ability to use BINARY instead of COMP, and PACKED-DECIMAL instead of COMP-3. This is nice, but old habits die hard. In developing example programs for this book, I continued to use COMP and COMP-3, and I plan to continue using them since they require fewer keystrokes.

The addition of POINTER, however, opens up new doors that will be explored in the next chapter. POINTER provides to COBOL programs the facility to treat addresses of data as data, a technique that was previously available only to assembler programmers.

Modifications to the VALUE clause.

The extension to VALUE that will be most appreciated is that it may now be used in OCCURS statements. In DOS/VS COBOL, a table could not be defined and initialized in the DATA DIVISION, requiring either a REDEFINES entry or a PERFORM VARYING statement in the PROCEDURE DIVISION. For example,

In DOS/VS COBOL

```
01  JOB-CODE-TABLE.
    05  JOB-CODE-ENTRIES OCCURS 8 TIMES INDEXED BY JOB-CODE.
        10  JOB-TITLE      PIC X(8).
        10  JOB-MAX-SAL    PIC S9(5)V99.
        10  JOB-MIN-SAL    PIC S9(5)V99.
            .
            .

    PERFORM 0100-INIT-TABLE VARYING JOB-CODE FROM 1 BY 1 UNTIL
        JOB-CODE > 8.
            .
            .

0100-INIT-TABLE.
    MOVE SPACES TO JOB-TITLE (JOB-CODE)
    MOVE ZEROS TO JOB-MAX-SAL (JOB-CODE)
                  JOB-MIN-SAL (JOB-CODE).
```

In COBOL II

```
01  JOB-CODE-TABLE.
    05  JOB-CODE-ENTRIES OCCURS 8 TIMES INDEXED BY JOB-CODE.
        10  JOB-TITLE      PIC X(8)     VALUE SPACES.
        10  JOB-MAX-SAL    PIC S9(5)V99 VALUE ZERO.
        10  JOB-MIN-SAL    PIC S9(5)V99 VALUE ZERO.
            .
            .
```

Techniques such as this can save procedural complexity and reduce programming efforts. Later on, you will see a new statement, INITIALIZE, which can replace the above PERFORM logic when needed in a program.

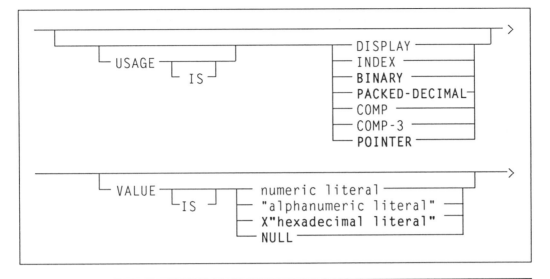

Figure 2.6. Example of USAGE and VALUE clauses (all options not shown).

Another option in the VALUE clause is that you may now code in hexadecimal, just as assembler programmers do (Note: The hexadecimal literal may now be used where other alphanumeric literals are valid, not just in the VALUE clause.) The literal must be preceded by *X* and the data must follow hexadecimal conventions (a multiple of two bytes, with values of 0 through 9 and A through F). Nice trick, but should you use this feature? One of the strengths of COBOL is its avoidance of machine dependencies. There are several situations, primarily between COBOL and non-COBOL modules, where hex literals may be effective, but I encourage you to be c-a-r-e-f-u-l. Here is an example of possible use:

```
05   WS5-PROCESS-SWITCH  PIC  X  VALUE X'01'.
     88  BIT-0-SET            VALUE X'80'.
     88  BIT-0-1-SET          VALUE X'C0'.
     88  BIT-0-2-SET          VALUE X'A0'.
     88  BIT-0-3-SET          VALUE X'90'.
     88  BIT-0-4-SET          VALUE X'88'.
     88  BIT-0-5-SET          VALUE X'84'.
          .
          .
```

This initializes the field to a binary value of 1 and provides 88-level entries to allow setting (covered later in this section) or testing of various bit combinations. This technique might be helpful if your system interacts with assembler programs that use one byte for multiple switches. This does *not* mean you can change individual bits. The down side of hex values is that it is easy to make mistakes with them and difficult to figure them out. For more information on bits and hexadecimal, see Chapter 7.

The new NULL option can't be explained without first laying some groundwork. NULL is related to POINTER. I'll show NULL and POINTER to you later.

The modifications to OCCURS DEPENDING ON.

With COBOL II, you may now have variable length data subordinate to variable length data, as demonstrated in Figure 2.7. Notice that the control fields (named here VALUE-A and VALUE-B) are in the fixed portion of the record and are not allowed to be in the variable portion. While this facility is now available, do you want to define files this way? The strong move towards data normalization has significantly reduced the number of variable-length records, and I applaud the change.

```
01   RECORD-NAME.
     05   1ST-GROUP-NAME.
          10   VALUE-A          PIC S9    COMP.
          10   VALUE-B          PIC S9    COMP.
     05   2ND-GROUP-NAME OCCURS 1 TO 10 TIMES
          DEPENDING ON VALUE-A.
          10   FIELD-C          PIC XX.
          10   FIELD-D   OCCURS 1 TO 30 TIMES
               DEPENDING ON VALUE-B.
               15 FIELD-E        PIC S9(5) COMP-3.
               15 FIELD-F        PIC XXX.
```

Figure 2.7. Example of nested OCCURS DEPENDING ON.

The COPY statement.

DOS/VS COBOL supported both the ANSI 1974 standard and the IBM extension to the ANSI 1968 standard. COBOL II supports the ANSI 1974 and the ANSI 1985 standard. The format of the COPY statement that met the ANSI 1968 standard is no longer allowed. That format was

```
01   data-name   COPY membername.
```

where data-name replaced the associated data-name from the copy member. See the example in Figure 2.8. COPY statements in DOS/VS COBOL that follow the ANSI 1974 standard should work satisfactorily.

An additional change in COBOL II is that you may have COPY statements imbedded within other COPY statements. This nesting was not allowed in DOS/VS COBOL. While writing this, my first thought was, "Why would anyone want to do this? Programming is hard enough without adding this complexity." I encourage you not to use it unless you have a very specific need for it.

COPYbook member EMPREC:

```
01  EMP-REC.
    05   EMP-NAME       PIC X(30).
    05   EMP-JOB-CODE PIC X.
```

COPY statement extension in DOS/VS COBOL:

```
01  WORK-REC   COPY   EMPREC.
```

Generated source code with DOS/VS COBOL:

```
01  WORK-REC.
    05   EMP-NAME       PIC X(30).
    05   EMP-JOB-CODE PIC X.
```

Generated source code with COBOL II (causes syntax error):

```
01  WORK-REC
01  EMP-REC.
    05   EMP-NAME       PIC X(30).
    05   EMP-JOB-CODE PIC X.
```

Example of allowable format:

```
COPY EMPREC.
```

Figure 2.8. COPY format that is no longer allowed.

Recommendation for using DATA DIVISION features.

Assuming you aren't using Report Writer or other no-no's, these changes in the DATA DIVISION do not require that you change the way you code COBOL programs (Exception: the COPY statement example I mentioned). Also, making any of these changes prevents your program from being compiled with DOS/VS COBOL again.

Some of these new opportunities are appropriate for only a small percentage of the programs you write. The two suggestions I offer are that you take advantage of the opportunity to omit FILLER and the opportunity to remove obsolete statements from your FDs and SDs. Anytime you can stop coding obsolete statements, the program becomes cleaner. Also, if you continue coding LABEL RECORDS ARE STANDARD and DATA RECORD IS, all the compiler will do with the statements is check the spelling. If you spelled them correctly, the compiler ignores them. If you didn't, you will get a syntax error. Is that any way to play the odds? So stop it, already.

2.3.4. PROCEDURE DIVISION

Changes to existing statements in the PROCEDURE DIVISION add several new options to your tool kit. Many of the changes qualify as all new. They are included here because they are extensions to existing statements. The issues that will require you to change any entries in this division were highlighted earlier in section 2.1 of this chapter (DOS/VS Features That Were Dropped in COBOL II).

Required entries (those that must always be present). None. (This would be true for a program within a run unit that consisted of no procedural code. I'll show you an example in Chapter 8.)

Obsolete, treated as comments. Not applicable in PROCEDURE DIVISION.

Obsolete and not allowed. References to CURRENT-DATE and TIME-OF-DAY, EXAMINE, EXHIBIT, READY/RESET TRACE, TRANSFORM, Report Writer statements, Communications statements, ISAM & BDAM statements, NOTE (use * in column 7, instead), ON statement (was used primarily for debugging), and OPEN and CLOSE obsolete options.

Enhanced elements. Scope Terminators, CALL, PERFORM, READ and RETURN, SET, SORT, and NOT ON SIZE ERROR and NOT INVALID KEY.

Scope terminators.

Scope terminators are the easiest of COBOL II's new PROCEDURE DIVISION enhancements to start using. Until now, the scope of a conditional statement extended for the duration of a sentence (i.e., the scope was terminated by a period). That sometimes caused clumsy coding practices. Consider the following from DOS/VS COBOL:

```
2100-PRODUCE-REPORT.
    PERFORM 2300-READ-RECORD
    IF NOT END-OF-FILE
        IF VALID-CONTROL-BREAK
            PERFORM 2400-WRITE-SUBTOTALS.
    IF NOT END-OF-FILE
        PERFORM 2500-ASSEMBLE-DETAIL-LINE
        PERFORM 2600-WRITE-DETAIL.
```

While you may have done this differently, the technique is not unusual and is an example in which a period is necessary to end the scope of the nested IF statement. Because there were additional processes dependent on the first IF statement, the statement had to be repeated. A scope terminator is a new COBOL II element that allows you to define the end of a conditional statement's scope without the need for a period. The syntax is straightforward: the letters *END-*, followed by the name of the affected verb. For example,

END-IF is the scope terminator for the IF statement.
END-COMPUTE is the scope terminator for the COMPUTE statement. (Remember, with an ON SIZE ERROR clause, any arithmetic statement can be conditional.)
END-READ is the scope terminator for a READ statement.

Any statement that has conditional elements may use a scope terminator if a period is not needed, and my philosophy is to never code anything that is not needed (More on this in the chapter on program design, Chapter 5). There is one exception to the first sentence in this paragraph: a new format for PERFORM has a mandatory scope terminator, yet it is *not* conditional. More on this later when new PERFORM features are addressed. For now, let's redo the previous example:

```
2100-PRODUCE-REPORT.
    PERFORM 2300-READ-RECORD
    IF NOT END-OF-FILE
        IF VALID-CONTROL-BREAK
            PERFORM 2400-WRITE-SUBTOTALS
        END-IF
        PERFORM 2500-ASSEMBLE-DETAIL-LINE
        PERFORM 2600-WRITE-DETAIL.
```

Notice how the logic is clearer. I finished the example with a period because it's the end of a paragraph, although an END-IF could have been coded if the logic flow were to continue. My preference is to code scope terminators every time I code a conditional statement and to avoid using periods except at the end of paragraphs. Scope terminators make the structure clear, and since I never use unnecessary periods, I never have to worry about an improperly placed one.

Changes to the CALL statement.

The opportunities that come with the new features in the CALL statement are not immediately apparent. The new features are extensions of, and do not conflict with, CALL statements from DOS/VS COBOL (Exception: In DOS/VS COBOL, you were allowed to have a paragraph-name as an identifier following USING. COBOL II does not allow this.) There are several changes, each of which needs clarification. Let's look at each option, keeping in mind that they can be combined within the same CALL statement.

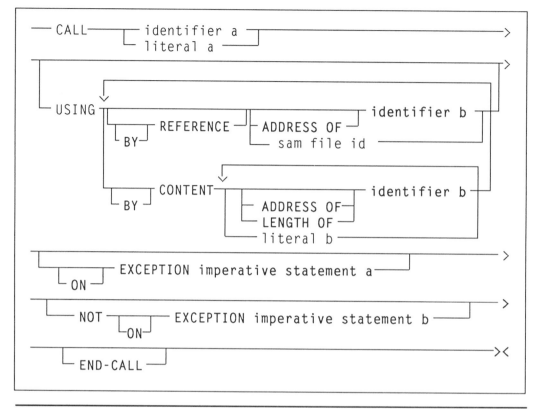

Figure 2.9. CALL Syntax in COBOL II.

Use of BY REFERENCE or BY CONTENT in CALL statement. This new option lets you control whether your program will let a subprogram have access to the data in your program or only the value of the data in your program. Confusing? Remember, in DOS/VS COBOL, a subprogram that accessed a passed parameter list (CALL USING . . .) was accessing the data directly within the CALLing program. That meant the subprogram could modify the data, even if you didn't want it modified. Now, by specifying BY CONTENT when you CALL a subprogram, the subprogram receives what appears to be your data area, but it is actually a separate area. If the subprogram changes it, your program's data area is not affected. If you code neither of these options, BY REFERENCE is assumed, since that is compatible with DOS/VS COBOL coding conventions.

Use of LENGTH OF clause in CALL statement. Did you ever want to pass data to a subprogram, but the length of the passed data varied? Now you can also pass the length of the data, so the subprogram can respond according to your intent. This is useful whenever variable data must be exchanged between programs. Errors can still occur, of course, if the program logic is incorrect, but now the information is available so such a program can be cleanly constructed. The LENGTH OF clause is not restricted to the CALL statement, as it is a new special register provided by COBOL II. The CALLed program must have an identifier defined in the LINKAGE SECTION with PIC S9(9) COMP. Here is an example of that technique:

```
CALL 'SUB1' USING WS3-WORK-REC
            BY CONTENT LENGTH OF WS3-WORK-REC
```

The subprogram, SUB1, would need the following:

```
LINKAGE SECTION.
01  LS1-WORK-REC.
01  LS2-LENGTH PICS9(9) COMP.
     .

     .

PROCEDURE DIVISION USING LS1-WORK-REC LS2-LENGTH.
```

Use of ADDRESS OF clause in CALL statement. This will be covered later, along with POINTER data elements. The ADDRESS OF clause is not restricted to the CALL statement since it is a new special register provided by COBOL II.

Use of ON EXCEPTION and NOT ON EXCEPTION in CALL statement. These are conditional expressions that receive control depending on whether the subprogram was accessed by your CALL statement. They apply only to dynamic CALLs. For example, your program periodically CALLs a large subprogram dynamically, but the partition may be of insufficient size. You might code:

```
CALL LARGE-PROG USING data-name
    ON EXCEPTION
        DISPLAY 'Program not loaded, increase partition'
        MOVE 16 TO RETURN-CODE
        STOP RUN
END-CALL
```

(DOS/VS COBOL had an option, ON OVERFLOW, that was equivalent to ON EXCEPTION. COBOL II supports that syntax, also.)

Changes to the PERFORM statement.
The PERFORM statement has always been one of my favorites and now it has even more flexibility, although the new features are a mixed blessing. First, I want to tell you about the new features and then I'll get back to my point about a mixed blessing.

PERFORM now has two major new syntax structures that can be useful if you do structured programming. The first is full implementation of the DO-UNTIL format (refresher: a DO-UNTIL statement executes the code before testing the condition, while a DO-WHILE tests the condition prior to executing the code). Until now, the PERFORM UNTIL (a DO-WHILE statement) had to serve both needs. Now you can specify the PERFORM UNTIL statement, add WITH TEST AFTER to it, and it becomes a DO-UNTIL format. (Note: If not coded on a PERFORM UNTIL statement, WITH TEST BEFORE is assumed for compatibility with existing code.)

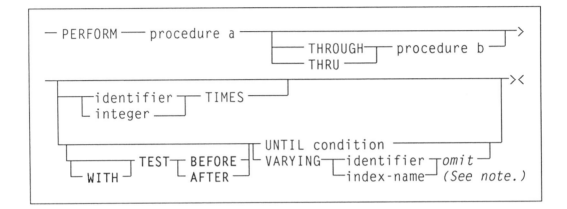

Figure 2.10.   Basic PERFORM syntax (Note: For clarity of new features, the syntax following VARYING is omitted from the diagram where *omit* appears. This includes FROM, BY, UNTIL and AFTER.)

For me, the big question was, "When would I ever need the WITH TEST AFTER clause?" I never found a satisfactory answer, but I can offer an example. WITH TEST AFTER has a potential advantage when you are using the VARYING clause to load a table and want the index-data-item to reflect the number of entries in the table, not a number one greater than the number in the table. Consider these two options:

```
PERFORM 3300-LOAD-PREMIUM-TABLE VARYING PREM-INDEX FROM 1 BY
    1 UNTIL END-OF-FILE

PERFORM 3300-LOAD-PREMIUM-TABLE WITH TEST AFTER VARYING
    PREM-INDEX FROM 1 BY 1 UNTIL END-OF-FILE
```

Assuming there were 1,000 premium entries to be loaded to the table, the contents of PREM-INDEX after the first statement would refer to a 1,001st entry, whereas the contents of PREM-INDEX in the second example would reflect that the table had 1,000 entries, not 1,001. Assuming the END-OF-FILE condition-name is not already set at the time the statements are executed, the choice becomes one of style.

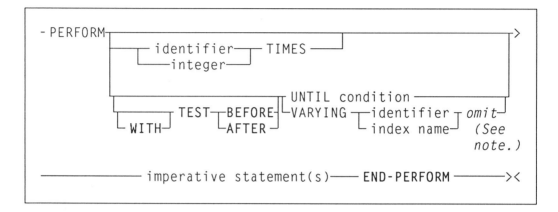

Figure 2.11. Inline PERFORM syntax (Note: For clarity of new features, the syntax following VARYING is omitted from the diagram, including FROM, BY, UNTIL and AFTER. This is where *omit* appears.)

The second option is the inline PERFORM with all PERFORMed code following the PERFORM statement. From the syntax in Figure 2.11, a sample inline PERFORM might be

```
PERFORM VARYING STATE-INDEX FROM 1 BY ONE UNTIL END-OF-FILE
    PERFORM 2100-READ-RECORD
    IF NOT END-OF-FILE
        MOVE STATE-DATA TO STATE-TABLE (STATE-INDEX)
    END-IF
END-PERFORM
```

Earlier, I mentioned that the PERFORM verb was an exception to my statement about using scope terminators on conditional statements. The END-PERFORM statement is the *only* scope terminator that applies to a nonconditional statement. Also, it must be coded at the end of all inline PERFORMs.

In my first paragraph on these PERFORM enhancements, I mentioned a mixed blessing. Although I admit it is a matter of style, I prefer not to use either statement. Why? From teaching programmers, I've learned that most programmers do best when they have a few simple tools. The PERFORM WITH TEST AFTER is so subtle in its difference that many novice programmers may not recognize what you are doing with the code. The inline PERFORM is nice in concept, but it can increase the density of paragraphs and reduce readability, especially when the code is to be maintained later by less experienced programmers. I speak more to this issue in Chapter 6 ("Coding Guidelines").

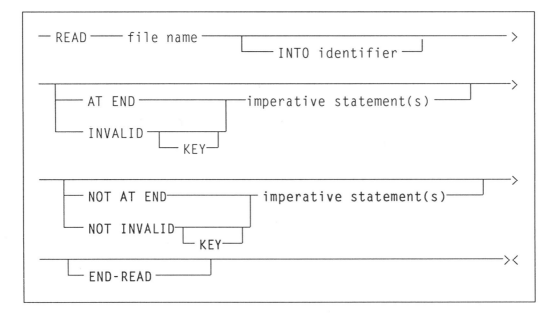

Figure 2.12. Basic READ syntax. Note: For clarity, I omitted little used options, such as NEXT RECORD. (AT END/NOT AT END cannot be intermixed with INVALID KEY/NOT INVALID KEY.)

Changes to READ and RETURN statements.

The changes to these two statements are so obvious and easy that one might wonder why these enhancements weren't done years ago. Anyway, they provide some interesting program structure opportunities (Example 8.2 in Chapter 8, "Sample Programs", is one). By adding a NOT AT END clause, much of the clumsiness of READs and RETURNs is eliminated. Consider this:

In DOS/VS COBOL, I typically had a paragraph similar to this

```
2300-READ-PAYROLL.
    READ FD3-PAYROLL-FILE
      AT END
        MOVE 'Y' TO FD3-EOF-SWITCH.
      IF FD3-EOF-SWITCH = 'N'
        ADD 1 TO FD3-RECORD-COUNT.
```

Now I can use the following replacement

```
2300-READ-PAYROLL.
    READ FD3-PAYROLL-FILE
      AT END
        MOVE 'Y' TO FD3-EOF-SWITCH
      NOT AT END
        ADD 1 TO FD3-RECORD-COUNT
    END-READ.
```

I think you will agree that the COBOL II approach is much cleaner. (Being the end of the paragraph, the END-READ wasn't required. I use it for clarity.) This feature also provides the opportunity to change a typical programming style that is common in structured programming. Consider this example:

Typical PERFORMed READ, followed by test for end of file

```
PERFORM 2300-READ-PAYROLL
IF FD3-EOF-SWITCH = 'N'
    imperative statements to process data
    .
    .
```

Opportunity for a different approach with COBOL II

```
READ FD3-PAYROLL-FILE
  AT END
    MOVE 'Y' TO FD3-EOF-SWITCH
  NOT AT END
    imperative statements to process data
    .
    .
```

It works, but I suggest you use the approach carefully. I prefer decomposition of a program to keep I/O statements in separate paragraphs. While the READ statement fits well in the previous example, it will tempt a maintenance programmer to add another READ statement in the future. Your shop may have standards on this, too.

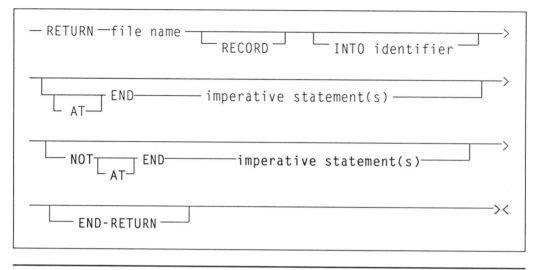

Figure 2.13. RETURN syntax.

SET enhancements.

Many programmers have never used this statement. Lack of use is indicative of a lack of experience with managing indexes in programs (more on this in Chapter 3, "Programming with COBOL II"). For now, let's look at a new capability. The SET statement may now reference 88-level condition names. Demonstrating is easier than explaining.

```
01   WS3-EMPL-DATA.
     05   EMPL-NAME              PIC X(30).
     05   EMPL-JOB-CODE          PIC X.
          88   PROGRAMMER        VALUE '1'.
          88   ANALYST           VALUE '2'.
          88   MANAGER           VALUE '3'.

01   FD2-PRINT-REC.
     05   FD2-EMPL-NAME          PIC X(30).
     05   JOB-TITLE              PIC X(10).
          88   PROGRAMMER-TITLE  VALUE 'PROGRAMMER'.
          88   ANALYST-TITLE     VALUE 'ANALYST'.
          88   MANAGER-TITLE     VALUE 'MANAGER'.
          88   UNKNOWN-TITLE     VALUE '**********'.
```

If the application is to interrogate EMPL-JOB-CODE and move the appropriate value to JOB-TITLE, in DOS/VS COBOL, you might code:

```
IF PROGRAMMER
    MOVE 'PROGRAMMER' TO JOB-TITLE
ELSE
    IF ANALYST
        MOVE 'ANALYST' TO JOB-TITLE
    ELSE
        IF MANAGER
            MOVE 'MANAGER' TO JOB-TITLE
        ELSE
            MOVE '**********' TO JOB-TITLE
```

In COBOL II, you can code:

```
IF PROGRAMMER
    SET PROGRAMMER-TITLE TO TRUE
ELSE
    IF ANALYST
        SET ANALYST-TITLE TO TRUE
    ELSE
        IF MANAGER
            SET MANAGER-TITLE TO TRUE
        ELSE
            SET UNKNOWN-TITLE TO TRUE
```

As you can see, this use of SET removes literals from the PROCEDURE DIVISION and moves them to the DATA DIVISION where they belong. Readability is improved, too, since all options appear beneath the data name. When you get to the EVALUATE statement in the next section, you will discover an even cleaner way to write the logic by using both the EVALUATE statement and the SET statement.

I haven't yet covered all the new features of the SET statement. I have more on SET in the next section, where I include it with a definition of POINTER data elements.

SORT enhancements.

People have debated with me on whether what I'm about to describe is an enhancement or not. To me, anything that makes a program cleaner is an enhancement. SORT hasn't changed, so what's the big deal? Well, COBOL II syntax does not require that procedural logic be organized by SECTION names. That's it. Why is that important? Anytime an unnecessary coding element is removed, you have the opportunity for a cleaner structure. This is what I call a style issue. If you consider that most programmers never use SECTIONs except when they do SORT programs, there is a tendency to use both paragraphs *and* SECTIONS. This practice creates programs that are unstructured and rife with

GO TOs. It is not unusual to find SORT programs when an INPUT PROCE-DURE is something like this:

```
1000-INPUT SECTION.
1010-INITIALIZE.
    initialization logic
    .

    .
1030-PROCESS-DATA.
    PERFORM 1040-READ-RECORD
    IF EOF-SWITCH = 'Y'
       GO TO 1050-EXIT.
    process record...
    .

    .
    GO TO 1030-PROCESS-DATA.
1040-READ-RECORD.
    input statements
    .
1050-EXIT.
    EXIT.
```

Have you seen programs like this? Often, they occur because the require-ment for a SECTION caused the programmer to think that all paragraphs had to be within the SECTION, mandating a GO TO statement. It wasn't true, but it happens frequently, and I've even seen corporate standards manuals that dic-tate this technique. Removing the requirement for SECTIONs lets programmers write simpler SORTS. (See Chapter 8, "Sample Programs," for an example.) (Note: Some people might say that the previous example is good structured code. Admittedly, the SECTION has one entry and one exit, but the paragraphs do not. This is a coding practice that COBOL II can help eliminate.)

NOT ON SIZE ERROR and NOT INVALID KEY clauses.

These are straightforward. Wherever you may currently place an ON SIZE ERROR clause (e.g., ADD, SUBTRACT), you may now also, or instead of, place the NOT ON SIZE ERROR clause. Likewise, whenever you could place an INVALID KEY clause (e.g., READ, WRITE), you may now also, or instead of, place the NOT INVALID KEY clause.

Recommendation for using PROCEDURE DIVISION features.

My first recommendation is that you rethink how you do nested IF statements and start restructuring with END-IF and other scope terminators. This quickly improves your program structure. Next, I suggest using EVALUATE and the expanded features of READ and RETURN, since they also improve structure and readability. Familiarity with the new option of SET comes quickly if you already use 88-levels. To help you change your approach to SORT programs, I included an example in Chapter 8 ("Sample Programs").

The extensions to CALL and PERFORM should be approached more cautiously. The CALL enhancements offer some opportunities for new systems you are developing, but make sure you're comfortable with the features before committing to a large project. As I indicated earlier, the PERFORM enhancements are powerful, but you may want to postpone using them until you have more experience with scope terminators.

2.4. NEW COBOL COMPONENTS

By now, you may feel that you've already read about the new features of COBOL II. New, yes, but the components described in the previous section were enhancements to existing COBOL elements. This section introduces new features with their own syntax. Making the decision to separate COBOL features this way was not easy. As I mentioned at the beginning of this chapter, my guiding light was to address the learning requirements of the maintenance or conversion programmer. By first learning what was dropped, followed by learning what is different, and ending by learning new features, you will be more productive more quickly than if I had glossed over differences and jumped here immediately.

While these elements are new, many benefit from being used in combination with each other or with the expanded capabilities described for current components.

2.4.1. Nested Programs/END PROGRAM Statement

I've picked nested programs first because it is an interesting concept that may take time to absorb, although your shop may decide never to use this approach to application development. From previous material in this book, you have probably surmised that program structure is more flexible with COBOL II (e.g., INITIAL in PROGRAM-ID and extensions to CALL and PERFORM statements). If so, you're right on target. This feature, and those that follow, support and expand on flexibility in program structure.

First, let's get our terms straight. A nested program is one that is contained within another program, a concept that did not previously exist in COBOL, although PL/1 and FORTRAN have always had such capabilities. Placing a program within another program requires that a means be defined to identify the end of a program. That new COBOL element is the END PROGRAM statement. See Figure 2.14 for an example.

```
IDENTIFICATION DIVISION. ←─────────────────
PROGRAM-ID. MAIN1.                    main program
ENVIRONMENT DIVISION.
    .
    .
DATA DIVISION.
    .
    .
PROCEDURE DIVISION.
    .
    .
    CALL 'SUB1' USING WS1-WORK-REC
    .
    .
IDENTIFICATION DIVISION ←──────────
PROGRAM-ID. SUB1.                 nested
DATA DIVISION.                    program
    .
    .
PROCEDURE DIVISION USING WORK-REC.
    .
    .
END PROGRAM SUB1.       ←──────
END PROGRAM MAIN1.←─────────────────
```

Figure 2.14. Sample of nested program. SUB1 is CALLed by MAIN1, yet exists within MAIN1.

In the example, MAIN1 calls SUB1. Notice how the END PROGRAM statements make clear to the compiler that SUB1 is within MAIN1. The program name in END PROGRAM must match that in the PROGRAM-ID statement or a syntax error occurs. Because SUB1 exists only within MAIN1, it has no identifier within the object module from a compile and is invisible to the Linkage Editor (i.e., SUB1 cannot be CALLed from separately compiled programs).

When used, END PROGRAM must be the last statement of a program. The statement may be used, if desired, for any program, even one that is not nested, as a means to let the compiler validate the last statement. Other terms that have meaning to nested programs are COMMON (in PROGRAM-ID) and GLOBAL (in FD and data descriptions).

You are probably wondering, "Why would I ever use such a structure?" When I first learned about nested programs, that was my question, too. At first, it appears to be an unwieldy structure with nothing positive about it. Actually, it is more a change in the way you build structure than in the way you write code. This is an exciting feature, one that will receive special treatment in Chapter 3 in the section titled Module Structures. For now, it is sufficient that you are aware of the concept and how the basic structure is formed. There is an example of a nested program in Chapter 8.

2.4.2. EVALUATE

The EVALUATE statement is an extension of the IF statement and provides the CASE concept for structured programming. Many programmers attempted to implement a form of CASE in earlier versions of COBOL by using the GO TO DEPENDING ON statement. That worked with limited success, but required many GO TO statements to support it and had other restrictions in its structure.

The EVALUATE can take one or more data elements or conditions and specify the action to take. The entries following the word EVALUATE specify what will be evaluated and how many evaluations will be made. For example,

```
EVALUATE WS1-SEX-CODE  ALSO  WS3-MARITAL-STATUS
```

The above statement specifies that there will be two evaluations, each against a data-name. Entries following WHEN could then specify values that might be in those fields. The number of comparisons following WHEN must match the number of entries following EVALUATE. For example,

```
EVALUATE WS1-SEX-CODE  ALSO  WS3-MARITAL-STATUS
WHEN         'F'        ALSO     'S'
    .
    .        imperative statement(s)
```

would be a possible entry. The imperative statement(s) following the entry would be executed if BOTH conditions were true. For example,

```
EVALUATE WS1-SEX-CODE  ALSO  WS3-MARITAL-STATUS
WHEN         'F'        ALSO     'S'
                 PERFORM 3100-SINGLE-FEMALE-EMP
```

The appearance of the next WHEN entry or END-EVALUATE terminates the scope of the WHEN clause. It is easier to understand the statement by looking at one, so I refer you to the following examples. Keep your use of EVALUATE simple at first while you build experience. You will find EVALU-ATE can make what would have been long IF statements more readable and easier to maintain.

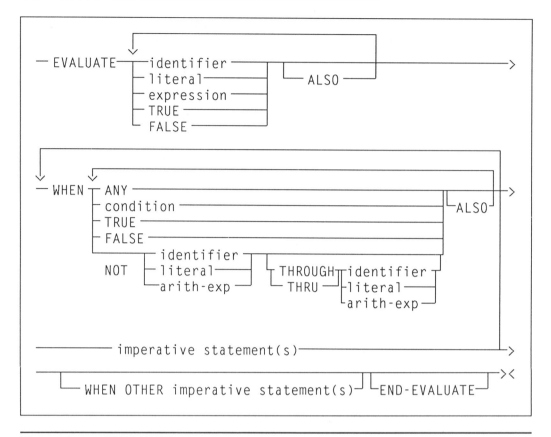

Figure 2.15. EVALUATE syntax.

Generally, the TRUE options provide more flexibility because a condition may be any valid COBOL condition (e.g., 88-levels, data-name followed by relational operator followed by literal or data-name, conditions separated by AND or OR). Although the syntax in Figure 2.15 may imply that you can mix and match, you cannot. The combination of possible entries must contain three components:

1. A value (e.g., data-name, expression or literal)
2. A value to compare to the first value
3. A condition (e.g., true or false)

For example, an 88-level-name defines a data-name and a value and could be used with TRUE or FALSE, but could not be combined with "literal" or "identifier" since those are already defined by the 88-level-name. Likewise, condition entries and 88-levels may not be used when a data-name follows the EVALUATE verb because it provides more than the three required components. The following examples do not include all options of the EVALUATE statement and are intended to show examples of concept, features, and format. There is an IF statement following each one for comparison purposes.

Testing value of a single field

```
EVALUATE WS1-SEX-CODE
    WHEN 'M' PERFORM 2100-MALE-APP
    WHEN 'F' PERFORM 2200-FEMALE-APP
    WHEN OTHER PERFORM 2300-ERROR-RTN
END-EVALUATE
```

IF equivalent:

```
IF WS1-SEX-CODE = 'M'
    PERFORM 2100-MALE-APP
ELSE
    IF WS1-SEX-CODE = 'F'
        PERFORM 2200-FEMALE-APP
    ELSE
        PERFORM 2300-ERROR-RTN
    END-IF
END-IF
```

Testing truth of a single 88-level or condition

```
EVALUATE   TRUE
    WHEN 88-level-name    PERFORM 2100-RTNA
                          PERFORM 2300-RTNB
                          MOVE 'Y' TO WS1-SWITCH
    WHEN 88-level-name2 OR condition-a
                          PERFORM 2500-RTNC
    WHEN OTHER            MOVE 'N' TO WS1-SWITCH
END-EVALUATE
```

IF equivalent:

```
IF 88-level-name
    PERFORM 2100-RTNA
    PERFORM 2300-RTNB
    MOVE 'Y' TO WS1-SWITCH
ELSE
    IF 88-level-name OR condition-a
        PERFORM 2500-RTNC
    ELSE
        MOVE 'N' TO WS1-SWITCH
    END-IF
END-IF
```

Testing more than one 88-level or condition

```
EVALUATE    TRUE         ALSO     TRUE
    WHEN 88-level-a   ALSO  condition-b
                            PERFORM 2100-RTNA
        WHEN condition-c  ALSO  88-level-d
                            PERFORM 2200-RTNB
        WHEN 88-level-e   ALSO   ANY
                            PERFORM 2300-RTNC
        WHEN OTHER          MOVE 'N' TO WS2-SWITCH
END-EVALUATE
```

IF equivalent:

```
IF 88-level-a AND condition-b
    PERFORM 2100-RTNA
ELSE
    IF condition-c AND 88-level-d
        PERFORM 2200-RTNB
    ELSE
        IF 88-level-e
            PERFORM 2300-RTNC
        ELSE
            MOVE 'N' TO WS2-SWITCH
        END-IF
    END-IF
END-IF
```

Testing more than one data field

```
EVALUATE
    WS1-SEX-CODE   ALSO WS2-MAR-STATUS
        WHEN 'M'       ALSO    'S'    PERFORM 3100-SGL-MALE
        WHEN 'M'       ALSO    'M'    PERFORM 3200-MAR-MALE
        WHEN 'F'       ALSO    'S'    PERFORM 3300-SGL-FEM
        WHEN 'F'       ALSO    'M'    PERFORM 3400-MAR-FEM
        WHEN OTHER                    PERFORM 3500-ERROR
END-EVALUATE
```

IF equivalent:

```
IF WS1-SEX-CODE = 'M' AND WS2-MAR-STATUS = 'S'
    PERFORM 3100-SGL-MALE
 ELSE
    IF WS1-SEX-CODE = 'M' AND WS2-MAR-STATUS = 'M'
```

```
                PERFORM 3200-MAR-MALE
        ELSE
            IF WS1-SEX-CODE = 'F' AND WS2-MAR-STATUS = 'S'
                PERFORM 3300-SGL-FEM
            ELSE
                IF WS1-SEX-CODE = 'F' AND WS2-MAR-STATUS = 'M'
                    PERFORM 3400-MAR-FEM
                ELSE
                    PERFORM 3500-ERROR
                END-IF
            END-IF
        END-IF
END-IF
```

Testing expressions and literals

This short example demonstrates that you may use EVALUATE for situations other than comparing data names to values. All other above combinations may also be used here:

```
EVALUATE   LOAN-BAL + NEW-LOAN-AMT
WHEN O THRU LOAN-LIMIT   PERFORM 3100-ISSUE-NEW-LOAN
WHEN LOAN-LIMIT + 1 THRU LOAN-LIMIT * 1.10
                           PERFORM 3200-WRITE-CHECK-DATA
WHEN OTHER                 PERFORM 3300-REJECT-LOAN
END-EVALUATE
```

The easiest way to learn the EVALUATE statement is to start using it. I have found that novice programmers pick this statement up quickly because it is easier (and quicker) to code than nested IF statements, and the logic is easier to see in the code.

2.4.3. CONTINUE

CONTINUE is a new statement that does nothing except meet the requirement of having a procedural statement where required. You might be thinking, "Wasn't that what NEXT SENTENCE did?" No. NEXT SENTENCE is really a GO TO statement that transfers control to an unnamed sentence following the current sentence. By now, you can probably guess that I don't like the NEXT SENTENCE clause for that very reason. A GO TO is a GO TO, even when it is a NEXT SENTENCE clause. In COBOL II, there is never a need for NEXT SENTENCE if you use the new features of COBOL II and use periods sparingly.

In the previous paragraph, I stated that the CONTINUE statement did nothing. Well, that's not exactly true. What it does is allow the procedural logic to continue to the next procedural statement within the program. Unlike NEXT

SENTENCE, it does not determine what that statement is. Let's look at some examples in which CONTINUE fills a gap.

Example 1

```
EVALUATE  FD3-SEX-CODE
WHEN  'M'  PERFORM 3200-PROCESS-MALE-APP
WHEN  'F'  CONTINUE
WHEN OTHER MOVE 'Y' TO FD3-INVALID-TRANS-CODE
END-EVALUATE
```

Here is a situation in which CONTINUE allows the EVALUATE syntax to contain a WHEN condition for code "F" when no processing is to be done on that condition, preventing the WHEN OTHER from being executed for what is a valid code.

Example 2

```
IF APPL-AGE > 17 OR APPL-PARENT-CONSENT = 'Y'
    CONTINUE
ELSE
    PERFORM 3100-ISSUE-REJECTION-NOTICE
```

This is a less obvious example. Often it is much clearer to code positive logic than to code negative logic, even when the processing is for the negative condition. If example 2 had been coded for the negative condition, it would have read:

```
IF APPL-AGE NOT > 17 AND APPL-PARENT-CONSENT NOT = 'Y'
    PERFORM 3100-ISSUE-REJECTION-NOTICE
```

The need for the two NOT conditions and the use of AND are sometimes lost on novice (and even senior) programmers. Turning the statement around is cleaner and the CONTINUE fills the requirement that a procedural statement be present.

Here is a more typical case, in which a nested IF has a condition that is not to be processed. Coding CONTINUE makes the logic clearer, since it denotes (in this example) that if SEX-CODE is 'M" and MARITAL-STATUS is other than "M', nothing is to process.

Example 3

```
IF SEX-CODE = 'M'
    IF MARITAL-STATUS = 'M'
        PERFORM 3100-MALE-MARRIED-APP
```

```
      ELSE
          CONTINUE
  ELSE
      PERFORM 3200-TEST-FEMALE-APPS
  END-IF
```

Note: Without CONTINUE, the following is also valid (just in case you were wondering if END-IF could work also):

```
IF SEX-CODE = 'M'
    IF MARITAL-STATUS = 'M'
        PERFORM 3100-MALE-MARRIED-APP
    END-IF
ELSE
    PERFORM 3200-TEST-FEMALE-APPS
END-IF
```

2.4.4. INITIALIZE

Have you ever had some initialization (or reinitialization) code in a program in which you had to reset a myriad of program switches or storage areas? It is usually tedious to code, and you always wonder if you remembered them all. That's where INITIALIZE can help.

First, you need to organize your data areas so one statement can reset all of them. I recommend placing all accumulators or switches that affect a particular logic path into a single 01-level entry. This is important because the INITIALIZE statement acts on data fields based on their data type, not their data name.

The function performed by INITIALIZE is to reset numeric fields to zero and alphanumeric fields to spaces, although there is an optional clause that does a REPLACING BY. The most common use of INITIALIZE is

```
INITIALIZE data-name.
```

Here are some examples. If you have the following data areas,

```
01  WS2-COMMON-ITEMS.
    05  WS2-TRANS-SWITCH    PIC  X.
    05  WS2-HEADER-SWITCH   PIC  X.
    05  WS2-LINE-COUNT      PIC  S999    COMP-3.
    05  WS2-TOTAL-DEP       PIC  S9.
    05  WS2-JOB-CODE        PIC  X.
01  WS3-PREMIUM-TABLE.
    05  WS3-PREM-ENTRY      PIC  S9(5)V99 COMP-3 OCCURS 100
                                 TIMES   INDEXED BY PREM-INDEX.
```

you can set all of them to appropriate spaces or zeros:

```
INITIALIZE  WS2-COMMON-ITEMS  WS3-PREMIUM-TABLE
```

Compare the simplicity of this with the extra coding you would need to do using DOS/VS COBOL. Your programs may never need to do this type of processing, but if your programs need that logic, this is the way to go.

I have been criticized by a few technicians for recommending INITIALIZE, since it generates a few more machine instructions than the proper number of MOVE statements. I mention it here because those technicians may also work at your shop. If machine cycles become more expensive than your time, I'll change my views. But I think the industry passed that mark two decades ago.

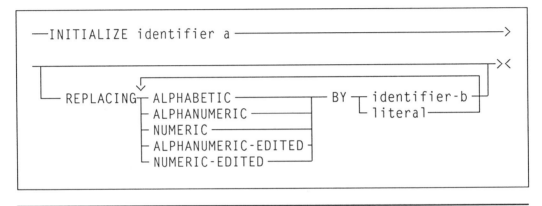

Figure 2.16. INITIALIZE Syntax.

2.4.5. TITLE

I like the ability to place comments in a document so they will be seen more than once. TITLE generates no code and is active only during the compile process. It serves to place a custom title line on your source listing on every page until another TITLE statement is encountered. Here is an example.

```
TITLE  'PREMIUM CALCULATION PROGRAM'
IDENTIFICATION DIVISION.
    .
    .
    .
PROCEDURE DIVISION.
TITLE  ' TERM POLICY CALCULATIONS'
    .
    .
    .
TITLE  ' WHOLE LIFE POLICY CALCULATIONS'
    .
    .
```

In addition to printing a title on your source listing, TITLE also causes a page eject to occur. If you're thinking, Doesn't the "/" in column 7 do that, too?, you're right. The difference is that the "/" causes the comment to appear only once, not on all the following pages. This simple line of text improves a program's documentation. As a matter of style, I like to use it just before the IDENTIFICATION DIVISION statement.

2.4.6. Data Manipulation Enhancements/Changes

I've saved these enhancements until the end because they add subtle opportunities for rethinking program structure and data manipulation techniques. Because they are different, your shop may not allow their use, so you may want to get the corporate scoop before using these particular features. Topics here relate to the many new ways data may be defined both for system management and for data manipulation. Most of the entries here are new features, although some changes may require that you change how you write some pre-COBOL II statements.

LENGTH OF and ADDRESS OF special registers.

You saw these two elements previously as part of the CALL statement. They are new special registers (some other special registers you may be familiar with are TALLY, RETURN-CODE, and several relating to SORT). Special registers are facilities provided by the compiler and not defined within the source program.

The LENGTH OF special register is a value kept by the generated code for each 01-level item. You may never have need for it in your programs, but it makes a significant improvement to CICS programs by eliminating the need to manipulate or specify LENGTH in EXEC CICS statements (covered in Chapter 3).

The ADDRESS OF special register is a value kept by the generated code for the address of each 01-level item in the LINKAGE SECTION. (Use of ADDRESS OF with POINTER is explained further in this topic.) In addition to being used in the CALL statement, it also simplifies CICS programs by eliminating the need for CICS programmers to use BLL cells (covered in Chapter 3).

GLOBAL and EXTERNAL data elements.

This is a major enhancement, providing extensive new options for program design. In DOS/VS COBOL, data elements were part of the source program in which they were defined. Access to the data elements from other programs could only be done via a CALL USING statement. No more. With COBOL II, data areas can be accessed separately from the program in which they are defined or where their definitions are coded (more on this in the section Module Structures in Chapter 3). GLOBAL and EXTERNAL provide these opportunities. Let's examine each term separately.

GLOBAL. When appended to a data or file definition (01-level or FD), that data element or FD may be referenced by any nested program within the run unit. I reviewed the concept of nested programs earlier, but didn't explain why it might have advantages. Here is one possibility, being able to define an FD or 01-level that is directly accessible from within other programs. See Figure 2.17 for an example. The module, SUB1, has no DATA DIVISION, yet can reference all defined GLOBAL entries in the program in which it is nested.

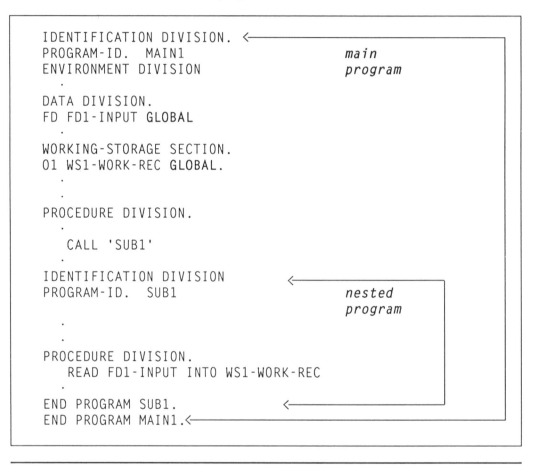

Figure 2.17. Sample of GLOBAL file and record definition.

That previous sentence is important. A GLOBAL item is global *only* to those programs that are contained within it. Programs that do not share the same parentage do not have access to the data. Examine Figure 2.18. While most COBOL code is missing from the example, the structure is

```
Outermost module: MAIN1.
```

MAIN1 may access data or FDs only from within itself. (MAIN1 isn't contained within any other module.)

```
Directly contained modules: SUB1 and SUB2.
```

SUB1 and SUB2 may access any data area or FD within their own programs or that are GLOBAL in their parent, MAIN1 (i.e., SUB1 may not access any data area or FD defined in SUB2).

```
Indirectly contained module: SUB2A.
```

SUB2A is directly contained within SUB2 and indirectly contained within MAIN1. It has no relationship to SUB1. Therefore SUB2A may access data areas within itself, that are GLOBAL within its parent SUB1, or within SUB1's parent MAIN1.

```
IDENTIFICATION DIVISION. <─────────────────────────────
PROGRAM-ID.   MAIN1                      main
DATA DIVISION.
FD FD1-INPUT GLOBAL
WORKING-STORAGE SECTION.
01 WS1-WORK-REC  GLOBAL.
PROCEDURE DIVISION.
    CALL 'SUB1'
    CALL 'SUB2'
IDENTIFICATION DIVISION <───────────────────────────
PROGRAM-ID.   SUB1                       nested
    This program has access to FD1-INPUT
      .                    and WS1-WORK-REC
    This program does NOT have access to WS5-DATA
END PROGRAM SUB1.        <───────────────────────────
IDENTIFICATION DIVISION <───────────────────────────
PROGRAM-ID.  SUB2                        nested
This program has access to FD1-INPUT
      .                    and WS1-WORK-REC
01 WS5-DATA GLOBAL.
    CALL 'SUB2A'
ID DIVISION.             <───────────────────────
PROGRAM-ID. SUB2A                       nested
This program has access to FD1-INPUT,
        WS1-WORK-REC and WS5-DATA
END PROGRAM SUB2A.<───────────────────────
END PROGRAM SUB2.       <───────────────
END PROGRAM MAIN1.<─────────────────────
```

Figure 2.18.   Sample of GLOBAL access by subprogram.

Use of GLOBAL is an excellent technique to maintain control of data accessibility and eliminate the need to code definitions of the FDs or data areas within each module.

EXTERNAL. The external clause may be used on FDs and 01-level entries also. Where GLOBAL applied to nested programs, EXTERNAL applies to traditional, external structures, in which each program in the run unit is separate, often separately compiled (and link-edited, if DYNAM is used). This can be advantageous if it is desirable for several programs to share the same files or data areas. Whereas GLOBAL elements were accessible only from programs that were contained within a program, EXTERNAL elements may be accessed from any program in the run unit that has the same definitions.

From a coding perspective, the difference between GLOBAL and EXTERNAL is that the EXTERNAL items must be coded in all programs exactly the same. If the element is spelled differently, for example, it compiles with no errors and executes, but the defined EXTERNAL element is unique and processing errors (ABENDs) will depend on the process attempted. Elements that will be EXTERNAL should be defined as COPYbooks to eliminate this possible error. Also, EXTERNAL 01-level items may not have a VALUE clause.

For an example of EXTERNAL, assume the following COPYbooks:

PAYSEL

```
    SELECT FD1-PAYROLL-FILE
        ASSIGN TO PAYMAST  FILE STATUS IS FD1-STAT.
```

PAYFD

```
    FD FD1-PAYROLL-FILE  EXTERNAL
        RECORD CONTAINS 100 CHARACTERS
        RECORDING MODE IS F.
    01 FD1-PAYROLL-REC.
        05  FD1-EMP-NUMBER   PIC X(5).
        .
        .
```

PAYWORK

```
    01   WS1-PAYROLL-WORK  EXTERNAL.
         05  FD1-STAT            PIC XX.
         .
         .
```

Using these three COPYbooks, you could develop the program structure in Figure 2.19. It helps to visualize the structure by considering that EXTERNAL elements are separate from programs. The true in-memory structure for the example in Figure 2.19 follows (assumes RENT option).

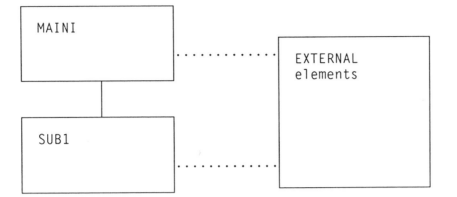

```
ID DIVISION.
PROGRAM-ID.  MAIN1.
ENVIRONMENT DIVISION.
INPUT-OUTPUT SECTION.              Unlike GLOBAL,
FILE-CONTROL.                      there is
    COPY PAYSEL.                   nothing unique
DATA DIVISION.                     about the
FILE SECTION.                      main program
    COPY PAYFD.                    regarding use
WORKING-STORAGE SECTION.           of EXTERNAL.
    COPY PAYWORK.
PROCEDURE DIVISION.
1.  OPEN INPUT FD1-PAYROLL-FILE
    CALL 'SUB1'
    .

END PROGRAM MAIN1.
ID DIVISION.                       This subprogram
PROGRAM-ID.  SUB1.                 could be
ENVIRONMENT DIVISION.              CALLed either
INPUT-OUTPUT SECTION.              statically or
FILE-CONTROL.                      dynamically.
    COPY PAYSEL.
DATA DIVISION.                     The linkage
FILE SECTION.                      is established
    COPY PAYFD.                    at run-time,
WORKING-STORAGE SECTION.           not during
    COPY PAYWORK.                  compile or
PROCEDURE DIVISION.                link-edit.
1.  READ FD1-PAYROLL-FILE
    .

END PROGRAM SUB1.
```

Figure 2.19. Example of EXTERNAL use.

As you saw, EXTERNAL and GLOBAL bring new structure opportunities to COBOL programs. Both offer their own advantages that may change the way you design programs. Also, you can use EXTERNAL and GLOBAL definitions together. Suggestions on when to use these features in program design are in Chapter 3 ("Programming with COBOL II").

NULL value, POINTER data items, SET, and ADDRESS OF.

Earlier in the book, while describing changes to the USAGE and VALUE clause, I mentioned that NULL and POINTER were new terms and would be explained later. I also postponed an addition to the SET statement and use of ADDRESS OF with the CALL statement. This is as good a place as any to discuss those features. The features here are needed to replace BLL manipulation in CICS programs and allow use of dynamic SQL (SQLDA) in SQL/DS programs (see Chapter 3). Some programmers will probably never need to code any of these entries, but they create interesting opportunities for new structures (also in Chapter 3).

All of these elements relate, since they all support manipulating addresses within an application. I don't foresee these options being used much (other than for CICS and SQL/DS), but they do offer unique opportunities. While they don't have to be used together, it will be simpler to grasp them that way. Let's start with ADDRESS OF. The term ADDRESS OF represents an internal register for each 01-level item in the LINKAGE SECTION. One of the new CALL formats uses it this way:

```
CALL 'SUB1' USING ADDRESS OF  WS3-DATA-AREA
```

This CALL statement passes the address of the data element *as data*. The CALLed subprogram must move it to where it can use the address to access the data the address points to. Here is an example of a CALLed subprogram, demonstrating the concept.

```
LINKAGE SECTION.
01  LS1-ADDRESS              POINTER.
01  LS2-DATA-AREA.
     .
     .

PROCEDURE DIVISION USING LS1-ADDRESS.
1.  SET ADDRESS OF LS2-DATA-AREA TO LS1-ADDRESS
     .
     .
```

Before the program can work with the data elements in LS2-DATA-AREA, it first establishes addressability to it. This is accomplished by the SET statement. The SET statement takes the passed address in LS1-ADDRESS and establishes it for addressability to LS2-DATA-AREA. LS1-ADDRESS is defined as a POINTER item. This occurs because it contains an address of data, not data. Notice there is no PIC clause.

    If this were the typical way of using POINTER items, it would be easier to code in the traditional way, since COBOL has always provided addressability to data areas in CALLing programs. For example,

Calling program

```
CALL 'SUB1' USING WS3-DATA-AREA
```

Called program

```
LINKAGE SECTION.
01  LS2-DATA-AREA.
        .
        .
    PROCEDURE DIVISION USING LS2-DATA-AREA.
```

    This typical structure passes the address of the data-name, but it does so as an address for the internal code to manage, not as data for the application logic to manage. Obviously, POINTERs are not intended for use in traditional CO-BOL-to-COBOL structures.

    While this technique isn't needed in typical COBOL applications, there is a use for it if your application must interact with assembler programs that pass addresses of addresses between programs rather than addresses of data. With CICS, for example, the list of BLL cells in a DOS/VS COBOL application is an address of addresses that requires attention before using the data areas.

    The example showed one form of the SET. Here are the two basic forms it takes when ADDRESS OF is used.

```
SET pointer-item TO ADDRESS OF data-name <—   This stores the
                                               address of the
                                               data-name in the
                                               pointer-item.


SET ADDRESS OF data-item TO pointer-item <—   This establishes
                                               addressability of
                                               the data-item
                                               within the COBOL
                                               program.
```

To summarize:

- NULL may appear in a VALUE clause for a POINTER item or within a SET (SET pointer-item TO NULL).
- POINTER items are valid only for use as one of the operands in the form of the SET statement using ADDRESS OF.
- ADDRESS OF exists only for elements in the LINKAGE SECTION.

Examples of these techniques are explored in Chapter 3 under the sections Module Structures and CICS-DL/1-SQL/DS Issues.

Class tests—alphabetic and numeric.

This is a good news/bad news situation. The good news is that you may now test for ALPHABETIC-UPPER and ALPHABETIC-LOWER when you are validating an alphanumeric field for all upper-case or all lower-case text. The bad news is that ALPHABETIC now allows both upper- and lower-case text. In DOS/VS COBOL, the statement

```
IF data-name ALPHABETIC
```

would only be true if the field contained characters *A* through *Z* and the space. Now, it will be true if the field contains *A* through *Z*, *a* through *z*, and the space. If you will be converting programs from DOS/VS COBOL to COBOL II, I suggest you change all occurrences of ALPHABETIC to ALPHABETIC-UPPER.

The NUMERIC situation is not as clear. The NUMERIC class test operates differently, depending on a compile-time option, NUMPROC. Your shop has set a default value for this option and your technical staff can probably assist you with questions on this issue. The NUMPROC option is explained in Chapter 3, along with all other compile options. The good news about the NUMPROC option is that it provides some performance improvements if your numeric data elements are always properly signed.

Reference modification.

Reference modification is another addressing technique that has been lifted from other languages. This is a technique in which you may access part of a data area without using the REDEFINES clause in the DATA DIVISION. For example, assume you have a data area defined that contains a phone number, including parentheses [e.g., (555) 555-1212]. Counting parentheses, spaces, and the hyphen, this comes to 14 positions. If the data area is defined:

```
05  FD3-EMPL-PHONE-NUMBER      PIC X(14).
```

you can access the area code (you know it is the second, third, and fourth characters in the field) by coding this:

```
MOVE FD3-EMPL-PHONE-NUMBER (2:3)  WS1-AREA-CODE
```

In case you didn't figure out the example, the first digit specifies the starting byte within the field. In this case 2 for the second byte. The digit following the colon represents the length of the field (in bytes) for this statement. In this case 3 because the area code is three bytes long.

Since reference modification applies to bytes, this technique should be used for alphanumeric fields. (It could be used for other data types, but would become a maintenance nightmare.) The complete syntax is

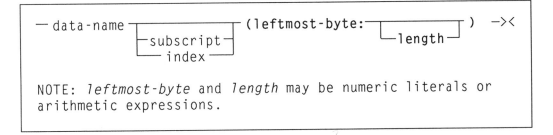

```
NOTE: leftmost-byte and length may be numeric literals or
arithmetic expressions.
```

Figure 2.20.   Reference modification syntax.

From Figure 2.20, you see that if subscripts or indexes are used, they are placed first, following the data name. The length operand is optional. When length is omitted, the compiler assumes a length that represents the remaining bytes in the field. Therefore, to use the previous example of a phone number, the code to move the seven-digit phone number and the hyphen would be

```
MOVE FD3-EMPL-PHONE-NUMBER (7:8)  TO WS3-LOCAL-PHONE
```

or

```
MOVE FD3-EMPL-PHONE-NUMBER (7:)  TO WS3-LOCAL-PHONE
```

As you can see, this can be nonproductive. Counting the bytes in the field to code this statement takes time and can be difficult to read. When not needed, I don't encourage this approach: it adds one more possible element to debug. Finally, if you use an arithmetic expression to compute the starting position and length at run-time, results may be unpredictable if your computations do not fall within the defined data field length (e.g., a starting position of -5 or a length of 0). A new compile option, SSRANGE, can assist in debugging. (SSRANGE also supports debugging OCCURS clauses and is covered in Chapter 3 under the section Specifying COBOL II Options, and in Chapter 4, "Debugging.")

De-editing numeric data.

The term *de-edit* means to be able to MOVE from a data element that is edited (i.e., it has PIC characters such as $, Z, and decimal points, as in PIC $,$$$.99) to a numeric data element that is not edited (i.e., it has PIC characters that depict a numeric value for computation, such as PIC S9(5)V99). This was impossible to do before. It can be handy if you are pulling numeric entries from a data entry screen (e.g., CICS) and want the screen to be edited for the terminal operator and also want it in numeric format for processing. This ability requires no special coding on your part. It is a capability for the MOVE statement that was not allowed in earlier releases of COBOL.

DAY-OF-WEEK.

Earlier, I explained that CURRENT-DATE and TIME-OF-DAY were replaced by a form of the ACCEPT statement. That capability existed in DOS/VS COBOL, as the ACCEPT statement is an ANSI 74 statement. Here are additional extensions to the ACCEPT statement you can use with COBOL II.

```
ACCEPT data-name FROM DAY-OF-WEEK
```

where the implicit PIC for DAY-OF-WEEK is PIC 9(1). The values range from 1 for Monday through 7 for Sunday. For example, the value 5 represents Friday.

Extended compiler limits.

Normally, you don't think about how large a data item can be. In fact, you probably never knew the limit when working with DOS/VS COBOL programs. I didn't. It didn't usually matter; data elements were used to store copies of data records in memory, so the limiting factor was usually the data record size. This has changed with COBOL II. Consider the following comparison:

	Maximum data size	
	DOS/VS COBOL	COBOL II
Working-Storage	1 megabyte	128 megabytes
01-level size	1 megabyte	16 megabytes
Linkage Section	1 megabyte	128 megabytes

Note: A megabyte is not one million bytes. It is 1,048,576 bytes. This means that 128 megabytes is really 134,217,727 bytes and 16 megabytes is really 16,777,215 bytes.

This extension offers possibilities for using an 01-level for an in-memory database, something you couldn't consider in DOS/VS COBOL. While there are always other considerations when designing a high-performance application, one option might be to load a database into a table in memory and then access it through an index. VSE/ESA offers applications the opportunity to reevaluate their use of memory, once considered more precious than other resources.

SUMMARY

This has been a hefty chapter of the book. I encourage you to read it more than once, highlighting and underlining those elements that affect your programming techniques. COBOL II is a major step forward for COBOL. You don't need to read the next chapter (and probably shouldn't) until you have experimented with several of these different features and developed a feeling of comfort for and enthusiasm with COBOL II. The language structure should feel natural before you start looking for new techniques.

3

Programming with COBOL II

This chapter is designed to provide tips and techniques for day-to-day programming assignments and for maximizing a program's design and performance. I assume you have read the previous chapter and that you have experimented with COBOL II. This chapter does not, however, focus solely on COBOL II components. Instead, it focus on whatever technique is appropriate to the topic. This will often include a new feature of COBOL II, but not always.

This chapter is not written to be read from beginning to end like the previous chapter was. Instead, use this chapter as a ready reference for COBOL techniques. You will find many topics are duplicated to some degree elsewhere in the book, and you may be wondering why some topics appear twice. I did this because, as a desk reference, you should find topics where you look for them, so some topics may appear in several places. I hope that they appear in enough locations to ease your use of the book.

3.1. USING STRUCTURED PROGRAMMING COMPONENTS

First, if you're not familiar with structured programming, see Chapter 5 ("Program Design Guidelines"). For the rest of you, you know whether or not you use structured programming practices. Structured programming contains

- no GO TOs (that's right, none)
- no EXIT statements

- no PERFORM THRU statements
- one entry and one exit for all statements/paragraphs/modules

If you coded those statements only in DOS/VS COBOL SORT or CICS programs, that's OK. There was often little choice. EXIT and PERFORM THRU don't explicitly violate structured programming concepts, but they do violate top-down design techniques since they do not decompose logic. This section is a brief review of COBOL statements that provide structured programming components (SEQUENCE, SELECTION, DO-WHILE, DO-UNTIL, and CASE).

3.1.1. SEQUENCE Component

SEQUENCE means that a statement's scope places it in sequence with the preceding statement. A set of sequence statements, therefore, all share the same scope. When you execute the first statement in a sequence, the structure takes you through all the statements. So, what does this mean? It means that you must *not* contain the scope by inserting any periods that aren't required. For example,

```
MOVE A TO B
MOVE C TO D
```

are two statements that meet the definition of SEQUENCE. The first is executed and then the second. If we were to precede those two statements by an IF statement

```
IF condition
    MOVE A TO B
    MOVE C TO D
```

we know that both MOVE statements would be executed. However, some programmers are in the habit of placing periods after *every* statement. Preceding such statements with an IF statement would give us this:

```
IF condition
    MOVE A TO B.
    MOVE C TO D.
```

Obviously, this would be an error. It has been this practice over the years that has sensitized many people to "always check for missing periods." In truth, the reverse is the proper approach. Instead of checking for missing periods, you should avoid placing unnecessary periods and periodically spot check for them. They are only appropriate at the end of a paragraph. Throughout this book, the approach is if you don't need it, don't code it.

3.1.2. SELECTION component

If you're thinking that this is accomplished by the IF and ELSE statement, you're correct—but there are many more selection statements. For example, other statements that provide selection options are

```
Statement    Selection clause

ADD          ON SIZE ERROR, NOT ON SIZE ERROR
CALL         ON EXCEPTION, NOT ON EXCEPTION
COMPUTE      ON SIZE ERROR, NOT ON SIZE ERROR
DELETE       INVALID KEY, NOT INVALID KEY
DIVIDE       ON SIZE ERROR, NOT ON SIZE ERROR
EVALUATE     WHEN
MULTIPLY     ON SIZE ERROR, NOT ON SIZE ERROR
READ         AT END, NOT AT END, INVALID KEY, NOT INVALID KEY
RETURN       AT END, NOT AT END
REWRITE      INVALID KEY, NOT INVALID KEY
SEARCH       WHEN
START        INVALID KEY, NOT INVALID KEY
STRING       ON OVERFLOW, NOT ON OVERFLOW
SUBTRACT     ON SIZE ERROR, NOT ON SIZE ERROR
UNSTRING     ON OVERFLOW, NOT ON OVERFLOW
WRITE        INVALID KEY, NOT INVALID KEY
```

Because all of these provide the SELECTION component, all of them also have scope terminators associated with them to avoid prematurely terminating the scope of the statement. (See SEQUENCE.) It is the extensive use of scope terminators for SELECTION statements that maintains the integrity of your structured program; scope terminators ensure the SELECTION components are eligible to be SEQUENCE components as well.

3.1.3. The DO-WHILE Component

Nothing new here. The PERFORM UNTIL statement accomplishes this. You have a choice of using the traditional approach, in which the executed code is in a separate paragraph, or use the new inline format where the executed code immediately follows the PERFORM statement. Remember, a DO-WHILE component tests a condition BEFORE executing the code, whereas a DO-UNTIL component tests the condition after executing the code. For example,

Traditional

```
PERFORM 2300-PROCESS-RECORDS UNTIL EOF-SWITCH = 'Y'
```

Inline

```
PERFORM VARYING TAB-INDEX FROM 1 BY 1 UNTIL END-OF-FILE
    PERFORM 2400-READ
    IF NOT END-OF-FILE
        MOVE FD1-REC TO WS3-TABLE (TAB-INDEX)
    END-IF
END-PERFORM
```

Remember, the inline PERFORM requires the scope terminator END-PERFORM.

3.1.4. The DO-UNTIL Component

This was never before available in COBOL and many analysts who develop programming specifications for COBOL applications avoid using DO-UNTIL. Anyway, you now have it with the **WITH TEST AFTER** clause appended to a PERFORM statement. You have a choice similar to that offered previously for the DO-WHILE component: either use the traditional PERFORM in which the executed code is in a separate paragraph or use the new inline format in which the executed code immediately follows the PERFORM statement.

Traditional

```
PERFORM 2300-PROCESS-RECORDS UNTIL EOF-SWITCH = 'Y' WITH
    TEST AFTER
```

Inline

```
PERFORM WITH TEST AFTER VARYING TAB-INDEX FROM 1 BY 1 UNTIL
    END-OF-FILE
    PERFORM 2400-READ
    IF NOT END-OF-FILE
        MOVE FD1-REC TO WS3-TABLE (TAB-INDEX)
    END-IF
END-PERFORM
```

This example seems identical to the earlier example for DO-WHILE. The difference is in the status *after* execution. Remember, the inline PERFORM requires the scope terminator END-PERFORM.

3.1.5. The CASE Component

This component is provided by the new EVALUATE statement. You can find many examples in the previous chapter. Do not use the GO TO DEPENDING ON statement to attempt this.

3.1.6. How to Avoid the GO TO Statement

There is additional material in Chapter 5, "Program Design Guidelines," that addresses this topic. I include the topic here because it is a common concern of programmers who have trouble with the concept. My approach is to concentrate on decomposing the program design and not to concentrate on GO TOs. The need for GO TO statements disappears in an application when each paragraph decomposes downward and outward to accomplish the scope of the paragraph.

When dealing with structure, I create analogies with an office environment in which the main module/paragraph is the manager and the other modules/paragraphs are subordinates or junior managers. For example, a manager wanting to review records for employees eligible for a pay raise in the current month would not say to a subordinate, "Please get me all the employee records." Instead, the manager would say, "Please get me the employee records for the employees eligible for a pay raise this month."

Sound simple? Compare this simple logic to a program that needs to read a file, but wants to process only certain records. Often, we see something like this:

```
2100-PROCESS.
    PERFORM 2300-READ-RECORD
    IF NOT END-OF-FILE
        IF ELIGIBLE-FOR-PAY-RAISE
            process, etc
                .
                .
        ELSE
            GO TO 2100-PROCESS.

2300-GET-READ-RECORD.
    READ
      AT END
          SET END-OF-FILE TO TRUE
    END-READ.
```

This is poor code, primarily because the process of getting input has not been decomposed. Why not try the office analogy approach and do this:

```
2100-PROCESS.
    PERFORM 2300-GET-VALID-RECORD
    IF NOT END-OF-FILE
        process, etc
          .
          .
2300-GET-VALID-RECORD.
    PERFORM UNTIL END-OF-FILE OR ELIGIBLE-FOR-PAY-RAISE
        READ FILE-ID
          AT END
              SET END-OF-FILE TO TRUE
        END-READ
    END-PERFORM.
```

This delegates the process of simple validation to a subordinate module, freeing the manager module to make processing decisions instead of doing simple edits as well. You will probably find your programs have more paragraphs, and smaller ones at that. You will probably also find that junior programmers can maintain them. The use of the GO TO statement will continue to be used by a portion of programmers, but it will always be indicative of either an inadequate or an incomplete program design.

3.2. MODULE STRUCTURES

This section contains suggestions and tips for when you are building a new application, adding a subprogram to an existing structure, or contemplating different ways to link your logic subsets together. If you're unfamiliar with combining programs, read the first two topics for an overview of the concept.

3.2.1. Main Modules and Submodules

This section introduces the term *run unit*, which appears throughout the book. A run unit is the logical collection of programs executed under control of a main program. This may be one or more programs in one or more languages formed into one or more phases. For example, in a batch environment a run unit is identified by the JCL EXEC statement.

A main program/module is one that is invoked from VSE (e.g., on JCL EXEC statement). A main program is to a great degree coded the same way as a subprogram. Differences lie in the way they are terminated (see next topic) and how they share data with other programs in the run unit (see topics Sharing Data and Sharing Files). For example, a main program using the PROCEDURE DIVISION USING statement is receiving data from VSE (via the JCL PARM parameter) in a format different from the same statement being used in a subprogram. Where a LINKAGE SECTION is used in a main program, it is typically to store the above mentioned PARM data from a JCL statement. The main program is the highest element in a run unit. As in other components of a run unit, a main program should have one entry and one exit. (Note: If the first COBOL program is CALLed from an assembler program, there are some differences. See that topic later in this section.)

Subprograms and submodules are invoked from another program (i.e., CALLed from another application or from a software environment). Subprograms use PROCEDURE DIVISION USING to accept data from a CALLing program in a format determined by the CALLing program. Subprograms can, in turn, also CALL other subprograms. As in other components of a run unit, a subprogram should have one entry and one exit.

Example of a batch main program and subprograms

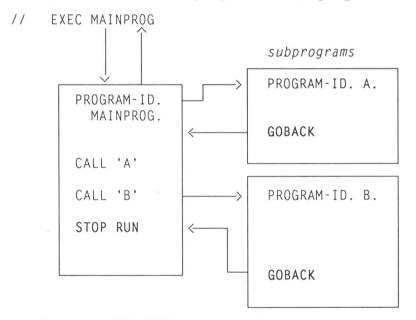

From the JCL, VSE gives control to MAINPROG. MAINPROG, in turn, transfers control first to program A and then to program B. The subprograms use GOBACK to return control, and the main program uses STOP RUN to return control to VSE.

3.2.2. Terminating a Program/Module

COBOL provides five ways to terminate an application.

1. **STOP RUN.** The STOP RUN statement, used by main programs, returns control back to the system environment. The system environment is normally established by VSE at the time the first program (the

main program) is initiated. Therefore, a subprogram should not use STOP RUN. Another function of the STOP RUN statement closes any files in the run unit that are still open. One STOP RUN, at most, should be within a run unit. While COBOL II has removed many of the restrictions on using STOP RUN for CICS applications, I don't recommend it. (Note: For other considerations on the "environment," see the topic on assembler language, below.)

2. **GOBACK.** The GOBACK statement returns control to the CALLing program and should be used by subprograms. (Note: GOBACK may also be used by main programs, but the resource cleanup that would have been done by STOP RUN is dependent on various installation defaults, primarily the RTEREUS run-time option. Check with your technical staff before standardizing on this approach.)

3. **EXIT PROGRAM.** The third option is the EXIT PROGRAM statement, which performs differently depending on whether it is executed from within a main program or from within a subprogram. If executed in a CALLed subprogram, it functions as GOBACK. If executed in a main program, it is ignored. Note: An EXIT PROGRAM statement is implicitly defined at the end of every COBOL program; therefore, if the last statement in a program falls through to the next available statement, an EXIT PROGRAM statement will be executed. This is avoided by PERFORMing paragraphs and not allowing fall-through logic (e.g., PERFORM THRU or GO TO). Most shops do not use EXIT PROGRAM; they use GOBACK instead. Because COBOL applications treat this statement differently depending on whether EXIT PROGRAM is in the highest level module or not, I don't recommend that you use it. Anytime a statement acts differently in different settings, it is only a matter of time before you are burned for using it incorrectly. This is a statement to avoid.

4. **EXEC CICS RETURN.** The fourth option applies to CICS programs. CICS provides a specific statement, EXEC CICS RETURN, to terminate run units in the CICS environment. CICS programs should use EXEC CICS RETURN in the highest level module when the run unit is finished and control is to be returned to CICS. Note: Under COBOL II, STOP RUN no longer crashes the CICS environment as it did in DOS/VS COBOL, but it lacks environmental cleanup functions of EXEC CICS RETURN, and if used by a subprogram violates structured programming concepts.

5. **ABEND.** The final option is to force an ABEND. While this isn't a clean technique, there may be times when you do not want the application to appear to have terminated with no errors. Any ABEND code you use should not be in the range of 1000 to 1999; those are used by the COBOL II run-time routines. Your shop may have some home-grown subprograms that do this, or for CICS, use the EXEC CICS ABEND

command. Otherwise, here is a sample assembler program, following COBOL linkage conventions:

This example produces a printed dump if there is a SYSLST JCL statement in the step. (NOTE: As with all other assembler examples in this book, this module is not reentrant.)

Sample assembler program to ABEND

```
ABEND     START  0
R1        EQU    1
R2        EQU    2
R12       EQU    12
R13       EQU    13
R14       EQU    14
R15       EQU    15
          USING  ABEND,R12
          SAVE   (14,12)
          LR     R12,R15
          LA     R14,SAVEAREA
          ST     R14,8(,R13)
          ST     R13,4(,R14)
          LR     R13,R14
          L      R1,0(,R1)
          LH     R2,0(,R1)
          DUMP   RC=(2)
SAVEAREA  DC     18F'0'
          END    ABEND
```

Here is an example of how the program would be CALLed. In this example, the User ABEND code is 0005.

```
05  WS1-ABEND-CODE   PIC  S9(4)  COMP  VALUE +5.
    .
    .

    CALL 'ABEND' USING WS1-ABEND-CODE
```

One benefit (drawback?) of this module is that, if it ABENDs, it does not activate any debugging function such as the FDUMP option. Be sure to assemble it with IBM's VSE/ESA Assembler product.

STOP RUN versus GOBACK.

Some people are confused by differences between STOP RUN and GOBACK. If a subprogram uses STOP RUN, it exits back *past* the program that CALLed it, defeating the concept of structured programming. (Note: it is also affected by RTEREUS run-time option.) Consider this example:

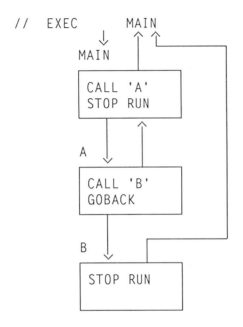

```
//  EXEC    MAIN
         ↓      ↑ ↑
       MAIN
      ┌───────────┐
      │ CALL 'A'  │
      │ STOP RUN  │
      └───────────┘

   A
      ┌───────────┐
      │ CALL 'B'  │
      │ GOBACK    │
      └───────────┘

   B
      ┌───────────┐
      │ STOP RUN  │
      └───────────┘
```

Module MAIN does a STOP RUN back to the system. That's proper. Module A executes a GOBACK to return control to the CALLing program. That's proper too. Module B executes a STOP RUN, bypassing all prior modules, creating a GO TO environment. This can cause structural problems in an application.

Some programmers writing in CICS code STOP RUN (in error) because they visualize their program as being the one that receives control from VSE. Actually, the program that receives control from VSE is the CICS control program, which in turn invokes the application program. A CICS application, then, is *always* a subprogram when viewed from VSE. If you're ever in doubt, GOBACK is safer than STOP RUN; it works with both main programs and with subprograms. CICS programs have a specific CICS statement, called EXEC RETURN, which should be used for the highest level module.

3.2.3. COBOL II to COBOL II

This is the simplest approach to a multi-module application. When all COBOL programs in a run unit are COBOL II, you may use all functions available from the COBOL II environment. This includes the ability to use reentrant code, use the SVA or GETVIS areas, and share data and files as documented later in this section. There are no special techniques to use here, but I mention it to encourage you to develop (or convert) all modules that constitute a run unit to COBOL

II to minimize any incompatibilities and to ensure you full access to COBOL II facilities. (Note: Mixing and matching is not allowed in CICS. All COBOL programs for a run unit must be either COBOL II or DOS/VS COBOL. See your technical support staff for more information.) See Figure 3.1 for graphic examples of sample structures.

3.2.4. Nested Programs in COBOL II

Nested programs were introduced in the previous chapter with examples. The primary advantage of using this approach is the extra features available to you in sharing data or files with other programs (explained later in this section). A secondary benefit is that the compiler sees the programs as one program, not several. This means the documentation from the compile process (e.g., cross-reference listings, program assembler code, or offset listings) is more thorough, and you never encounter the situation in which one of the modules has several different object copies and the Linkage Editor used the wrong copy. You also receive a listing from the compiler showing the hierarchy of your structure, which can be helpful to a maintenance programmer who is unfamiliar with the application.

From a structured programming point of view, the benefit of nested programs is that you can insert new subprograms quickly. One technique I encourage is putting subprograms in COPYbooks, which makes it simpler to share them across an application.

The debugging advantage is that there is only one true program. The added complexity of doing hex arithmetic to determine in which module the ABEND occurred is history.

From this discussion, you probably feel I think it is a good approach. I do. Having all the code together, getting one cross-reference listing, not having to pass data back and forth to subprograms, not having to remember to insert COPY statements for all the common items are big benefits to a maintenance staff. Let's look at an example.

If we have a new application that has been designed to use several subprograms and share a common file and table data, the traditional approach is to develop several COPYbooks, develop the various applications using the COPY statements, compile and link them, and then test to see if they communicate together. Whew! Here is a nested way.

Develop all common data and files and place them in one master COPYbook, something like this:

COPYbook   Name: PAYMAST

```
IDENTIFICATION DIVISION.
PROGRAM-ID.  PAYMAST.
ENVIRONMENT DIVISION.
```

```
INPUT-OUTPUT SECTION.
FILE-CONTROL.
    SELECT FD1-PAY-FILE  ASSIGN TO PAYFILE
       FILE STATUS IS PAY-STAT.
DATA DIVISION.
FILE SECTION.
FD FD1-PAY-FILE   GLOBAL
    .
    .
    .
WORKING-STORAGE SECTION.
01  WS1-PAY-WORK  GLOBAL.
    .
    .
    .
PROCEDURE DIVISION.
1.  CALL 'PAYRUN01'
    STOP RUN.
```

Now, all you need to do to use this program is to code

```
COPY  PAYMAST
ID DIVISION.
PROGRAM-ID.  PAYRUN01.
PROCEDURE DIVISION.
    .
    .
    .
END PROGRAM PAYRUN01.
```

This is much simpler than coding all the normal entries for a program and remembering which COPY statements to code. If the nested programs are to CALL each other in the same fashion, specify COMMON on their PROGRAM-ID statements.

The down side of nested programs is that you must recompile all of them even when you change only one of them. Whether this issue is more important than the other benefits is something for your shop to decide. Note to CICS users: A nested program, including all nested CALLed modules, must be processed as one unit by the CICS translator.

3.2.5. Assembler Language to COBOL II

Assembler language has special considerations because it is outside the COBOL environment. By COBOL environment, I am referring to the run-time modules that are invoked to provide integrity from one COBOL module to another. There are specific differences, depending on whether the assembler program is the CALLing or the CALLed module.

Assembler programs as subprograms.

It is no problem for COBOL programs to CALL assembler programs, provided that the assembler programs follow standard IBM linkage conventions. (See the following sample programs for an example.) If you are migrating a DOS/VS COBOL application to COBOL II and the application CALLs some assembler modules, those modules may need to be reassembled using IBM's VSE/ESA assembler product. Your shop probably has a technical staff already familiar with the coding adjustments, and actual coding of assembler is beyond the scope of this book.

Assembler programs as main programs.

First, let's identify the concern. COBOL II programs operate in a COBOL environment that is normally established when the COBOL main program is initiated. This environment stays active throughout the run unit, without needing to be reinitialized for entry/exit of each COBOL module. If an assembler program is the main program, the possibility exists that, while the programs will function properly, the run-time environment will be reinitialized frequently and affect performance. Using assembler language, therefore, can create a performance issue if it is the highest level module in the run unit. (Note: In a CICS environment, assembler programs may not CALL a COBOL program.) Improving the environmental performance is usually accomplished by ensuring the COBOL II run-time library remains OPEN between CALLs to COBOL modules (the LIBKEEP option) and by forcing the initialization of the COBOL II environment.

There are four ways of initializing the environment.

1. Use the RTEREUS run-time COBOL option (documented later in this chapter). This is probably your shop's default setting for non-CICS applications (RTEREUS is ignored by CICS). (The section on compiler options shows a way to determine what this setting is.) This is the easiest approach, for it requires nothing on your part. If RTEREUS is not your shop's default and does not conflict with your shop's standards, your systems programmers can establish the option for your particular program (more information on this facility, IGZEOPT, is in the section on compile options). Doing so requires a modification to your link-edit control statements (documented later in this chapter).

2. Use a COBOL program as the main program. Where RTEREUS is not the default and there are reasons not to establish it, this is the next simplest approach. By creating a small stub driver program, you cause the environment to be initialized for the run unit. It need only be

```
ID DIVISION.
PROGRAM-ID.  DRIVER.
PROCEDURE DIVISION.
1.   CALL 'assembler-program-name'
     STOP RUN.
```

The following chart depicts the possible structure.

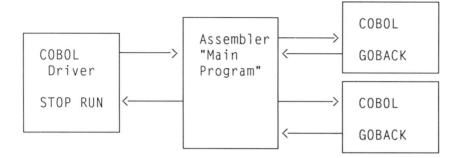

3. Modify the assembler program to initialize the run-time environment before the first CALL. IBM provides a module called IGZERRE that does this. (Note: This technique is not recommended for CICS applications.) The main assembler program would need to include these statements:

Prior to first CALL

```
LA    1,1
CALL  IGZERRE
```

After **last** CALL:

```
LA    1,2
CALL  IGZERRE
```

Simple assembler program to CALL a COBOL module

This is a simple program that initializes the COBOL environment and CALLs a program called MAINPROG.

```
          TITLE  'CALL COBOL subprogram and Initialize '
CALLCOB   START  0
          BALR   12,0
          USING  *,12
          LA     13,SAVEAREA
          LR     3,1
          LA     1,1               A '1' in register 1 will
          CALL   IGZERRE                initialize environment
          LTR    15,15
          BZ     OKAY
          WTO    'IGZERRE Error',ROUTCDE=(11)
```

```
              B        QUIT
    OKAY      LR       1,3
              CALL     COBPROG       Call PROGRAM-ID of 'COBPROG'
              LA       1,2           A '2' in register 1 will
              CALL     IGZERRE          terminate environment
              LTR      15,15
              BZ       QUIT
              WTO      'IGZERRE Error',ROUTCDE=(11)
    QUIT      EOJ
    SAVEAREA  DC       18F'0'
              END      CALLCOB
```

For more information on parameter lists for IGZERRE, see *IBM COBOL II Application Programming Guide* (Chapter 9, "Related Publications").

4. Use the DOS/VS COBOL assembler interface ILBDSET0 instead of IGZERRE. I include this because you might encounter CALLs to that module in your current assembler programs. If so, that module is still supported by IBM, so there is no need to change it, other than relinking the phase to INCLUDE the COBOL II module IGZEBST (for RES) or IGZENRI (for NORES). Otherwise, it will continue to initialize the DOS/VS COBOL environment, not the COBOL II environment.

STOP RUN considerations when CALLed by an assembler program.

As stated elsewhere in this book, subprograms should use GOBACK to return control to the CALLing program. That applies here, too, even if the CALLing program is written in assembler. However, there may be a reason you want to use STOP RUN at the highest level COBOL program and still treat it as a subprogram. The problem you face is that the STOP RUN statement normally returns control to either the program that CALLed the program that initiated the environment or to VSE, if VSE initiated the environment. To get around this, you need an additional assembler program between the high-level assembler program and your program. This will make it appear that the CALLing assembler and the CALLed COBOL program are communicating directly. (You also face *severe performance problems* if the COBOL program is CALLed frequently, since it must be reinitialized each time because STOP RUN does resource cleanup.)

Anyway, assuming you're determined, here is a sample program that can be tucked between the assembler main program and your COBOL main program. This example assumes the RTEREUS option is invoked. If not, use the previous example that included CALLs to IGZERRE. This works, but I don't recommend it. Here is the flow, showing both STOP RUN processing and GOBACK processing:

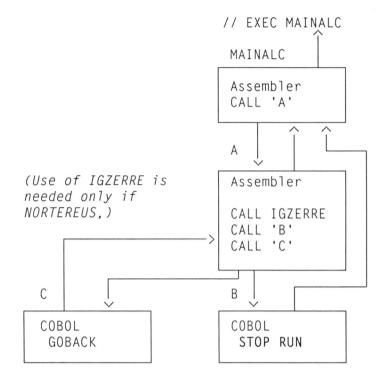

Sample program to CALL COBOL program without initialization

```
          TITLE  'CALL COBOL Main Program '
CALLMAIN  START  0
          SAVE   (14,12)
          USING  CALLMAIN,12
          LR     11,13
          LR     12,15
          LA     13,SAVEAREA
          ST     13,8(0,11)
          ST     11,4(0,13)
          CALL   MAINPROG          Call PROGRAM-ID of MAINPROG
          L      13,SAVEAREA+4
          RETURN (14,12),RC=(15)
SAVEAREA  DC     18F'0'
          END    CALLMAIN
```

The COBOL program in the previous diagram, module B, returns control at STOP RUN, not to module A that CALLed it but to MAINALC, the program that CALLed the program that CALLed B. The complexity of this solution may cause you to rethink why you prefer STOP RUN. As I mentioned earlier, GOBACK eliminates the need for the intermediate program.

All the considerations for assembler language are not addressed here. My goal is merely to make you aware of issues to address if you are developing or maintaining such an application. If you are developing COBOL applications with no non-COBOL modules, your shop's run-time environment considerations have already been addressed by your technical staff.

This treatment of the topic is elementary at best. If your shop is heavily into assembler interfaces, the complexities could fill several books. Check with your technical support staff for more assistance and direction before using these sample programs. Using non-COBOL languages with COBOL, especially if CICS is involved, often requires involvement and tuning considerations that are beyond this book.

3.2.6.   COBOL II to DOS/VS COBOL

If you are maintaining an application in which some of the modules in a run unit have been migrated to COBOL II while others remain in DOS/VS COBOL, you have some special considerations. You should view a mixed environment as a temporary approach, since there is performance degradation when both COBOL versions are used. First, if it is a CICS transaction, either keep all modules DOS/VS COBOL or convert them all to COBOL II. A mixed approach is not supported in CICS (other than by EXEC CICS LINK, which introduces its own performance degradation).

Since DOS/VS COBOL modules may not reside in SVA, you must use appropriate COBOL II compile options for downward compatibility to the DOS/VS COBOL module. The compile option is NORENT and the structure *must* be a static CALL. (See the topic Static and Dynamic CALLs in this section for more information.) See Figure 3.1 for a depiction of some (not all) sample COBOL II-to-DOS/VS COBOL structures and COBOL II-to-COBOL II structures.

In the examples in Figure 3.1, the data areas (WORKING STORAGE) will be allocated in GETVIS for RENT phases. The other phases have the data areas within the object module by specifying NORENT. No changes are needed for an DOS/VS COBOL module if it was compiled with RES and the appropriate CALL statement. Of the three structures, only the one with RENT (in SVA) offers any COBOL II VSCR advantages. Notice that the RES option does not by itself dictate a structure.

If the DOS/VS COBOL program were compiled with NORES, you would have one or more additional steps, since my assumption is that you will want to use RES for all COBOL II programs. (COBOL II requires that all modules in a run unit share the same RES option.) Your choices are

1. Convert the DOS/VS COBOL program to COBOL II for a complete solution (all modules in run unit are COBOL II).

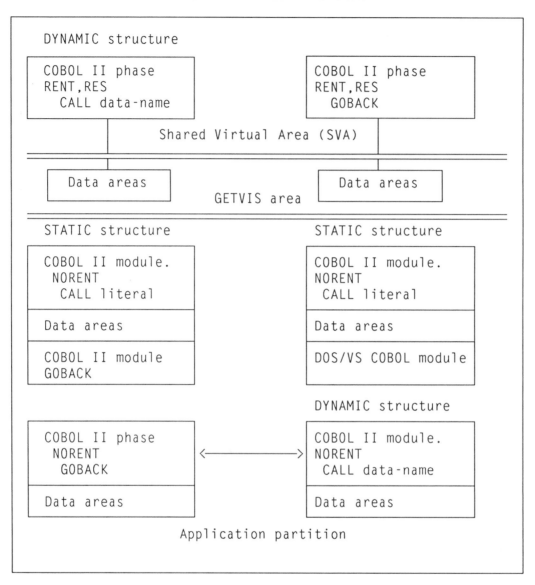

Figure 3.1. COBOL II and DOS/VS COBOL structures.

2. Recompile and link the DOS/VS COBOL program with the DOS/VS COBOL compiler, specifying RES, for a temporary solution.
3. Compile the COBOL II program with NORES for a temporary solution. (You give up the performance opportunities provided by VSE/ESA, since NORES requires NORENT.) This requires step 4 also.
4. If the DOS/VS COBOL program is not to be converted or recompiled with RES, ensure that during the link-edit process all DOS/VS COBOL ver-

sions of the ILBDxxxx modules are replaced by their equivalent modules from the COBOL II subroutine library. (See the section Creating a Phase for more information on link-editing.) This step can be combined with step 3 for a NORES environment or with step 5 for a mixed environment.

5. If your choices from the above options cause you to have a mixed environment (a combination of RES and NORES), use the COBOL II run-time option MIXRES until the DOS/VS COBOL modules have been converted.

If your choices included option 5 (MIXRES), you must ensure that MIXRES is specified as a run-time option. The section on compile options explains how to determine your shop default options. My guess is that it is not set to MIXRES. If it is not, you must ask your systems programming staff to assemble a special run-time module for you (IGZEOPT). You must explicitly include the IGZEOPT module in the link-edit process for any phases in the run unit that contain the NORES option. See the section Specifying COBOL II Options in this chapter for more information.

After reading this information, I hope you agree that converting the DOS/VS COBOL applications to COBOL II is the preferred approach if it is at all possible. The effort to create a coexisting environment of COBOL II and DOS/VS COBOL modules will almost always be more costly than migrating the older programs to COBOL II and getting it finished.

3.2.7. Using RETURN-CODE

Every time a program returns control to a CALLing module, a return code is passed back to the CALLing module. At the highest level, this return code is made available to VSE. With the ON and IF JCL statements (e.g., // ON $RC<8 CONTINUE, // IF $RC>7 THEN), this value can be tested. This technique may also be used within applications (even those with a mix of assembler and COBOL II, or COBOL II and DOS/VS COBOL). This is because in every COBOL program there is a special register called RETURN-CODE. It is initialized to zero at program initiation, and the value is updated following each CALL statement. RETURN-CODE is implicitly defined as PIC S9(4) COMP VALUE ZERO. (Note: Prior to COBOL II, this was not allowed for CICS applications. Since EXEC CICS commands affect the RETURN-CODE, you need to test or change its value with this in mind.)

Using this special register requires no special coding on your part. What it does require is a disciplined set of values to be used within your application. The most widely known set of disciplined values are those developed by IBM for use by its language processors and utility programs. For example, we all know that

- A return code of 0 means "no errors."
- A return code of 4 means "minor warnings."
- A return code of 16 means "serious error."

This is not magic. It just proves that when everyone on a project agrees to use certain values, communication improves. To send a value in RETURN-CODE to a CALLing module, all you need do is code:

In subprogram

```
MOVE numeric-literal  to RETURN-CODE
GOBACK
```

In CALLing program

```
CALL 'subprogram'  ...
IF RETURN-CODE = numeric-literal...
      .
      .     insert appropriate processing here
      .
```

In the previous example, the CALLing module must also include logic to set the value of RETURN-CODE before returning control via GOBACK or STOP RUN. Otherwise, it will contain the last value returned.

3.2.8.   Sharing Files Among Modules

Sometimes, it is desirable to have several modules in an application have access to a file. I don't recommend it. I prefer to keep tighter control on the read/write process. However, I recognize the need for it, since there are probably situations when good functional decomposition dictates it. There are different considerations for file sharing, one for assembler programs and two others for COBOL II programs.

Sharing files with assembler programs.

You have very little control here and there is the (mostly theoretical) possibility that IBM will redo the format of the Data Control Block. Anyway, if the file is SAM, you can share it with an assembler program by specifying the file name in the CALL statement. (DON'T try this with COBOL subprograms.) The format is

```
CALL 'program-name" USING fd-name
```

This passes the address of the I/O control block to the assembler program. This can work if there is clear agreement on which program OPENs, CLOSEs, READs, and WRITEs to the file. The file must be OPENed prior to the CALL.

Sharing files with COBOL II programs.

There are two ways to share files with other COBOL II programs. One technique works with nested program structures and one with traditional, separately compiled structures. Since a program can have both nested modules and separately compiled modules, the two techniques may appear in a single run unit. (If any terms in this topic are unfamiliar, reread the sections on nested programs and on GLOBAL and EXTERNAL data elements in Chapter 2.) In both applicable cases, the logical processing of the file must not be violated. The options presented still require, for example, that the shared file be OPENed prior to issuing a READ to it.

For nested programs

In a nested program, use the GLOBAL clause on the FD, e.g.,

```
FD   FD2-PAYROLL-MASTER  GLOBAL
     RECORD CONTAINS 100 CHARACTERS.
01   FD2-PAYROLL-REC    PIC X(100).
```

If this is specified in an outer program, all contained programs (both directly and indirectly) can access the file just as if the FD appeared in each contained program. Any program within the subset may issue any valid I/O statement for the file and has access to the 01-level entry for it, as well.

For separate programs

For separate programs, each participating program must have a common DATA DIVISION entry for the shared files and shared I/O areas. The FD entry must be similar to this:

```
FD   FD2-PAYROLL-MASTER  EXTERNAL
     RECORD CONTAINS 100 CHARACTERS.
01   FD2-PAYROLL-REC    PIC X(100).
```

The file description entries must be an *exact match*, even to the spelling. This is best done by COPYbook entries. There are examples of this in the topic GLOBAL and EXTERNAL Data Elements in Chapter 2.

3.2.9.   Sharing Data Among COBOL II Modules

Sharing data other than files has many options, all of which can be combined with file sharing techniques if desired. Let's start with the simplest and proceed to the more complex:

Pass selected data via CALL BY REFERENCE statement.

This is the most common approach to sharing data, as a CALL statement uses by default the BY REFERENCE format. Until COBOL II, this was the only way to pass data to another program, so I encourage you to also consider the other options. In this approach, the original data exists within the CALLing module and it makes the data available to the CALLed module with something like:

```
CALL 'proga' USING data-name
```

Actually, this passes not the data, but *addressability* to the data, to the CALLed program. The CALLed program can not only reference the data, but it can change it as well. This approach is well documented, as the CALLed program must establish a LINKAGE SECTION to describe all data being passed from the CALLing program. The problem with this approach is when the two programs have different definitions of the data. Consider:

CALLing module

```
01   WS1-REC        PIC X(24).
01   WS2-REC        PIC X(80).

     CALL 'SUBA' USING WS1-REC
```

CALLed module

```
LINKAGE SECTION.
01   WORK-REC       PIC X(50).

PROCEDURE DIVISION USING WORK-REC.
100-PROCESS.
    MOVE ZEROS TO WORK-REC
    GOBACK.
```

Examine what happens in this simple example. The CALLing program passes addressability of WS1-REC to SUBA. The CALLed subprogram uses this addressability to address, not the intended 24-byte record, but the 24-byte record PLUS 26 bytes of WS2-REC in the CALLing program. This happens because the PIC clauses have different values. By moving zeros to WORK-REC, both WS1-REC and much of WS2-REC are set to zeros.

This is not untypical if the CALL statement is used and is a major cause for problems created by CALL statements. My recommendation is to use COPYbooks for passed data items and to have walk-throughs of all CALL statements and associated ENTRY or PROCEDURE DIVISION USING statements. (Although I included reference to the ENTRY statement, I don't recommend it. It gives more than one entry point to a COBOL program, a violation of structured programming rules. If you're thinking it is required, such as for DL/1 programs, it is not.)

Passing selected data via CALL BY CONTENT statement.

Similar to the previous example, this approach is desirable if your program must pass selected data to another program, but the other program has no need to update the data. It also ensures some added control. The downside is that there is additional overhead, since the system makes a copy of the data for the CALLed program. The format is

```
CALL 'suba' USING BY CONTENT  data-name
```

With this format, the subprogram can change the data, but doing so does not change the data in the CALLing program and the potential problem in the previous example is avoided. This format, BY CONTENT, may be mixed with the previous approach, BY REFERENCE, i.e., passing some fields by reference and others by content.

Passing variable selected data by CALL statement.

This technique may be combined with either of the two previous examples. This approach is useful if the data being passed to may have a varying length. The format requires the clause BY CONTENT LENGTH OF data-name. A sample CALL:

```
CALL 'suba' USING WS1-WORK
            BY CONTENT LENGTH OF WS1-WORK.
```

The subprogram must be prepared to receive two data items:

```
LINKAGE SECTION.
01  LS-WORK.
        .

        .

01  LS-LENGTH      PIC S9(9)   COMP.
PROCEDURE DIVISION USING LS-WORK  LS-LENGTH.
```

The procedural code of the subprogram must include logic to interrogate LS-LENGTH and act appropriately according to application specifications.

Sharing data areas within a nested program.

This technique uses the GLOBAL clause discussed in Chapter 2 for files. If you use my earlier recommendation to use GLOBAL file structures, this complements the approach, making a complete set of data accessible from one program or COPYbook. The format applies to 01-level entries in WORKING-STORAGE. The format is

```
01 data-name  GLOBAL.
   05  ...
      .
      .
```

GLOBAL may be combined with EXTERNAL, if desired.

Sharing data areas externally.

This technique uses the EXTERNAL clause we discussed in Chapter 2. The advantage is that there is no need to pass data with the CALL statement, which can be a plus if specifications change for an application. The clause may only be used at the 01-level in WORKING-STORAGE. The format is

```
01 data-name  EXTERNAL.
   05  ...
      .
      .
```

Caution: With EXTERNAL, the generated run-time code allocates a new data area if the EXTERNAL element cannot be located. (Remember, even the spelling must match. This is why I recommend COPYbooks for all such elements.) If, for example, a data item were spelled differently in a subprogram, the CALLed subprogram would access a new, uninitialized data area (VALUE clause isn't allowed for EXTERNAL) instead of the intended EXTERNAL data area. This causes no warning message to occur, as COBOL II cannot detect what the spelling should have been. This may or may not cause an ABEND, depending on how the program accesses the data. Finally, any indexes specified in an INDEXED BY clause are treated as local, not as EXTERNAL.

Accessing data within a CALLed subprogram.

I include this technique not because I anticipate frequent use of it, but to demonstrate that it is possible. This technique is appropriate if there are data areas in a CALLed subprogram that the CALLing program wishes to access or you have decided that the data should not be EXTERNAL. Before COBOL II, this was impossible to do.

The technique is to establish a POINTER element in the CALLing program and have the CALLed program return the proper address for it. We accomplish this by using a combination of the POINTER data element and the SET statement with the ADDRESS OF clause. In the following example, note that the two SET statements are slightly different.

In this example, there are three programs.

1. MAINPROG, which desires direct addressability to the table in SUBPROG called PREM-TABLE. It CALLs SUBPROG, passing it the POINTER item in which the address of the PREM-TABLE is to be stored.

2. SUBPROG, which is CALLed by MAINPROG and contains a premium table that needs to be shared. It CALLs SETADDR, passing it PREM-TABLE and a data element in which to receive the address.

3. SETADDR, a necessary subprogram to establish the address of PREM-TABLE in SUBPROG. This process *must* be done in a separate program because the ADDRESS OF value exists **only** for entries in the LINKAGE SECTION. Since PREM-TABLE is in WORKING-STORAGE for SUBPROG, a third subprogram was needed. This program, upon receiving control from SUBPROG, uses the SET statement to store the address of PREM-TABLE.

The structure:

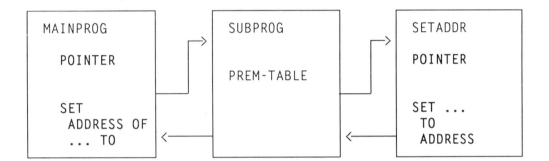

The code:

```
TITLE 'Main Program'
IDENTIFICATION DIVISION.
PROGRAM-ID.  MAINPROG.
DATA DIVISION.
WORKING-STORAGE SECTION.
01  WS1-WORK                      POINTER.
LINKAGE SECTION.
01  SUBPROG-AREA.
    05  SUBPROG-DATA-ITEM         PIC X(5) OCCURS 100.

PROCEDURE DIVISION.
1.
    CALL 'SUBPROG' USING WS1-WORK
    SET ADDRESS OF SUBPROG-AREA TO WS1-WORK

    ·   MAINPROG may now access the area, SUBPROG-AREA,
    ·   directly, without further CALLs to SUBPROG
    STOP RUN.
END PROGRAM MAINPROG.
```

```
TITLE 'Subprogram with sharable data area"
ID DIVISION.
PROGRAM-ID.  SUBPROG.
DATA DIVISION.
WORKING-STORAGE SECTION.
01  PREM-TABLE.
    05  PREM-TABLE-ITEM      PIC X(5)    OCCURS 100.
01  MY-POINTER               PIC S9(9)  COMP.
LINKAGE SECTION.
01  MAIN-POINTER             PIC S9(9)  COMP.

PROCEDURE DIVISION USING MAIN-POINTER.
1.
    CALL 'SETADDR' USING PREM-TABLE  MY-POINTER
    MOVE MY-POINTER TO MAIN-POINTER
    GOBACK.
       .
       .
END PROGRAM SUBPROG.

TITLE 'Subprogram that locates addresses'
ID DIVISION.
PROGRAM-ID. SETADDR.
DATA DIVISION.
WORKING-STORAGE SECTION.
LINKAGE SECTION.
01  LS-POINTER               POINTER.
01  LS-WORK.
    05                       PIC XXXXX.
PROCEDURE DIVISION USING LS-WORK  LS-POINTER.
1. SET LS-POINTER TO ADDRESS OF LS-WORK
    GOBACK.
END PROGRAM SETADDR.
```

Note that SETADDR did not need to properly define the layout of PREM-TABLE, since it only needs to SET its address. SETADDR could be used to SET the address of any data area in any program, making this a reusable program.

While this technique has power, remember that MAINPROG's access to the premium table is dependent on SUBPROG. For example, if SUBPROG were dynamically CALLed and later CANCELed, MAINPROG would ABEND if it attempted to access the area.

Receiving data via a JCL PARM.

This technique is only valid for a main program, executed from the JCL EXEC statement. (Exception: An assembler main program could make this data available to subprograms.) Other than the previous example, this is the only time a main program has a LINKAGE SECTION.

First, we need an understanding of what a PARM is. Unlike other passed data, where we receive a pointer directly to the data, a PARM requires a different technique. The data from the PARM= parameter on the EXEC statement is preceded by a half-word binary field containing the number of bytes of data in the PARM. This data element is dynamically allocated and any attempt to access a larger PARM than that provided results in an ABEND (usually 0C4). For example, if we code

```
//   EXEC progid,PARM='07/24/91'
```

the data passed will be

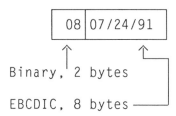

If we omitted the PARM, one is still allocated by VSE that looks like this:

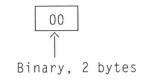

The main program would need something like this:

```
LINKAGE SECTION.
01   PARM-DATA.
     05   PARM-LENGTH    PIC S9(4)  COMP.
     05   PARM-CONTENT   PIC X(8).
PROCEDURE DIVISION USING PARM-DATA.
1.   IF PARM-LENGTH = 8
         MOVE PARM-CONTENT TO ...
     ELSE

... Reminder: If PARM-LENGTH had a value less than 8, there
would be a data error and a possible ABEND.
```

3.2.10. Static versus Dynamic CALL Structures

The choice of using static CALLs to modules versus using dynamic CALLs has many elements. First, let's clarify the terms.

Static CALL: A static CALL is where the CALLing and the CALLed modules are bound together in the same phase during link-edit processing (see the section, Creating a Phase, for more information on the process).

Dynamic CALL: A dynamic CALL is one that is not resolved until the run unit needs to transfer control to the CALLed module. In this case, the CALLing and the CALLed modules are each processed separately by the Linkage Editor. (See the section CICS-DL/1-SQL/DS Issues for applicability in CICS.)

You can combine the two, using both static and dynamic CALLs within a run unit.

Considerations of a static CALL.

Static CALLs are used at most shops. When you do static CALLs, you can improve the performance of your application. This is because all programs, being in the same phase, are loaded into memory together. (Note: The jury is still out on this. Some systems performance experts believe that, while static CALLs improve a single application, dynamic CALLs are better for overall computer throughput.)

An additional benefit is that all modules are located and their references resolved during the link-edit process. Assuming you check your listings from the Linkage Editor, you are assured that all modules are in place. Finding that a module is not available is preferable now, rather than during run-time when you might ABEND. Having a complete listing of all modules of the application can also be useful documentation.

If the Linkage Editor is not able to locate a requested module, it can still finish creating the phase (depending on the options used), but it prints a warning message about the missing module. The phase will execute properly *unless* the logic causes it to CALL the missing module. If that occurs, you will normally get an 0C1 ABEND, with a PSW (Program Status Word) showing the address of the ABEND somewhere around 00000004. This occurs because the CALL transferred control to location zero and VSE attempts to locate the next sequential instruction from zero. Some programmers attempt to correct this situation by changing the LIBDEF PHASE because "the system didn't find the needed module." Don't fall into this trap. Remember, a static CALL must be resolved at link-edit time, not at run-time. (The LIBDEF technique is valid, however, for dynamic CALLs.)

Static CALLs may be done by coding (full syntax not shown):

```
CALL 'literal'
```

where 'literal' is the PROGRAM-ID if the desired program and you have specified NODYNAM as a compile option.

Considerations of a dynamic CALL.

Dynamic CALLs are the most flexible because you control them at run-time, not at link-edit time. Their use also introduces more complexity into the application logic. Because each module is a separate phase, every application that uses it will get the same version, a definite plus if a program is used by several applications. With static CALLs, all affected modules need to relink-edit when changes are made. In a dynamic CALL, no relinks of all modules are needed.

An additional benefit, depending on your shop's system environment, is that you can control memory requirements depending on which modules are needed. For example, if you have a large module that is rarely needed, it doesn't take up memory during the times it isn't used.

Since dynamic CALLs are resolved at the time the CALL is executed in the run unit, the Linkage Editor is unaware of the need for the module. That means the link-edit listing that is so useful for static CALLs has little use here. More important for dynamic CALLs is to know in which sublibraries the needed modules are stored. With this information, you can code the proper entries in a LIBDEF PHASE JCL statement. (Reminder: VSE will search the system sublibraries after searching the sublibraries in the LIBDEF statement.)

If, at run-time, a needed module is not located, you will receive an ABEND message, including a message with the name of the needed module (i.e, you do not need to read the dump to solve this). You will also ABEND if the module is too big to fit into memory. These problems are corrected by locating the appropriate phase sublibrary and making corrections to your LIBDEF JCL statement or by scheduling your application in a larger partition. There is no need to recompile or to relink-edit. (Note: For dynamic CALLs, you can protect against these ABENDS by using the ON EXCEPTION or NOT ON EXCEPTION clauses of the CALL statement. For more information, see the previous chapter.)

Earlier I mentioned that dynamic structures introduce complexity. That occurs because the application may now have both application logic in it and memory management logic in it. For example, while the CALL statement causes a dynamic module to be loaded into memory and given control, the CANCEL statement is used to release it from memory. A program CALLed again after being CANCELed will be in its initial state, with no saved values. Statements such as

```
CALL program-a USING data-namea
ON EXCEPTION
    CANCEL program-b
    CALL program-a USING data-namea
    END-CALL
END-CALL
```

can get you into trouble if CANCELing program-b did not free up sufficient memory or wasn't even in memory. These techniques can work well, but keep the added complexity of such techniques in mind.

An optional way to CANCEL a program is to define the program with the INITIAL clause on the PROGRAM-ID statement. For example,

```
PROGRAM-ID.  program-name  INITIAL.
```

This specifies that the program must be CALLed in its initial state. If the program is also CALLed dynamically, it is CANCELed when the GOBACK is executed. Note: This can have severe performance degradation. If a module requires reloading each time it is called, it requires electro-mechanical processes (to the DASD phase sublibrary) that are much slower than electronic processes. My recommendation when a program must always be in its initial state is to write the procedural logic to initialize all work areas each time the program is entered.

Dynamic CALLs are done by coding:

```
CALL 'literal'
```

where 'literal' is the PROGRAM-ID of the desired program and you have specified DYNAM as a compile option

or

```
CALL data-name
```

where *data-name* is a data element of PIC X(8), containing the name of the desired program. The setting of DYNAM or NODYNAM has no bearing on this syntax. This is the only acceptable format for dynamic CALLs in CICS.

As a final comment on managing dynamic CALLs, remember that the affected phases must share appropriate attributes. This is normally done by using the same RENT and RES compile-time options. Otherwise, you can get some weird ABENDs because the modules won't be able to interface to each other correctly. (For more information, see the sections Creating a Phase and Specifying COBOL II Options.)

Converting a static CALL to a dynamic CALL.

Creating a dynamic structure once required that the decision be made prior to compiling the affected programs. Now, with COBOL II, you can convert a run unit with static CALL statements to one with dynamic CALLs. While you should recompile and relink programs to create a dynamic CALL structure when possible, the conversion approach is still an option (normally desired if source code is not accessible). The "conversion" is done by supplying an intermediate module between the CALLing program and the dynamically CALLed programs.

To convert a structure, IBM provides a module called IGZBRDGV. This is an assembler language macro program that, when supplied with the proper parameters, generates an object module with ENTRY points for the names of the modules you want to be dynamically CALLed. The syntax for the macro is

```
name    IGZBRDGV  ENTNMES=(prog1,prog2,...progn)
```

where

> name = the name you assign to the intermediate module (This can be any valid 8-character CSECT name.)
>
> proga though progn = names of the phases that you want to dynamically CALL (These names must already appear within the CALLing program as CALL 'literal.')

Using the macro will require that you get assistance from your systems programmers. (They usually control access to IBM-supplied software and use of assembler macros.) The steps required are

1. Run IGZBRDGV to create the interface module.
2. With the Linkage Editor, create phases of all CALLed programs that are to be dynamically CALLed.
3. With the Linkage Editor, create a phase consisting of the CALLing module and the IGZBRDGV-created module.

3.3. DEFINING, INITIALIZING, AND USING DATA AREAS

One of the main ways in which the professional programmer is distinguished from the novice programmer is the way in which data areas are defined and accessed. The approach used can affect memory allocation, the number of instructions generated, run-time efficiency, and program readability. Each of those topics is addressed in the following material.

3.3.1. Efficiencies in Data Definitions

This topic applies to two categories: memory efficiency and processing efficiency. Some of the guidelines have changed since DOS/VS COBOL, especially for binary (COMP) data items. This section concentrates on the popular data formats: alphanumeric, packed-decimal, zoned decimal, and binary, with implications for virtual storage allocation. While floating point data (COMP-2) does receive limited use, it is not addressed in this book.

Memory efficiency.

With the amount of memory available in mainframes today, attaining memory efficiency may not seem to be an issue anymore. While this is true for small, independent applications, it remains an issue for larger, corporate systems. The following topics might assist you.

Virtual storage constraint relief. The term *Virtual Storage Constraint Relief* (VSCR) refers to the process of reallocating memory from problem partitions into the SVA and GETVIS areas. As mainframes increase memory, the increase will be in this address space, and applications that don't take advantage of it will not benefit from the potential improvement. Realizing VSCR for an application includes allocation of both program memory and data memory. As this material is covered in more depth in specific topics, the following is a brief summary of that information.

Allocation of memory for programs. Whether or not a program is loaded in the SVA area is dependent on the RENT compile option and the Linkage Editor PHASE statement parameters. All program modules in a phase must have RENT for this to work. NORENT is primarily for compatibility with older programs. NORES also affects memory use, since it requires all COBOL II run-time modules to share the partition with the application code. See the sections Module Structures and Creating a Phase for more information. (See Figure 3.1 for an example of memory use.)

Allocation of memory for data. Data areas are allocated in the GETVIS area if RENT is specified. (The use of the DATA(31) compile option has no meaning in VSE, but ensures upward compatibility at the object code level with MVS/XA and MVS/ESA.) With RENT, the DATA DIVISION is separate from the phase, but it is within the phase for NORENT. (See Figure 3.1 for an example of memory use.)

Alignment. First, remember that eight (8) bytes are the minimum allocated to 01-level entries (double-word alignment). Thus,

```
01  REC-A    PIC X.
01  REC-B    PIC X.
```

requires 16 bytes, not 2. That is why I recommend that switches and accumulators be combined into common 01-level items, not only to improve readability, but also to reduce unnecessary memory use.

Packed-decimal field sizes. Another concern is the number of bytes allocated for COMP-3 items. If you recall that packed-decimal items contain 1 decimal digit in the rightmost byte and 2 decimal digits in all other bytes, you will know that the right technique is to always specify an odd number for COMP-3 items. For example,

```
05  FLDA    PIC S9(4)  COMP-3   VALUE +5.
```

appears in memory as:

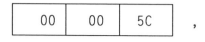

which is what would be assigned if the PIC had been S9(5). The difference is that additional instructions will be generated to truncate the high-order digit due to the even-numbered PIC clause.

Processing efficiency.

Although you may have been adept at determining processing efficiency for DOS/VS COBOL programs, you will find some differences here. How you define data elements, in addition to what compile options you select, will make a noticeable impact on your processing efficiency.

Processing efficiency by sign definitions.
With DOS/VS COBOL, my recommendation was to put S in the PIC clause for every numeric item. Now, I have a different recommendation, but let me first share some background information. COBOL II has the facility to be forgiving with signs (the new NUMPROC compile option), which means it can generate inefficient code on demand. Many shops, fearing that some of their programs potentially misuse signed data, opted for the least efficient NUMPROC option, NUMPROC(NOPFD), which is explained later. If you want to use the most efficient option, NUMPROC(PFD), you must establish data in the following format:

1. If the data will never be signed, omit the S in the PIC. For example, PIC 99. If such a field has a plus (C) or minus (D) sign, you will get incorrect results on IF NUMERIC.
2. If the data is always signed with C or D (never F), place the S in the PIC clause. (Note: A MOVE from a PIC 9 to a PIC S9 field will set the sign to C.)

If all your data qualifies, you may specify NUMPROC(PFD) for your compiles. If you are unsure about $C, D,$ and F, specify NUMPROC(MIG) and test the results. Here are some examples of the number of instructions generated, depending on the selected option:

```
05   DISP-1        PIC 999.
05   DISP-2        PIC S999.
05   DISP-3        PIC 999.
05   PACKED-1      PIC S9(15)    COMP-3.
05   PACKED-2      PIC S9(15)    COMP-3.
```

This table lists the number of instructions generated for each compile option for these example statements.

MIG	NO PFD	PFD	
3	3	2	MOVE DISP-1 TO DISP-2
2	2	2	MOVE DISP-2 TO DISP-1
2	2	1	MOVE DISP-1 TO DISP-3
4	6*	4	ADD 1 TO DISP-1
5	7*	5	ADD DISP-1 TO DISP-2
3	4*	3	COMPUTE PACKED-1 = PACKED-1 * PACKED-2

The items in the NOPFD column with * included a CALL to a COBOL II run-time subroutine for additional validation and adjustment.

This table may indicate that MIG and PFD are alike because they generate the same number of instructions in these few examples. Don't assume this will occur, as these examples demonstrate only a few situations, and the choice of these options also affects how conditional statements are processed (e.g., IF NUMERIC, IF POSITIVE). For information on this subject, see the section Handling Conditional Statements in this chapter.

Processing efficiency considerations with binary data. This was an easy decision to make with DOS/VS COBOL. Using DOS/VS COBOL, you had a compile option choice of TRUNC or NOTRUNC. With COBOL II, this option is replaced by TRUNC(BIN), TRUNC(STD), or TRUNC(OPT). One IBM manual states that TRUNC(BIN) is the equivalent of NOTRUNC. Another IBM manual states that TRUNC(OPT) is the equivalent of NOTRUNC. Unfortunately, both are correct. In DOS/VS COBOL, NOTRUNC caused the data to be stored as a full or half-word (not truncated) and *also* generated the least amount of code.

In COBOL II, the process of generating the most efficient code and the process of not truncating data have been separated into two different compile options. If you use binary arithmetic for efficiency and do not have a concern for truncation, use TRUNC(OPT). If you use binary arithmetic to store the maximum number of bits in the half or full-word, use TRUNC(BIN). Here are some examples of the instructions generated for different options.

```
05  BIN-F1          PIC S9(9)   COMP.
05  BIN-F2          PIC S9(9)   COMP.
05  BIN-H1          PIC S9(4)   COMP.
05  BIN-H2          PIC S9(4)   COMP.
05  BIN-F3          PIC S9(6)   COMP.
05  BIN-F4          PIC S9(6)   COMP.
```

This table lists the number of instructions generated for each compile option for these example statements.

BIN	STD	OPT
17	1	1
4	1	1
19	4	3
19	6	3
20	11	10
7	6	3
11*	4	3

```
MOVE BIN-F1 TO BIN-F2
MOVE BIN-H1 TO BIN-H2
COMPUTE BIN-F1 = BIN-F1  * BIN-F2
COMPUTE BIN-H1 = BIN-H1  * BIN-H2
ADD BIN-F1 TO BIN-F2
ADD BIN-H1 TO BIN-H2
COMPUTE BIN-F3 = BIN-F3  * BIN-F4
```

The BIN option generated 11 instructions, in addition to a CALL to a COBOL II run-time subprogram for further data validity.

From this data, there are clearly performance differences. If you rarely use COMP data, the choice of compile options for your applications may not be critical, but if your applications require COMP data, you should be sensitive to the performance implications.

Processing efficiency considerations for field sizes. When considering data efficiencies, we often think only of the arithmetic statements. Too often over-looked is the importance of field sizes where the MOVE instruction is used. For example, if the data types, sizes, and signs match, you will get more efficient data moves than if they are different. A small point, but significant if your application does a lot of MOVE instructions.

3.3.2. Coding Literals

Literals may be numeric, nonnumeric, or hexadecimal. I encourage removing as many literals from the procedural code as possible, except for simple situations, such as where a zero or one is obvious (e.g., . . . VARYING FROM 1 BY 1 UNTIL . . .). Here is a brief summary of common literal usage.

Numeric literals.

Length from 1 to 18 decimal digits, sign is optional, as is a decimal point. Number is assumed positive if sign is omitted.

Nonnumeric literals.

Length from 1 to 160 bytes, any EBCDIC character combination, enclosed in quotes or apostrophes, depending on choice of APOST compile option. If a quote or apostrophe must appear within the literal, it must occur twice, as in 'DON''T GET CONFUSED'.

Hexadecimal literals.

Length from 2 to 320 hexadecimal digits (1 to 160 bytes), enclosed in quotes/ apostrophes (depending on choice of compile options) and preceded by X, as in X'C8C5E7', which occupies 3 bytes, and in EBCDIC is 'HEX'.

3.3.3. Defining a Table

If tables are new to you, you might consider reading the first four subtopics here; they provide additional information on tables. This topic will explain how to define a table in WORKING-STORAGE. You may have heard terms such as two dimensional, three dimensional, or even four dimensional. Let's simplify those terms. The dimensions for a table are the number of search arguments that must be used to get a result. We'll take several examples to demonstrate this.

One-dimensional tables.

A one-dimensional table consisting of a single element type is merely a list. If unordered, I call it a laundry list, because the only way to find something is to read every item. This approach is useful if you have data that must be validated and the validation itself affects the logic. For example, if you know one of your company's products is legal in 10 states and not legal in 40, then a purchase order from any of the 40 states should not be processed. To validate purchase orders, a table such as this one might be defined using these sample two-character state codes:

```
01   LEGAL-TABLE-ENTRIES.
     05      PIC X(22)
        VALUE 'ALAZCOFLIDKSMAMONYOHZZ'.
01   LEGAL-TABLE REDEFINES LEGAL-TABLE-ENTRIES.
     05   VALID-STATE   PIC XX, OCCURS 11.
```

Or, you could code this:

```
01   LEGAL-TABLE-ENTRIES.
     05      PIC XX        VALUE 'AL'.
     05      PIC XX        VALUE 'AZ'.
     05      PIC XX        VALUE 'CO'.
     05      PIC XX        VALUE 'FL'.
       .
       .
     05      PIC XX        VALUE 'ZZ'.
01   LEGAL-TABLE REDEFINES LEGAL-TABLE-ENTRIES.
     05   VALID-STATE   PIC XX, OCCURS 11.
```

Notice how the redefinition does not need to follow the PIC clause format as long as it is faithful to the number of bytes represented. There is an eleventh entry here, ZZ (although any unique code would do). The purpose of including an extra entry for tables is to allow better procedural control. For example, a control field, such as ZZ, is for tables in which the last entry can't be otherwise predicted or in which the size of the table is subject to frequent change (e.g., using the previous example, the number of states in which the product is legal will probably change periodically).

Another type of one-dimensional table contains multiple data element types, usually a search element and a data component. For example, an insurance company might have a table by age, containing premium amounts. That could be shown:

```
01   PREM-TABLE.
     05   PREM-ENTRY    OCCURS 99   TIMES
                                    ASCENDING KEY IS PREM-AGE
                                    INDEXED BY AGE-INDX.
          10  PREM-AGE           PIC 99.
          10  PREM-MALE          PIC S9(5)V99   COMP-3.
          10  PREM-FEMALE        PIC S9(5)V99   COMP-3.
```

This table has more depth and structure than the previous one. Also, whereas the previous table only needed to be searched for a match to make processing decisions, that isn't true of this one. Searching the table presents different amounts to charge for the insurance policy. The ASCENDING KEY clause specifies that this table must be in ascending order by age *if* a SEARCH statement is used to process against it (covered in the topic Improving Table Searches). The INDEXED BY clause specifies an index-name. This is covered in the topic on subscripting. Searching the previous table requires knowledge of one variable: age.

Two-dimensional tables.

A two-dimensional table is a one-dimensional table with an added dimension. Let's take the table in the previous topic and add a new dimension, a smoking/ nonsmoking premium. Searching this table will require two variables, age and smoker/nonsmoker status. Here is one way of constructing the table.

```
01   PREM-TABLE.
     05   PREM-ENTRY    OCCURS 99   TIMES
                                    ASCENDING KEY IS PREM-AGE
                                    INDEXED BY AGE-INDX.
          10   PREM-AGE          PIC 99.
          10   PREM-SMOKE-OPTION  OCCURS 2.
               15   PREM-MALE        PIC S9(5)V99   COMP-3.
               15   PREM-FEMALE      PIC S9(5)V99   COMP-3.
```

This structure gives us four premium amounts for each age: two for smokers (male and female) and two for nonsmokers. Whether adding an INDEXED BY clause for the smoking option will improve performance will be addressed in

Subscripting versus Indexing. Tables of any complexity are usually initialized by reading a file of data and inserting data elements in the appropriate table entry. The PERFORM VARYING statement is effective here.

3.3.4. Initializing a Table

Initializing a table can be done in a variety of ways, usually dependent on how frequently the data changes and how complex it is. Here are some examples,

Redefine the table and store variable data

```
01   LEGAL-TABLE-ENTRIES.
     05     PIC X(22)
       VALUE 'ALAZCOFLIDKSMAMONYOHZZ'.
01   LEGAL-TABLE REDEFINES LEGAL-TABLE-ENTRIES.
     05 VALID-STATE   PIC XX, OCCURS 11.
```

Initialize the table to spaces or zeroes with VALUE clause

```
01   LEGAL-TABLE.
     05 VALID-STATE   PIC XX   OCCURS 11   VALUE SPACES.

     Note: This feature did NOT exist in DOS/VS COBOL.
```

Initialize the table to spaces or zeros at run-time

```
INITIALIZE LEGAL-TABLE

     Note: INITIALIZE was reviewed in Chapter 2. With one
statement, you can reset a table.
```

Some programmers accomplish this by something like the following, which should be avoided:

```
     PERFORM 3400-RESET-TABLE VARYING STATE-CODE FROM 1 BY
        1 UNTIL STATE-CODE > 11
     .

     .

3400-RESET-TABLE.
     MOVE SPACES TO VALID-STATE (STATE-CODE).
```

It works, but it is unnecessary with COBOL II, it is inefficient, and it is clumsy to code.

Initialize the table with variable data from a file

```
PERFORM VARYING AGE-INDX FROM 1 BY 1 UNTIL EOF OR
   PREM-AGE (AGE-INDX - 1) = 99
      READ  FD3-PREM-FILE
         AT END
            SET EOF TO TRUE
         NOT AT END
            MOVE FD3-PREM-AGE TO PREM-AGE (AGE-INDX)
            MOVE FD3-ML-PREM-SM TO PREM-MALE (AGE-INDX, 1)
            MOVE FD3-FM-PREM-SM TO PREM-FEMALE (AGE-INDX, 1)
            MOVE FD3-ML-PREM-NOSM TO PREM-MALE (AGE-INDX, 2)
            MOVE FD3-FM-PREM-NOSM TO PREM-FEMALE (AGE-INDX, 2)
      END-READ
END-PERFORM
```

This assumes that each record on the file contains the four premiums for an age group. Here an inline PERFORM can be effective because the logic is contained within a few eye scans and does one function.

3.3.5. Improving Table Searches

One of the problems with tables is that as we become familiar with them, we forget that a lot of computer time is spent calculating addresses and making comparisons that prove false. For example, if a table is unordered, the only way to locate a valid entry is to start at the beginning and test each variable until the end of the table is reached or a match is found. If this is done rarely, it may not be worth the effort to improve the process. However, many tables are used frequently. Improving the process will reduce costs and resource use. Here are some options that can improve table searches.

Use SEARCH statement. The SEARCH statement has several benefits over the PERFORM VARYING when the task is searching tables that are unordered or where the key elements are sequenced. One, the SEARCH statement is complete, able to increment the subscript value, make the comparison, test for the end of the table, and execute valid conditions, all with only a few lines of code. Each dimension in a table requires a separate SEARCH statement. The SEARCH statement isn't new with COBOL II, although many programmers have never used it before. Also, the SEARCH statement requires that the table be defined with an INDEXED BY clause. This is advantageous; it relieves you from needing to specify it, as you would with a PERFORM VARYING statement. Here are examples using basic syntax. (There are other options.)

A sequential search

```
SET AGE-INDX TO 1
SEARCH PREM-ENTRY
   AT END    SET  AGE-ERROR TO TRUE
   WHEN PREM-AGE (AGE-INDX) = APP-AGE
      PERFORM 3300-EXTRACT-PREMIUMS
END-SEARCH
```

Equivalent code with the PERFORM would require

```
SET AGE-ERROR TO TRUE
PERFORM VARYING AGE-INDX FROM 1 BY 1 UNTIL
 AGE-INDX > 99
   IF PREM-AGE (AGE-INDX) = APP-AGE
      PERFORM 3300-EXTRACT-PREMIUMS
      SET AGE-INDX TO 99
      SET AGE-OKAY TO TRUE
   END-IF
END-PERFORM
```

The above SEARCH statement searches the table from beginning to end until the AT END condition is met or the WHEN condition is met. (There can be multiple WHEN conditions.) The PERFORM accomplishes this also, but it requires several extra statements that may not appear obvious, and if omitted, this can cause errors in processing.

A binary search

```
SEARCH ALL PREM-ENTRY
   AT END    SET  AGE-ERROR TO TRUE
   WHEN PREM-AGE (AGE-INDX) = APP-AGE
      PERFORM 3300-EXTRACT-PREMIUMS
END-SEARCH
```

This format of SEARCH appears similar to the sequential SEARCH statement, but it is quite different. It requires that the table entry have the ASCENDING/DESCENDING KEY clause specified and that the variable following WHEN be that data-name.

The benefit is increased processing speed for large tables. This is accomplished by a technique called a *binary search*. To get an appreciation of the technique, assume you have a table with 10,000 entries. Sequentially searching the table for a match would, on average, require about 5,000 comparisons per attempt. For example, if your match value were the 5,061st entry, the SEARCH (or PERFORM VARYING) would execute the comparison 5,061 times before finding the match. This is both expensive and time consuming. A binary search divides the remaining elements in half and checks for high or low. For the example mentioned, it would start at the 5,000th entry and test for high or low. Since ours is the 5,061st, it would test higher than the 5,000th entry. (Remember: the ASCENDING KEY or DESCENDING KEY is required for this option.) The logic would then split the remaining items and test the 7,500th entry. The process would continue, splitting and testing high or low until the 5,061st entry were matched.

While computers may use slightly different numbers, the example is still valid. The concept is to narrow the remaining entries, based on discoveries already made. In my theoretical example, the 5,061st entry is located on the twelfth compare, not the 5,061st.

Since the SEARCH statement is dependent on indexes, you will want to check a later topic, Subscripting versus Indexes.

Arrange tables by probability of occurrence. Sometimes, you know that, of all the possible entries in a table, the majority of matches will match a subset of the table entries. In that case, you may want to use a sequential search and initialize the table with the most frequently used data elements at the beginning. For example, if you have 100 job titles in a human resources table, but 95% of the employees have the title Programmer, it wouldn't make sense to do a binary search to locate job title. Put the Programmer job title as the first entry in the table and do a sequential search.

There is a drawback to this easy approach. Over time, the most probable job title may change. If in our example the department were restructured and programmers were reclassified as Programmer/analysts, the performance of the application would suffer until changes were made to the table.

Arrange tables for direct access. This technique can rarely be used, but for that reason it is often overlooked when it is the best approach. Consider the case in which you want to print the name of the month, but only have the number of the month. I've actually seen people do this inefficient technique:

```
01   MONTH-CONTENTS.
     05          PIC X(10)   VALUE '01JANUARY'.
     05          PIC X(10)   VALUE '02FEBRUARY'.
     05          PIC X(10)   VALUE '03MARCH'.
         .
         .
         .
01   MONTH-TABLE REDEFINES MONTH-CONTENTS.
     05  MONTH-ENTRIES   OCCURS 12
             ASCENDING KEY IS MONTH-CODE
```

```
                INDEXED BY MONTH-INX.
     10   MONTH-CODE    PIC  99.
     10   MONTH-NAME    PIC X(8).
        .
        .
        .
SET MONTH-INX TO 1
SEARCH MONTH-ENTRIES
   AT END
      DISPLAY ' INVALID MONTH'
   WHEN MONTH-CODE (MONTH-INX) = REP-MONTH
      MOVE MONTH-NAME (MONTH-INX) TO REP-TITLE
END-SEARCH
```

This works, but it uses much unnecessary processing. A better and much simpler approach is to acknowledge that the appearance of entries within the table corresponds to the search argument (e.g., the seventh entry in the table happens to represent the seventh month). That gives us this simple approach:

```
01   MONTH-CONTENTS.
     05          PIC X(8)   VALUE 'JANUARY'.
     05          PIC X(8)   VALUE 'FEBRUARY'.
     05          PIC X(8)   VALUE 'MARCH'.
        .
        .
        .
01   MONTH-TABLE REDEFINES MONTH-CONTENTS.
     05  MONTH-NAME      PIC X(8)  OCCURS 12.
        .
        .
        .
   IF REP-MONTH > 0 AND < 13
      MOVE MONTH-NAME (REP-MONTH) TO REP-TITLE
   ELSE
      DISPLAY ' INVALID MONTH'
   END-IF
```

This is a case where indexes are not beneficial, since the entry within the table is extracted in one statement. More on this concept in the next topic.

3.3.6. Subscripting versus Indexes with Tables

If you work with tables, you've probably encountered discussions on the pros and cons of using indexes to subscript through tables. (Not using indexes is generally just called subscripting.) First, let's identify the issue. Each time you request access to a table element, the run-time code must calculate the location of the data. Consider the following data description:

```
01  MONTH-TABLE.
    05  MONTH-NAME   PIC X(8)   OCCURS 12.
```

If this statement is encountered,

```
MOVE MONTH-NAME (REP-MONTH) TO REP-TITLE
```

the compiler will generate appropriate code to take the value of REP-MONTH and compute how many bytes the proper data element is beyond the starting point of the table. For example, if REP-MONTH contained the value 07, the generated code would need to do the following (approximately):

1. Convert REP-MONTH to COMP format, if necessary.
2. Subtract 1 from the value (7 − 1 = 6).
3. Multiply the value by the length of MONTH-NAME (8 ∗ 6) to get the offset in the table.
4. Add the result to the memory location of MONTH-TABLE.
5. Store the value temporarily as a base address and execute the MOVE statement.

The resulting object code from compiling the statement may not generate the code quite this way, but my intent is to demonstrate that some work is needed **every time** a table element's address must be calculated. **All of the above** must be done each time the contents of the search argument, REP-MONTH, is changed, whether subscripting or indexing is used. With indexes, however, the result is saved for future use. With subscripting, the calculations are repeated for every access if there is the possibility that the value has changed. (Note: This is dependent, but only to a degree, on the OPTIMIZE compile option.)

So, what are your choices? If the table is accessed only once for each change of the search argument, it makes no difference which method you use. That is rare, however. Usually, you will access the table several times before changing the search argument, meaning that indexes will serve you better. Here is an example in which the table search argument does not change for several statements:

```
IF MONTH-CODE (REP-MONTH) > 3 AND MONTH-CODE (REP-MONTH) < 7
    MOVE MONTH-TITLE (REP-MONTH) TO REP-TITLE
    MOVE '2ND QUARTER' TO PAGE-TITLE
END-IF
```

In this simple example, the calculations would be done three times (once for the first comparison, again for the second comparison, and once again for the move) if REP-MONTH is not defined as an index. If REP-MONTH were an index, no computations would be needed, since the offset would have been previously calculated. This can mean much to an application. (The OPTIMIZE compile option minimizes some of this, but the need to do a computation of some degree still remains when indexes are not used.)

The main issue, then, is how many statements are executed after changing the value of an index. Indexes can be changed by three statements: (1) the SET statement, (2) the SEARCH statement, and (3) the PERFORM VARYING statement.

Together with the ASCENDING KEY and INDEXED BY clauses of the DATA DIVISION, this gives good documentation and efficiency to an application. If you haven't used these statements before, I believe you will find that they complement each other.

3.3.7. Using Large Table Space as a Database

This is a simple technique that was introduced in the previous chapter. There are no special coding requirements, other than some form of table management technique. The big change is that you may define an 01-level item up to 16 million bytes. For example, if you are processing a keyed VSAM file, it may be much quicker to load the database into a table and use the SEARCH ALL statement instead of reading randomly from DASD. The limits of 01-levels changed considerably from DOS/VS COBOL, giving this capability.

3.4. HANDLING CONDITIONAL STATEMENTS

With COBOL II, you need to be sensitive to a few changes in conditional statements. While these differences appear elsewhere, they are summarized here for ease of access.

3.4.1. ALPHANUMERIC Tests

In DOS/VS COBOL, you could code IF ALPHABETIC and know you were testing for upper-case alphabetic characters. In COBOL II, you must use IF ALPHA-BETIC-UPPER for the same results. IF ALPHABETIC still works, but it accepts both upper- and lower-case text as valid.

3.4.2. NUMERIC Tests

IF NUMERIC works the same for most situations. The difference depends on your choice of the compiler NUMPROC option. Here is an example of where the difference lies:

```
05  DATA-FLD   PIC  S999.
    IF DATA-FLD NUMERIC
```

will be true with all options if DATA-FLD contains a signed positive or negative number. This means the sign would be either 'C' or 'D'. If DATA-FLD contains an unsigned value (sign of 'F'), the test will be true for NUMPROC(MIG) and NUMPROC(NOPFD), but it will fail for NUMPROC(PFD). These same considerations should also be used when using the IF POSITIVE, ZERO, or NEGATIVE tests. (See an earlier topic, Efficiencies in Data Definitions, for more information.)

If you define data elements with the 'S' (e.g., PIC S999), regardless of whether you anticipate a sign, you may want to use the NUMPROC(MIG) option to maintain compatibility with that coding technique.

3.5. MAKING A PROGRAM MORE EFFICIENT

Making a program more efficient can be tough work, especially if major flaws exist in the design or if the program is already written. This section summarizes techniques that can improve a program's performance. None of these techniques go beyond COBOL (i.e., if the file is poorly structured or if the logic flow is inefficient, you'll need more than some performance tuning to resolve the problem). Several of these topics will refer you to other topics for more information.

3.5.1. File Blocking of SAM Datasets

I'm still amazed at how frequently this old-fashioned technique is ignored. Increasing the block size of a sequential file reduces the number of physical I/O requests that must occur, thereby reducing the elapsed time and cost of a program. Years ago, many shops had standard guidelines, such as "always block by 10." This may have been good advice in the early 1970s, but it is no longer. A programmer doing small tests will not see the difference, but a full-scale productional run can be significantly affected. (Note: When I speak of large block sizes, I refer to numbers greater than 20,000—don't be stingy.)

An additional consideration for SAM files on DASD is achieving efficient use of each track (e.g., a block size of 30,000 on a device with a track size of 40,000 would cause 10,000 bytes to be not used—a loss of 25%). While there are complicated formulas to calculate an efficient block size, I suggest you do it the easy way: buy a reference card from IBM for the DASD device in question (e.g., the reference card for the IBM 3380, order no. GX26-1678, sells for less than $1). Don't waste valuable time when a solution is available for pennies.

3.5.2. Data formats

This topic is covered under an earlier topic, Efficiencies in Data Definitions. Here are my general guidelines:

- Always use packed-decimal for computational fields.
- Always specify an odd number of digits for PIC clause.
- Always specify sign in PIC clause for computational fields.
- Always use indexes for tables. (If you refuse to accept my earlier arguments about indexes, then at least use COMP items for subscripts to minimize the inefficiencies.)
- Use COMP every time it is specified in application or IBM documentation, since that normally means that either VSE or an application program expects it. (Be careful of misuse of the SYNC clause; misuse forces boundary alignment that may change desired record alignment.)

If you're skeptical about guidelines beginning with the word *Always*, so am I. Even so, by following simple guidelines, I can concentrate on the programming assignment at hand instead of worrying about minor differences in performance. If you're convinced that binary arithmetic (COMP) is superior, review the earlier topic, Efficiencies in Data Definitions.

3.5.3. COMPUTE statement

Years ago, I was advised to avoid the COMPUTE statement because it was inefficient. In hindsight, I was given poor advice. In test after test, the COMPUTE statement has been at least as efficient as other instructions, whether replacing a simple ADD with COMPUTE X = X + 1, or something more complex. The additional advantage of COBOL II is that, with OPTIMIZE specified, the compiler looks for sequences of arithmetic and saves those intermediate values for later use . The sequences can either begin the computation or be bound in parentheses to ensure they are identified. This can often create what appears to be amazing efficiency on a statement-by-statement basis. Consider this example:

```
COMPUTE A = A * (B / C)
  .
  .
COMPUTE Z = F * G + (B / C)
  .
  .
COMPUTE E = B / C
```

In all three statements, there is the sequence, B / C. If the compiler determines the logic flow of the program cannot change the values of B and C between any two of the three statements, it saves the result of the division so it can be reused. In the last statement, for example, no division takes place. The generated machine code simply moves the result into field E.

While I encourage use of the COMPUTE statement, you need to be sensitive to the possibility of incurring large intermediate values that exceed machine capacity. (See Chapter 7 for more information on machine capacities.) As a general guideline, you can add the 9s in the PIC clauses to determine the largest intermediate value for multiplication or division. For example,

```
05  A   PIC  S9(15)    COMP-3.
05  B   PIC  S9(15)    COMP-3.
05  C   PIC  S9(15)    COMP-3.
05  D   PIC  S9(15)    COMP-3.
    .
    .
        COMPUTE A = A * B
```

will have an intermediate result of 30 digits (15 + 15), and it is within the machine capacity for packed decimal arithmetic. The generated machine code (using LIST compile option) would look something like this:

```
Assembler instructions        Compiler comments

ZAP  376(16,13),19(8,9)       TS2=0        B
MP   376(16,13),11(8,9)       TS2=0        A
ZAP  11(8,9),384(8,13)        A            TS2=8
```

You don't need to know assembler language to understand that this represents three instructions. The first one moves B to a temporary work area, the second multiplies the temporary work area by A, and the third moves the result to A. Very efficient. Now let's look at a different example:

```
COMPUTE A = A * B * C * D
```

This will have an intermediate result of 60 digits (15 + 15 + 15 + 15). Since this is a number too large for the machine, extra code must be generated to programmatically extend and validate the intermediate values. Explaining the generated assembler code for this is too complex for this book, but I show it here to highlight what pattern of assembly language indicates less efficient code (again, using the LIST compile option):

```
Assembler instructions             Compiler comments

    ZAP  360(16,13),11(8,9)        TS1=0        A
    MP   360(16,13),19(8,9)        TS1=0        B
    ZAP  376(16,13),19(8,9)        TS2=0        C
    L    2,92(0,13)                TGTFIXD+92
    L    15,188(0,2)               V(IGZCXMU )
    LA   1,782(0,10)               PGMLIT AT +766
    BALR 14,15
```

```
         CLC   401(8,13),0(12)          TS2=25              SYSLIT AT +0
         BC    2,484(0,11)              GN=13(0005E4)
         BC    15,494(0,11)             GN=14(0005EE)
GN=13    EQU   *
         L     15,460(0,2)              V(IGZEMSG )
         LA    1,754(0,10)              PGMLIT AT +738
         BALR  14,15
GN=14    EQU   *
         MVC   360(16,13),408(13)       TS1=0               TS2=32
         NI    360(13),X'OF'            TS1=0
         ZAP   376(16,13),27(8,9)       TS2=0               D
         L     15,188(0,2)              V(IGZCXMU )
         LA    1,782(0,10)              PGMLIT AT +766
         BALR  14,15
         ZAP   11(8,9),416(8,13)        A                   TS2=40
```

Instead of three instructions, you generate 20. However, that is just the visible portion. The **highlighted instructions** are the key to alert you to possible inefficiencies you may want to avoid. They represent the assembler language equivalent of CALL statements. The first is a CALL to module IGZCXMU, the second is a CALL to IGZEMSG, and the final CALL is to IGZCXMU again. While I have no idea how large those IBM-supplied programs are, I assure you they are each much larger than these 20 instructions. The guideline is not to look for these specific modules in arithmetic statements, but to watch for the pattern. (Note: You will see similar patterns in other, nonarithmetic instructions. In those instances, they are necessary for proper operation and may be ignored.) Whenever you have this pattern of instructions in COMPUTE statements and performance is important to you, consider using several COMPUTE statements, such as:

```
COMPUTE A = A * B
COMPUTE A = A * C
COMPUTE A = A * D
```

The preceding information is presented to sensitize you to possible inefficiencies. Yes, you can often avoid the appearance of these inefficiencies by coding many MULTIPLY and DIVIDE statements. They generate more code on average, however, since each MULTIPLY or DIVIDE statement edits and stores intermediate results, and they make the equation more difficult to read.

3.5.4. Compiler Options for Run-Time Efficiency

Some of these compile options have been discussed earlier. This topic summarizes the impact on performance of various options and does not explain their functions in detail. A full discussion appears later under the section Specifying COBOL II Options.

RECOMMENDED. Options that give maximum productional performance (some of them have implications on your data definitions):

Compile-time options

```
OPTIMIZE
NUMPROC(PFD) or NUMPROC(MIG)
TRUNC(OPT)    (has potential implications for CICS and SQL/DS)
NOSSRANGE
AWO
NODYNAM
FASTSRT
NOTEST
```

Run-time options

```
NOAIXBLD
NOWSCLEAR
NOSSRANGE
LIBKEEP
RTEREUS   (IF main program is non-COBOL and frequently CALLs COBOL
             programs.)
```

RECOMMENDED. Options that generate maximum flexibility in the run-time environment, both for the application and for the computer:

```
RESIDENT   (required for CICS)
RENT       (required for CICS)
```

3.5.5. CALLs

A CALL statement generates a significant amount of executable code, often invisible. By invisible, I mean that the executed code is buried in the initialization code of the CALLed module, not in the CALLing module. Where a program is small (e.g., 50 statements or less), consider imbedding it in the parent program or using a nested structure. Either has the opportunity to minimize or eliminate some overhead code. If this isn't feasible, the most efficient CALL structure is the CALL BY REFERENCE format, with the NODYNAM compile option. Don't worry about the GLOBAL and EXTERNAL options for data reference: their use does not affect performance.

By including this information, I am not suggesting that you not use the CALL statement. I use it regularly. It has many benefits if a shop has reusable code or large applications. Just be aware that of all COBOL statements, the

CALL statement will normally execute the most overhead (nonproductive to the application logic) instructions.

3.5.6. SORTs

This chapter has a separate topic on SORT techniques, in addition to a topic on control statements for sorts. SORT design and coding techniques receive special treatment in Chapters 5 and 6. For a more thorough discussion of the opportunities, read those topics. What appears here is a brief summary.

First, assess your application data flow to see if the new sorted structure is needed in several places. If so, you will usually incur less cost by sorting the data once and saving to a permanent file, eliminating the need to resort the data later.

Second, consider using SORT/MERGE II to do the sort instead of COBOL. SORT/MERGE II is more efficient and the control statements can be done in a matter of minutes, not hours or days. This is explained later in the chapter.

Third, never use the COBOL SORT statement format, SORT USING . . . GIVING. . . . Doing so accomplishes nothing more than SORT/MERGE II could do in less time with less coding and testing effort.

Fourth, consider using SORT/MERGE II control statements to replace an INPUT or OUTPUT PROCEDURE on those occasions when SORT/MERGE II cannot do all the necessary processing. This could be situations in which an INPUT PROCEDURE is to do simple data selection or will reformat the data before sorting. This type of situation is much simpler to code with SORT/MERGE II control statements than by writing an INPUT PROCEDURE. (This technique has been available for years, yet many programmers are unaware of it.) A program using this approach is presented in Chapter 8 ("Sample Programs").

Fifth, always use the FASTSRT compile option. If your SORT is anything other than SORT INPUT PROCEDURE . . . OUTPUT PROCEDURE . . . , you will receive improved performance.

3.5.7. SEARCH ALL

This is described under the previous topic, Improving Table Searches. If your application searches tables, see that topic. It explains and demonstrates the binary search process.

3.5.8. Indexes and Subscripts

This is described under the previous topic, Subscripting versus Indexes. If your application searches tables, see that topic. It explains and demonstrates the differences between use and nonuse of indexes to provide addressability to tables.

3.5.9. Data Structures and System Environments

There is no COBOL solution to this problem. I included the topic because you might be looking for a solution here. A poor data architecture can defeat the best written programs. Your data architecture should be designed before writing the programs that access them. If you believe your performance is being affected by poor data architecture or environmental considerations, see your shop's data specialists about conducting a design review or your shop's technical staff to conduct performance monitoring of your application.

Some issues that may affect performance:

1. For VSAM files, check the control interval sizes, the free space allocations, alternate indexes, buffers, and keys. If you are using the defaults from Access Method Services, this should be investigated by a person familiar with VSAM. For more VSAM assistance, which is beyond the scope of this book, you might want another QED book *VSAM: The Complete Guide to Optimization and Design.* (See Chapter 9.) This book addresses all issues that might affect VSAM performance.

2. For CICS applications, check your module structure, the number of EXEC LINK or EXEC XCTL commands that may occur within a transaction, and the number of I/O operations generated within a transaction. For more thorough information on CICS performance and design considerations, see the QED book *How to Use CICS to Create On-Line Applications: Methods and Solutions* (Chapter 9). This book covers all issues and tasks for building and executing CICS applications with COBOL.

3. For DL/1 applications, review how often your logic makes a CALL to DL/1. (This is not the same as how many CALLs are in your program.) By restructuring your SSAs (and your logic), you might be able to reduce the number of CALLs. Usually simpler programs require more CALLs, while sophisticated programs require fewer CALLs. A thorough coverage is in a more appropriate QED book *IMS Design and Implementation Techniques.* (see Chapter 9.) This book is appropriate, not only for addressing DL/1 performance issues, but also for its complete coverage of hierarchical data base design.

4. For SQL/DS data structures, their complex performance issues are such that I can only refer you to your shop's data specialists.

5. For information on SQL, see the QED book *SQL for DB2 and SQL/DS Application Developers* (Chapter 9, "Related Publications").

Earlier in this book I mentioned that COBOL II was not just a language, but an environment. By *environment*, I meant that it is involved not only with the compilation, but also with the execution. The other subjects mentioned in this topic are also full environments. While your COBOL II program is the heart of the application logic, how the program interacts within these other environments affects the quality, value, and performance of your applications.

3.6. MAKING A PROGRAM RESISTANT TO ERRORS

Is it really possible to make a program bullet proof? I don't think so, but I do know you can take steps in developing a program that will minimize the ABENDs and other errors that occur. In this topic, I have summarized various techniques that can help prevent an error.

3.6.1. FILE STATUS

If you use VSAM files, this technique is old hat to you. But what about those SAM files? COBOL II provides special services to SAM files that use the FILE STATUS clause in the SELECT statement. For one, the program does not ABEND (honest!) even if the JCL file assignment is absent. Of course, your program is expected to check the file status after each I/O to determine status and take appropriate action (e.g., after detecting that a file did not OPEN properly, your logic should ensure that no READ or WRITE went to that file). For FILE STATUS codes, see Chapter 7. Here is a simple example showing the fundamentals (highlighted) to improve SAM file integrity (some parts of the program are omitted). This example assumes that the absence of the file is acceptable (e.g., a file that is not always present). For that reason, the word *optional* appears in the SELECT statement, although this is primarily to indicate that absence of the file is anticipated. OPTIONAL also causes the status code to be different and supports CLOSE processing.

```
INPUT-OUTPUT SECTION.
FILE-CONTROL.
    SELECT FD1-WEEKLY OPTIONAL
      ASSIGN TO WKFILE   FILE STATUS IS WS1-FD1-STAT.
DATA DIVISION.
FILE SECTION.
FD  FD1-WEEKLY
    BLOCK CONTAINS 0 RECORDS
    RECORDING MODE IS F
    RECORD CONTAINS 100 CHARACTERS.
        .
        .
        .
WORKING-STORAGE SECTION.
01  WS1-FD1-STATUS.
    05  WS1-FD1-REC-CT   PIC S9(4)  COMP  VALUE 0.
    05  WS1-FD1-STAT     PIC XX.
    05  WS1-FD1-EOF-SW   PIC  X            VALUE 'N'.
```

```
          88 FD1-EOF                          VALUE 'Y'.
       .
       .

PROCEDURE DIVISION.
1.   PERFORM 1000-INITIALIZE
     PERFORM 2000-PROCESS UNTIL FD1-EOF
     PERFORM 3000-WRAPUP
     IF RETURN-CODE > 15
         DISPLAY 'SERIOUS I/O ERROR ON WKFILE'
     END-IF
     STOP RUN.

1000-INITIALIZE.
     OPEN INPUT FD1-WEEKLY
     IF WS1-FD1-STAT NE '00'
         SET FD1-EOF TO TRUE
     END-IF
       .
       .

2000-PROCESS.
     PERFORM 2100-READ
     IF WS1-FD1-EOF-SW  = 'N'
         .
         .         process the data record here
         .
2100-READ.
     READ FD1-WEEKLY
        AT END
            SET FD1-EOF TO TRUE
        NOT AT END
            IF WS1-FD1-STAT NE '00'
                SET FD1-EOF TO TRUE
                MOVE 16 TO RETURN-CODE
                DISPLAY 'FD1-WEEKLY I/O STAT ' WS1-FD1-STAT
            END-IF
     END-READ.
```

Notice that if an OPEN error occurs, the READ statement is not executed. This allows for different settings of the RETURN-CODE: 4 meaning that the weekly file was not present, and 16 meaning that it was present but an I/O error occurred.

3.6.2. ON SIZE ERROR

There is nothing new here with COBOL II, just an old standby that is rarely used. If your applications could conceivably cause an overflow or divide by zero, this should be considered.

3.6.3. PARM Processing

Validating PARM lengths was discussed earlier under the section Module Structures. For more information, see that section.

3.6.4. CALL Statement (LENGTH OF, ON EXCEPTION, and BY CONTENT)

These are all new features of COBOL II. The LENGTH OF clause lets a CALLed program validate the anticipated length of the passed data. The ON EXCEPTION clause is good for DYNAMically CALLed module structures, allowing you to prevent ABENDs.

The BY CONTENT clause has some performance implications, but could be advantageous if your program CALLs other programs that need data from your program, but they are not to modify it. This not only protects your data, but it also prevents a CALLed program from inadvertently overwriting parts of your program through addressability to your DATA DIVISION.

All these options of the CALL statement are explained in Chapter 2, and earlier in this chapter under the section, Module Structures.

3.6.5. Data Validation

The 0C4, 0C7, 0C9, and 0CB ABENDs are probably the most familiar ABENDs in all shops, yet they can usually be prevented. Let's take them separately:

0C4: This ABEND is usually caused by a runaway subscript or index, attempting to access unallocated memory. While it can occur for other reasons, the majority of programs ABENDing with 0C4 have an OCCURS clause. This can be prevented by testing the range of the subscript before use. During program testing, this can be supplemented by the SSRANGE compile option.

0C7: Caused by using nonnumeric data in an arithmetic statement. It can be prevented by using the IF NUMERIC test. (See the earlier topic Data Definitions for the implications of the NUMPROC compile option.) Don't attempt to do your own range test for these two reasons.

1. If the field is PIC 99, you could get an 0C7 in your attempt to prevent one. This occurs because the generated code converts the data to numeric format and then compares it to other numeric values.
2. If the field is PIC XX, you could be accidentally approving nonnumeric data, getting an 0C7 anyway. Consider the following:

```
05  DATA-ITM   PIC  999.
05  NEW-DATA-ITM  REDEFINES DATA-ITM  PIC XXX.

    IF NEW-DATA-ITM > '000' AND < '100'
       ADD DATA-ITM TO ...
```

In this innocent example, you need to be familiar with the EBCDIC collating sequence (Chapter 7). If you check it, you will find that '01 ' (a one and a blank) are between '001' and '099'. In fact, hundreds of nonnumeric values are in that range (e.g., '03<', '0Z#') and several could cause the ADD statement to cause an 0C7 ABEND.

0C9 and 0CB: These are, in fact, the same ABEND, a divide by zero. One is packed-decimal and the other is binary. They can be detected by an ON SIZE ERROR clause or by validating the divisor before the DIVIDE statement.

3.6.6. COPYbooks

The more data definitions, file definitions, common procedural statements, and program-to-program interfaces that you put in COPYbooks, the less exposed you will be to programming errors. If you give the same programming specifications to 20 programmers, expect at least one of them to make a simple error that affects processing or ABENDs the program.

COPYbooks will not only reduce your exposure to misinterpretations, but they will also improve overall program documentation and communications among a project team.

3.6.7. RETURN-CODE Tests

While reviewed earlier in the section, Module Structures, RETURN-CODE is another technique to improve resistance to error. Anytime you CALL a program or PERFORM a paragraph that could have a conditional outcome, ensure the program specifications include a status code to be returned. Doing so improves readability of the program, improves communication between the two modules, and provides incentive for the person writing the CALLed or PERFORMed code not to use a GO TO or issue an intentional ABEND. (Issuing an intentional ABEND is covered in the topic Terminating a Program/Module in this chapter.)

3.7. VSAM TECHNIQUES

This is not a treatment on VSAM programming techniques, but a summary of new facilities available to you in COBOL II. COBOL II does not change the way VSAM files are handled, and all of these changes appear in Chapter 2. They are also included here for quick reference.

First, COBOL II provides a VSAM status code field to allow you to interrogate status codes from Access Method Services. Those codes are defined in *VSE/VSAM Commands and Macros.* (See Chapter 9.) This is in addition to the standard FILE STATUS field. (See Chapter 7 for FILE STATUS codes.) An example of a VSAM SELECT statement follows:

```
SELECT FD2-MASTER
    ASSIGN TO MASTFL
    ORGANIZATION IS INDEXED
    RECORD KEY IS FD2-KEY
    FILE STATUS IS WS1-FD2-STATUS
      WS1-FD2-VSAM-STAT.
      .
      .

05  WS1-FD2-VSAM-STAT          COMP.
    10   STAT-RETURN-CODE      PIC 99.
    10   STAT-FUNCTION-CODE    PIC 99.
    10   STAT-FEEDBACK-CODE    PIC 99.
```

These data elements may be checked in addition to the normal FILE STATUS field. Notice that the VSAM status field is the *second named field* in the FILE STATUS clause. The FD for a VSAM file need be only

```
FD   file-name
     RECORD CONTAINS nn CHARACTERS.
```

In the above FD, the RECORD CONTAINS clause is optional. I suggest using it, primarily for its documentation function.

Another new feature of COBOL II that could affect VSAM processing is the addition of NOT AT END and NOT INVALID KEY to the I/O statements. These are explained under the topic Scope Terminators in Chapter 2.

The final new technique available to the COBOL II programmer is that the START statement has an additional option for the KEY clause that improves readability. That option is GREATER THAN OR EQUAL TO. For example, instead of coding this:

```
START file-name KEY NOT LESS THAN data-name ... ,
```

you can code this:

```
START file-name KEY GREATER THAN OR EQUAL TO data-name ... .
```

Although a small item, this option lets you think positively instead of negatively to state the same condition. Anytime you can avoid using *NOT*, you reduce the odds that a rookie programmer will make an error in the future when maintaining your program. For more specific VSAM considerations beyond those addressed within the scope of COBOL II, QED publishes *VSAM: The Complete Guide to Optimization and Design*. See Chapter 9, "Related Publications," for information on this and other related IBM VSAM publications.

3.8. SORT TECHNIQUES

A COBOL SORT requires several considerations not only to work correctly, but also to work efficiently. Additional sort information may be found in these sections: Making a Program More Efficient (in this chapter), JCL Requirements (in this chapter), plus sections in Chapter 5 and Chapter 6. First, let's review how the sort takes place. Let's use a simple SORT statement, such as

```
SORT SD-SORT-FILE ASCENDING KEY FIELD-A
   INPUT PROCEDURE 2100-PROCESS-INPUT
   OUTPUT PROCEDURE 3100-PROCESS-OUTPUT
```

3.8.1. SORT Logic Flow

A common perception of the logic flow is an implied PERFORM UNTIL state-ment of 2100-PROCESS-INPUT, followed by the sort, followed by an implied PERFORM UNTIL of 3100-PROCESS-OUTPUT. If this were true, you could view the process as similar to any other PERFORM structures. Instead, here is what happens:

1. When the SORT statement is executed, it does not transfer control to an INPUT PROCEDURE. Instead, it dynamically loads the SORT utility program (SORT/MERGE II, the same one used for standalone sorts) into memory and transfers control to that application, passing the addresses of any INPUT or OUTPUT PROCEDURES, plus the address of some sort control statements. (For efficiency, you should allocate more memory to the run unit than the application itself requires.)

2. SORT/MERGE II is now in control. The first thing SORT/MERGE II does is check for the existence of a control data set that might have standalone control statements (system name would be SYSIPT or the name of a VSE Librarian member (member type must be "C") and specified in the SORT-CONTROL special register). If present, SORT/MERGE II includes these control statements with those received from your SORT statement. Next, it does an implied PERFORM of your INPUT or OUTPUT procedure. This means your code is running subor-dinate to SORT/MERGE II, not subordinate to your parent paragraph with the SORT statement, and certain programming practices should not be done. These include such statements as STOP RUN, GOBACK, or (horrors!) a GO TO to a different logic path in the application. For the application to terminate cleanly, you must return control back by the same path, following normal structured practices. (If you're wondering how to stop a sort in progress, I'll get to that shortly.)

3. As each RELEASE statement is executed, SORT/MERGE II feeds the next record into the sorting process, which is occurring concurrently

with your INPUT or OUTPUT processing. Likewise with the RETURN statement, each execution causes SORT/MERGE II to pass back the next record available from the sort. An important point I'll explain shortly is that SORT/MERGE II also checks contents of a special register called SORT-RETURN each time it receives control from a RELEASE or RETURN.

4. As your code exits the INPUT or OUTPUT paragraph, SORT/MERGE II uses this as a signal to finish that sort phase or to return control back to the statement following the SORT statement. When control is returned to the statement following the SORT statement, SORT/MERGE II exits memory. If an error occurred at any time, SORT/MERGE II sets a nonzero value in the SORT-RETURN special register.

The following diagram is a symbolic representation of what is happening. The dotted lines represent the conceptual flow. The solid lines represent the actual flow.

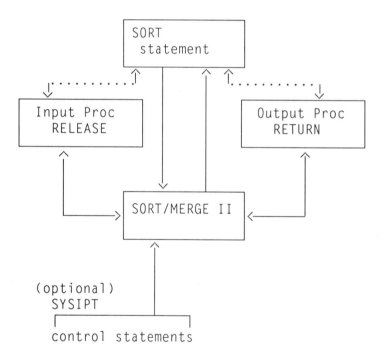

3.8.2. SORT Components

A COBOL SORT requires several components: a SELECT statement, an SD definition, an INPUT PROCEDURE of procedural code if the data is to be modified or selected prior to the sort, and an OUTPUT PROCEDURE of procedural code if the data is to be modified or otherwise processed after the sort. The optional INPUT PROCEDURE requires a RELEASE statement to transfer a record to the sort process, and the optional OUTPUT PROCEDURE requires a RETURN statement to read records back from the sort process. An example sort program is included in Chapter 8 ("Sample Programs"). Let's look at each of the SORT components.

The SELECT statement. Since sort work files are defined within the SORT/MERGE II programs, this is treated as a comment. Use

```
SELECT sort-file-id ASSIGN TO SORTWK.
```

The SD statement. Because the actual sort files are defined by SORT/MERGE II, your goal here is to use the minimum acceptable syntax to COBOL II. All data fields that will be keys for the sort process must be defined within the 01-level. Specify,

```
SD  sort-file-name
    RECORD CONTAINS nn CHARACTERS.
01 sort-record-name.
  05 sort-key-a    PIC  ...
  05 sort-key-b    PIC  ...
   .
   .
```

The PROCEDURE DIVISION. First, a SORT statement must be used. Usually, there will be one or both of the possible PROCEDURES. The INPUT PROCEDURE, if used, needs to have a RELEASE statement somewhere within the logic flow (i.e, the RELEASE statement does not have to be in the named paragraph). This also applies to the OUTPUT PROCEDURE, in that the RETURN statement need not be physically within the named paragraph.

3.8.3. SORT Performance Tips

Terminating a SORT.

Earlier, I reviewed the logic flow of a sort. You may recall that I stated that SORT/MERGE II checked the status of SORT-RETURN after receiving control through a RELEASE or RETURN statement. This is the key. If you are in an INPUT or OUTPUT procedure and decide to terminate the sort or the application itself, do it by these steps:

1. Set a flag so SORT/MERGE II knows to terminate. Do this by a statement such as: `MOVE 16 TO SORT-RETURN`.
2. Next, RETURN or RELEASE one more record. Since SORT/MERGE II checks SORT-RETURN first, that next record will not be processed.

Instead, SORT/MERGE II will shut down and return control to your statement following the SORT statement.

3. Those two steps cause the sort process to terminate. Now, you can terminate the application or whatever is appropriate. Use something such as this, following your SORT statement:

```
IF SORT-RETURN > 0
    your error termination process goes here
ELSE
    your normal next process goes here
END-IF
```

Improving performance of a SORT.

Much of this was covered in an earlier section, Making a Program More Efficient. Here are some specifics.

1. Use an INPUT PROCEDURE (or the SORT-CONTROL interface) to restructure your input records so only the fields needed are sorted. Since much of the sort process occurs in memory, this increases the number of records that can be sorted this way. (How to use SORT-CONTROL is explained in the next topic.)

2. Use selection logic to ensure no records are sorted that are not needed. For example, why sort 100,000 records when the OUTPUT PROCEDURE (or the following program) has logic that bypasses many of the records. This logic can be in either an INPUT PROCEDURE or the SORT-CONTROL interface.

3. Specify the FASTSRT option. This improves I/O for any USING or GIVING clauses (i.e., ignored for programs with both an INPUT and an OUTPUT PROCEDURE).

4. Never use a SORT USING... GIVING... statement. A standalone sort is quicker and easier to code.

5. Schedule the application in a larger partition than you think you need. Because SORT/MERGE II is a smart program, it does the best it can with what it gets. That doesn't mean it is working efficiently, only functionally. Your technical staff may have guidelines for your shop.

6. Don't specify many SORT work files in your JCL. Modern sort techniques generally work best with fewer, not more work files.

Using SORT/MERGE II control statements (SORT-CONTROL).

Although seldom used, the SORT control statements may be used from within COBOL SORT programs. The advantage is that they are easy to code and can eliminate the need for an INPUT or OUTPUT PROCEDURE, depending on complexity of requirements. They can also supplement processing if the program already has INPUT or OUTPUT PROCEDURES. For example, an INCLUDE or OMIT statement could determine what records are sorted or an OPTION statement could provide special performance information to SORT. When used within the job-stream, the statements must be in SYSIPT. This can be specified by the SORT-CONTROL register in a COBOL program (i.e., MOVE 'SYSIPT' TO SORT-CONTROL). The syntax for control statements is identical to that used in a standalone sort. (Remember, it is the same program.)

Your choice of statements must coincide with processing steps of the application. For example, if you use an INREC statement to realign data fields, the data fields must appear in the SD record description as they will appear after the realignment. (Note: Don't show a smaller record size in the SD record description, however, as SORT/MERGE II opens the file before processing the INREC statement, which generates a run-time error.) Likewise, use of OUTREC would change the record's description. For that reason, you cannot use both INREC and OUTREC in an application (nor would you need to). The format of each statement is in the section JCL Requirements. Here are some suggested uses.

1. To select records for the sort: Use the INCLUDE statement.
2. To omit records from the sort: Use the OMIT statement.
3. To realign and shorten (lengthen) records prior to the sort process: Use INREC.
4. To realign and shorten (lengthen) records after the sort process: Use OUTREC.

A coding example is in the section JCL Requirements. For additional information on using SORT/MERGE II, see your appropriate reference manual (Chapter 9, "Related Publications").

CONTROL STATEMENTS (in order of processing)

OPTION	provides temporary overrides to defaults
INCLUDE or OMIT	specifies what records to sort
INREC	reformats input records
SORT or MERGE	<— *provided by COBOL II SORT statement*
SUM	creates summary records & totals
OUTREC	reformats output records

Syntax on the SORT/MERGE II control statements is in the section JCL Requirements in this chapter.

3.9. CICS-DL/1-SQL/DS ISSUES

Some of the material presented here appears in various other places. The material here is presented with the assumption that you know how to program applications for CICS, DL/1, or SQL/DS. In all cases, refer to your technical staff for specifics for your shop. These are complex system environments and there may well be differences from what is written here. There is also a topic in the next chapter ("Debugging") about debug considerations for CICS.

3.9.1. CICS Considerations

CICS receives major performance improvements from COBOL II, and DOS/VS COBOL programs do not require specific program changes to benefit from them (exception: programs using BLLs). COBOL II simplifies several CICS processes and provides some features that weren't previously allowed.

Issues regarding module structure and compile options

1. Some features of COBOL II are only available by specifying the option ANSI85 to the CICS translator. Those features are lower-case characters in COBOL statements, batched compilations, nested programs, GLOBAL variables, and reference modification.
2. A run unit must not have a mix of DOS/VS COBOL and COBOL II.
3. Programs must use NOCMPR2, RES, RENT, NODBCS, and NODYNAM compile options.
4. IBM recommends that you use TRUNC(BIN), but I doubt you need this inefficient option, since VSE is a 24-bit operating system (i.e., all valid system addresses can be represented by PIC S9(8)). Unless your application is dependent on having no truncation for binary data (the TRUNC(BIN) option), you will realize more efficiency by selecting one of the other choices (explained in a previous section in this book). Note: If you are compiling for XA-Mode Portability, you should follow IBM's recommendation, since XA machines use 31-bit addresses.
5. Programs may not be CALLed from assembler programs, although they may CALL assembler subprograms.
6. While the DYNAM option is not allowed, the use of CALL *identifier* is valid with NODYNAM for dynamic CALLs to COBOL II subprograms.
7. If the FDUMP, TEST, or SSRANGE compile options are used, the formatted information will be written to the temporary storage queue, CEBRxxxx.
8. The ON EXCEPTION and NOT ON EXCEPTION clauses are not allowed with CICS.
9. Programs that use macro-level CICS code will not compile with CO-BOL II, nor will those using BLL cells.
10. If a COBOL II program CALLs another COBOL II program that will also execute EXEC CICS statements, pass the DFHEIBLK and DFHCOMMAREA as the first two parameters. The CICS translator

will insert the appropriate data definitions and adjustments to the PROCEDURE DIVISION USING statement for the CALLed program. Exception: When the CALLed module is a nested program, the PROCEDURE DIVISION USING statement must be manually coded. (Note: CALLing another program that also executes EXEC CICS statements was not allowed prior to COBOL II.) The LINK and XCTL commands may still be used for other forms of program transfer.

11. Dynamically CALLed subprograms may not contain EXEC CICS commands.

12. If the program(s) will use reentrant features, specify SVA on the PHASE statement for link-edit processing. (See the section, Creating a Phase.)

Programming techniques that apply to CICS are

1. If you use EXEC CICS HANDLE statements, the HANDLE is suspended when CALLing a separately compiled COBOL II program (reinstated upon return), but it remains active when CALLing a nested program. If the CALLed program will issue any EXEC statements, it must first issue an appropriate HANDLE statement to protect against possible ABENDs.

2. Do not use BLL cells. Instead, if SET or ADDRESS parameters reference BLL cells, specify the ADDRESS OF special register for the actual data area (see following example).

3. Do not write code that provides addressability for areas greater than 4K (usually done in DOS/VS COBOL by adding 4096 to the value of a BLL cell). This function is provided for you by COBOL II (see following example).

4. The TIME and DATE functions (via ACCEPT statement) are not allowed for CICS programs.

5. The SERVICE RELOAD statement is treated as a comment, so there is no need to code it.

6. The LENGTH parameter is not needed, although it may be coded if desired. (CICS uses the LENGTH OF special register from COBOL II to access the length of the data area.)

7. STOP RUN is now a supported statement, but I encourage you to continue using EXEC CICS RETURN or GOBACK for compatibility. (STOP RUN returns control directly to CICS, bypassing any higher modules in the application.)

8. INSPECT, STRING, and UNSTRING are COBOL statements that may be used in COBOL II CICS applications. (They were not allowed with DOS/VS COBOL.)

9. You will improve transaction response time and use less virtual memory by converting EXEC CICS LINK commands to COBOL CALL statements.

10. If any EXEC CICS commands include reference modification, be sure to include the length parameter. Otherwise, the CICS translator generates incorrect code. (Reference modification was explained in Chapter 2.)

If your shop has a CICS-to-COBOL II conversion software package, converting BLL cells can be done automatically for DOS/VS COBOL programs. Check with your technical staff. Here are some elementary (and incomplete) comparisons of how COBOL II replaces BLL processing. All differences are highlighted.

Accessing an area in LINKAGE SECTION

DOS/VS COBOL

```
LINKAGE SECTION.
      .
01   BLL-CELLS.
     05  FILLER              PIC S9(8)   COMP.
     05  DATA-REC-POINTER    PIC S9(8)   COMP.
01 DATA-REC.
   .

   .
     EXEC CICS ADDRESS CWA(DATA-REC-POINTER)
   .
```

COBOL II

```
LINKAGE SECTION.
     .
01 DATA-REC.
   .

   .
     EXEC CICS ADDRESS CWA(ADDRESS OF DATA-REC)
   .
```

Reading a File

DOS/VS COBOL

```
WORKING-STORAGE SECTION.
   .
01   WS1-FILE-WORK.
     05  WS1-REC-LEN    PIC S9(4)  COMP  VALUE 100.
   .

   .
```

```
01  WS2-DATA-RECORD      PIC X(100).
        .
        .
        .
    EXEC CICS READ DATASET('fileid')
        INTO(WS2-DATA-RECORD)
        RIDFLD(keyfield)
        LENGTH(WS1-REC-LEN)
        .
```

COBOL II

```
WORKING-STORAGE SECTION.
        .
01  WS2-DATA-RECORD      PIC X(100).
        .
        .
        .
    EXEC CICS READ DATASET('fileid')
        INTO(WS2-DATA-RECORD)
        RIDFLD(keyfield)
        .
```

Processing a large storage area

DOS/VS COBOL

```
WORKING-STORAGE SECTION.
        .
01  WS1-FILE-WORK.
    05  WS1-REC-LEN      PIC S9(4)  COMP  VALUE 5000.
        .
        .
LINKAGE SECTION.
        .
01  BLL-CELLS.
        .
    05  ADDR-1           PIC S9(8)     COMP.
    05  ADDR-2           PIC S9(8)     COMP.
        .
        .
01  DATA-REC-A           PIC X(5000).
        .
        .
    EXEC CICS READ DATASET('fileid')
        RIDFLD(keyfield)
        SET(ADDR-1)
        LENGTH(WS1-REC-LEN)
    END-EXEC
    SERVICE RELOAD ADDR-1
```

```
            COMPUTE ADDR-2 = ADDR-1 + 4096
            SERVICE RELOAD ADDR-2
```

COBOL II

```
        LINKAGE SECTION.
            .
        01  DATA-REC-A          PIC X(5000).
            .
            .
            EXEC CICS READ DATASET('fileid')
                RIDFLD(keyfield)
                SET(ADDRESS OF DATA-REC-A)
            END-EXEC
```

If you have a CICS application that accesses a DL/1 database, see the next topic for additional information.

3.9.2. DL/1 Considerations

There are no special changes for DL/1 applications that affect the applications programmer. Where DL/1 databases are processed by CICS applications, follow the guidelines in the previous topic. Although not specific to COBOL II, the main programming concerns for DL/1 are that you do not need to code ENTRY DLITCBL. Use PROCEDURE DIVISION USING instead. It is easier to code and provides better readability. The suggested compile options are RENT and RES.

For CICS applications, you may use EXEC DLI instead of the CALL statement. As noted above, however, BLLs are not allowed. Once the scheduling CALL is completed, there are no other differences for CICS DL/1 applications. Here is an example of the differences when using the scheduling CALL statement (sometimes referred to as a PCB CALL). Differences are highlighted. See the previous topic on CICS for explanations of the differences.

Differences for a scheduling CALL for CICS/DLI programs

DOS/VS COBOL

```
        LINKAGE SECTION.
            .
        01  BLL-CELLS.
            05  FILLER          PIC S9(8)    COMP.
            05  DLIUIB-BLL      PIC S9(8)    COMP.
            05  PCB-ADDR-BLL    PIC S9(8)    COMP.
            05  PCB-1-BLL       PIC S9(8)    COMP.
            05  PCB-2-BLL       PIC S9(8)    COMP.
```

```
01  DLIUIB.
    05  UIBPCBAL              PIC S9(8)     COMP.
       .

01  PCB-ADDRESSES.
    05  PCB-ADDR-1            PIC S9(8)     COMP.
    05  PCB-ADDR-2            PIC S9(8)     COMP.
       .

01  PCB-1.
       .

01  PCB-2.
       .

    CALL 'CBLTDLI' USING PCB-SCHEDULE
                         psb-name
                         DLIUIB-BLL
    MOVE UIBPCBAL      TO PCB-ADDR-BLL
    MOVE PCB-ADDR-1    TO PCB-1-BLL
    MOVE PCB-ADDR-2    TO PCB-2-BLL
```

COBOL II

The following example uses the POINTER technique described earlier in this chapter and in Chapter 2. This can be done by modifying the DLIUIB COPYbook or by using a REDEFINES statement to place the POINTER.

```
LINKAGE SECTION.
       .

01  DLIUIB.
    05  UIBPCBAL              POINTER.
       .

01  PCB-ADDRESSES.
    05  PCB-ADDR-1            POINTER.
    05  PCB-ADDR-2            POINTER.
       .

01  PCB-1.

01  PCB-2.
       .

    CALL 'CBLTDLI' USING PCB-SCHEDULE
                         psb-name
                         ADDRESS OF DLIUIB
    SET ADDRESS OF PCB-ADDRESSES TO UIBPCBAL
    SET ADDRESS OF PCB-1 TO PCB-ADDR-1
    SET ADDRESS OF PCB-2 TO PCB-ADDR-2
```

An alternative way to code the last three statements follows. Because this technique uses EXEC CICS commands, the DLIUIB COPYbook does not need to be changed.

```
EXEC CICS ADDRESS SET(ADDRESS OF PCB-ADDRESSES)
          USING(UIBPCBAL)    END-EXEC
EXEC CICS ADDRESS SET(ADDRESS OF PCB-1)
          USING(PCB-ADDR-1)  END-EXEC
EXEC CICS ADDRESS SET(ADDRESS OF PCB-2)
          USING(PCB-ADDR-2)  END-EXEC
```

A sample DL/1 program is included in Chapter 8. The sample was written to be compatible with both DOS/VS COBOL and COBOL II.

3.9.3. SQL/DS Considerations

While there are issues to address with CICS and DL/1, SQL/DS is hardly a concern. I include this topic to reassure SQL/DS programmers that I didn't overlook them. If your SQL/DS application operates within the CICS environment, those considerations will apply. Other than that, here are the few considerations:

1. Whereas no types of dynamic SQL statements were allowed with DOS/VS COBOL, you may use them with COBOL II.
2. If you used an SQLDA (Structured Query Language Data Area) with DOS/VS COBOL, you needed to write an assembler program to manage the address pointers. This is not needed with COBOL II. Instead, you may use POINTER variables with the SET statement. You will also need to define your SQLDA because the SQL INCLUDE for COBOL does not provide the code for it. Examples of an SQLDA, along with other information about dynamic SQL statements, are in *IBM SQL/DS Application Programming for VSE*. (See Chapter 9.)
3. The COBOL II options that affect the SQL/DS environment are TRUNC and NOCMPR2. IBM suggests TRUNC(BIN) for SQL/DS, as it does for CICS. If your application does not use binary arithmetic extensively, follow IBM's recommendation. If you do use binary arithmetic (COMP), you may want to test other options of TRUNC if performance is an issue. See the previous topic on CICS for more information regarding use of TRUNC(BIN). NOCMPR2 is required because of changes in COBOL II. (See the section Specifying COBOL II Options for more information.)
4. SQL/DS statements used by COBOL II are OPEN, CLOSE, PREPARE, DESCRIBE, and FETCH.
5. Non-SELECT statements, as well as fixed-list and varying-list SELECT statements, may be used with COBOL II.

3.10. CREATING A PHASE

Creating executable code (called a *phase* in VSE) requires that the output from the compile(s) be processed by the Linkage Editor. This is because IBM language compilers generate a standard format data set of machine code that includes nonexecutable tables of reference (e.g., list of CALLed modules that must be resolved). Certain compile options affect this process, and there are other items you can specify for your program at the time of the link.

The Linkage Editor is an intelligent software product and can do many things with the object code it processes. However, because the Linkage Editor does not know the logic structure of the application, or which program should get control at run-time, there are specific concerns you must address for a successful link-edit. This section addresses all Linkage Editor considerations except JCL and options for the Linkage Editor. The JCL and options for the Linkage Editor are in a later section (JCL Requirements: Compile, Link, and Execute).

3.10.1. Static Versus Dynamic CALLS

The concept of static CALLs and dynamic CALLs was explained in the section Module Structures. If you have static CALLs to resolve, you must have the needed modules, in object or phase format, accessible to the Linkage Editor through JCL statements. If you use dynamic CALLs, there are no concerns to the Linkage Editor in resolving these CALLs.

3.10.2. RESIDENT and REENTRANT Options

REENTRANT. At run-time, VSE checks to see what attributes a phase has so it can manage the phase correctly. Those attributes are placed in the phase by the Linkage Editor and are sometimes dependent on attributes specified by the language compiler. For example, by specifying RENT at compile-time, the COBOL II compiler generates different object code so the program will be reentrant. This, however, does not cause the module to be treated as reentrant: that is done by the Linkage Editor.

When this option, SVA (on PHASE statement), is specified to the Linkage Editor, the Linkage Editor sets an attribute bit so VSE will *assume* the module is reentrant. When VSE loads a run unit into the SVA that is marked reentrant, it schedules the run unit to take advantage of this feature, whether the run unit is or isn't reentrant. Don't make the mistake, then, of assuming that you can specify SVA at link-edit time and not specify RENT at compile-time. Each serves a different purpose. Here is a definition of reentrant code to help you determine when SVA needs to be specified to the Linkage Editor.

Reentrant code. By being reentrant, a phase is capable of being loaded once into memory so multiple transactions can execute concurrently, using the one copy. This feature can be useful for high-performance on-line transactions, but is of no benefit for batch transactions. Usually, your technical staff that supports on-line transactions can assist you with this. The decision has some dependency on how the on-line environment is initialized.

RESIDENT. The RES option affects the size of your phase, the size of your Linkage Editor listing, and how your phase accesses the COBOL II run-time modules. Since RES means that COBOL run-time modules will be resident in the system and not in your phase, there are no CALLs in your object module to COBOL routines for the Linkage Editor to resolve. (Exception: There is always a CALL to IGZEBST that must be resolved by the Linkage Editor.)

3.10.3. Using the Linkage Editor

Despite its simple design, the Linkage Editor is one of the least understood of IBM's software. This is not an extensive treatment of the subject, but it should suffice for most applications. The JCL options are in the section JCL Requirements. The control statements, however, are here. If your knowledge of the Linkage Editor JCL is minimal, you might prefer to read that section first.

Linkage Editor concepts.

First, Let's review terms to be sure we're in sync. See Figure 3.2 for a simple compile and link-edit for a two-module application.

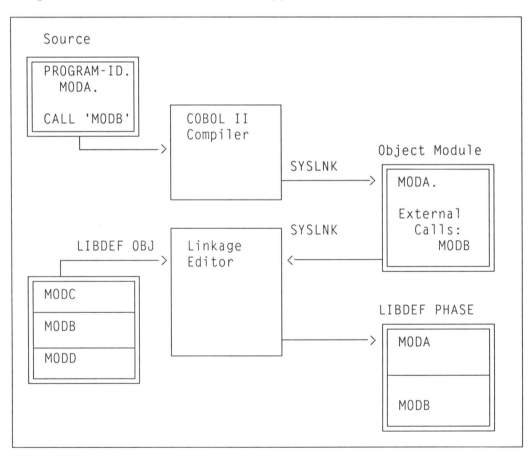

Figure 3.2. Sample flow of compile and link.

In Figure 3.2 (the datasets are double-lined), program MODA with a CALL to MODB is compiled. The output object module is written to SYSLNK. The object module has a table in it (referred to as a dictionary), listing all external references that the Linkage Editor must resolve.

When the Linkage Editor reads this as input (SYSLNK), it strips nonexecutable tables from the code and searches for any external references, in this case MODB. If the Linkage editor cannot locate MODB elsewhere (this is explained later), it searches those files described by a LIBDEF OBJ JCL statement, and, in the example, locates it (this automatic search facility is referred to as AUTOLINK in VSE). The module is read and combined with MODA into an executable phase.

The Linkage Editor has no idea which module should receive control at run-time. Unless specified elsewhere, it assumes the first module read from SYSLNK should get control (in this case MODA).

Now, let's back up and review the process in detail. Here are the basic logic steps as executed by the Linkage Editor, presented in a fashion to help you determine what, if any, special considerations need to be made.

1. First, it OPENs and READs SYSLNK. That data set may contain object module(s), control statements, or both. If it contained only object modules, all decisions would use Linkage Editor defaults (e.g., which module gets control at run-time, temporary versus permanent status). If it contained only control statements (covered later), they would need to specify which modules to process. Since INCLUDEd modules may contain 1) control statements and 2) object modules (which may contain tables that identify the name of all modules CALLed by them), this would become additional input to the Linkage Editor.

   The Linkage Editor continues to read (and process in the order of appearance) control statements and object modules until end-of-file is reached on SYSLNK or an ENTRY statement is read.

2. If all the object code needed to create a phase is in SYSLNK, the Linkage Editor searches no other libraries, but follows any control statement instructions and is then finished with that phase (see step 4, below).

3. If, after reading all input from SYSLNK, there were missing modules, the Linkage Editor has a priority of search to locate the missing module(s). That priority is
   * Were there INCLUDE control statements specifying additional modules? If so, the Linkage Editor will search the LIBDEF OBJ sublibraries. An INCLUDE statement identifies modules that contain a) object code that is to be included in the new phase or b) INCLUDE statements for additional input for the phase (INCLUDE statements may be nested up to a depth of 5). Note: Modules specified on INCLUDE statements are included in the phase, whether needed or not. The Linkage Editor is just following your instructions.

- Was NOAUTO specified on the ACTION statement? If so, the Linkage Editor does no further searching for the missing modules (the AUTOLINK function). If AUTO is specified, the LIBDEF OBJ sublibrary is searched.

4. After processing all the modules, the Linkage Editor produces the listing to SYSLST. It then creates the phase, based on the following criteria:
   - Was OPTION CATAL specified? If so, there must be a PHASE statement that names the phase and there must be a LIBDEF PHASE statement with CATALOG specified. The Linkage Editor writes the new phase into the named sublibrary.
   - Was OPTION LINK specified instead? If so, no PHASE or LIBDEF PHASE,CATALOG=... statement is needed, as the phase will be stored temporarily, for possible execution later in this JOB (i.e., // EXEC). Note: Only one phase may be stored at a time in this fashion within the job.
   - If end-of-file on SYSLNK has been reached, the Linkage Editor terminates. If the processing in step 4 was caused by the appearance of an ENTRY statement, that should be the last statement in SYSLNK, since the VSE Linkage Editor can create only one independent phase per execution.

That wraps up Linkage Editor processing. The Linkage Editor's only function is to locate and bind all modules that you (or the object module) identified as being needed in a phase. Whether the modules are needed or not, whether control is given to the right module, whether the modules are reentrant or not, are decisions the Linkage Editor cannot make. It only follows instructions and makes assumptions in the absence of those instructions.

Linkage Editor control statements.

These are the control statements, presented with the options most commonly used. For the options that are specified via the ACTION statement to the Linkage Editor, see the section JCL Requirements.

Control statements follow traditional IBM syntax (i.e., they must begin at or after column 2, must not exceed column 71, must have a nonblank character in column 72 if continued to a following statement, and must begin in column 16 on any continued statements). In most cases, the examples shown can be combined into one statement, if desired. The examples shown are the most common format.

```
INCLUDE   modulename      <— Forces inclusion of a module
```

This statement is a demand that the named module be included in the new phase. The Linkage Editor will search available sublibraries to locate and include it. The Linkage Editor includes the module, even if there are no CALLs to it and even if it is a duplicate of modules already located. Example:

```
// LIBDEF   OBJ,SEARCH=(PROJX.OBJSUBLIB)
// OPTION LINK
   INCLUDE MODB
// EXEC LNKEDT
```

In this case, the Linkage Editor would search the sublibrary specified in the LIBDEF statement and look for a member named MODB. MODB might contain control statements or object code.

```
PHASE   phasename,* [,NOAUTO] [,SVA]   <- Names a phase
```

If used, this must be the first control statement for a phase. This statement names the phase and all following object code becomes part of this phase. The Linkage Editor should read only one PHASE statement per execution. (Note: If one is not provided, VSE provides a dummy PHASE statement to allow for testing with the LINK option.) If OPTION CATAL was specified, the PHASE statement is required and the phase will be placed in the sublibrary identified by the CATALOG parameter on the LIBDEF PHASE statement. The NOAUTO option is identical to that on the ACTION statement (in the section JCL Requirements), except that here it means that AUTOLINK should not be used for this phase. The SVA option should be specified for phases that are to be placed in the SVA. These would normally be phases that are high-volume, on-line transactions that were compiled with RENT.

Note: COBOL II has the ability, based on the compile option, NAME, to create this Linkage Editor control statement for you. You will need to code it manually when NOAUTO or SVA needs to be on the statement. When done by the compiler, the PHASE statement format is PHASE program-id,*. The statement is generated when the compile options OBJECT and NAME are used. (Warning: If you specify the combination of OBJECT and NAME compile options, there will be a PHASE statement at the beginning of every module. When doing that, you should be compiling only one module [i.e., no batch compiles]. With batch compiles, the Linkage Editor output would be multiple, dependent phases.)

```
ENTRY   externalname        <- Specifies logical beginning of
                               phase
```

where externalname can be PROGRAM-ID name or ENTRY name from the source program.

When the logical beginning of the program might be other than the first module's PROGRAM-ID name (CSECT name), use the ENTRY statement. This is useful when you are combining modules in different sequences and can't predict their order of appearance to the Linkage Editor. When used, the ENTRY statement must be the last statement for the phase. This statement is never needed on single-module phases that have no ENTRY statement in the PROCE-

DURE DIVISION, or where the module that is the logical beginning of the phase is the first module to be processed by the Linkage Editor. Note: VSE places an ENTRY statement with a blank entry point at the end of SYSLNK, guaranteeing the presence of an ENTRY statement (this defaults to giving control to the first module). It is for this reason that you do not need an ENTRY statement unless the logical beginning of the phase is other than the first module.

Consider an example where PROGA CALLs PROGB. Both have been previously compiled. Now, PROGB is being recompiled due to a needed change. Since the Linkage Editor assumes the first object module read in through SYSLNK is the entry point, an ENTRY statement is needed, such as the following:

```
// OPTION LINK,NODECK
// EXEC IGYCRCTL,SIZE=IGYCRCTL        <— COBOL II compiler
        ID DIVISION.
        PROGRAM-ID.  PROGB.
             .                         <— instream source program
             .
/*
  INCLUDE PROGA                        <— placed in SYSLNK
  ENTRY    PROGA
// EXEC LNKEDT
   .
   .
```

Physically, PROGB will precede PROGA in the phase, although, because of the ENTRY statement, PROGA will be the logical beginning point. Note: This could cause debugging complications if you assume that the entry point identified in a dump is the beginning of the phase.

Here is an example, using statements where an object module is created in the first step:

```
// LIBDEF OBJ,SEARCH=(PROJX.SUBLIB)
// LIBDEF PHASE,CATALOG=(PROJX.PHASELIB)
// OPTION CATAL
   PHASE MAINA,*,SVA                   <— placed in SYSLNK
// EXEC IGYCRCTL,SIZE=IGYCRCTL         <— COBOL II compiler
        ID DIVISION.
        PROGRAM-ID.  PROGA.
             .                         <— instream source program
             .
/*
  INCLUDE PROGC                        <— placed in SYSLNK
  INCLUDE PROGD
// EXEC LNKEDT
/&
```

Contents of SYSLNK at beginning of LNKEDT:

```
PHASE MAINA,*,SVA
  object text-PROGA
    .
    .
INCLUDE PROGC
INCLUDE PROGD
ENTRY
```

In this example, the phase will be named MAINA, from the PHASE statement. The phase will contain PROGA, plus whatever is in PROGC and PROGD (even if not referenced). The module that gets control at run-time will be the first module, as no ENTRY statement was provided, leaving only the one generated by VSE.

This section on the Linkage Editor was not intended to give you all possible information for using it. Instead, it was intended to help you understand the flow and to determine when you need various JCL and control statements. JCL for the Linkage Editor is defined under the section JCL Requirements. Also, the order of appearance of the control statements is explained in that section.

3.11. SPECIFYING COBOL II OPTIONS

The COBOL II compile options are referenced throughout this book, often with partial explanations or examples of use. This section is somewhat more academic, explaining what each option does and typical uses, rather than describing tips and techniques.

3.11.1. Options Available

The options available fall into four categories: (1) those you may specify at compile-time, (2) those you may specify at run-time, (3) those you can not specify at compile or run-time, and (4) those that are ignored. I make you aware of that third category because, if your attempts to override an option aren't working, it is because your company has prevented it. This ability to enforce compile options is new with COBOL II. The fourth category may sound strange, but COBOL II provides some options that do not take effect with VSE, but are for XA-Mode Portability, in case you later migrate the code to an MVS environment.

COBOL II compile-time options.

Since those specified at compile-time are the most common, let's look there first. Figure 3.3 lists them by some general categories. Several options appear in more than one column. The categories are:

Performance: These are options that affect resource usage, either at compile-time or at run-time. "R" means the option affects run-time. "C" means the option affects compile-time. "O" means the option affects input/output of the compiler, other than to SYSLST.

Documentation: These are options that affect the SYSIPT input or SYSLST output (normally, printed listings) from the compile.

Structure: These are options that affect the module-to-module structure, and the residency and addressing facilities of the run-time module.

Standards: These options provide opportunities your company may wish to use to monitor or enforce standards.

Test-debug: These options provide debugging capabilities, but at the expense of extra resource usage. "C" is for compiler debugging, for use by systems programmers.

Run-time effect: These are options that have an effect on the run-time environment (either in required JCL, data formats, application logic, or options) that may be changed from that specified at compile-time.

In reviewing the following list, you may want a list of the defaults at your company. You can get that by submitting any program for a compile, if you have included the SOURCE compile option. If, at the same time, you want a list of all COBOL II error messages, use this two-statement program:

```
ID DIVISION.
PROGRAM-ID. ERRMSG.
```

```
ADV        Options:  ADV, NOADV
              Abbreviations:  None
```

This option is used with WRITE AFTER ADVANCING statement. It adds 1 byte to the length of 01-level entry. For example, to write a 133-byte physical record with the first byte for carriage control would require a 132-byte record definition with ADV and would require a 133-byte record definition (with the first byte not referenced) with NOADV. ADV gives better performance and retains device independence.

```
APOST      Options:  APOST, QUOTE
              Abbreviations:  APOST, Q
```

This option determines whether you will enclose literals with the apostrophe (') or with quotation marks (").

```
AWO          Options: AWO, NOAWO
             Abbreviations: None
```

This option specifies APPLY WRITE ONLY for any physical sequential datasets with blocked, V-mode records. AWO gives a better performance.

```
BUFSIZE      Options: BUFSIZE(integer)
             Abbreviations: BUF(integer)
```

This option specifies how many bytes may be allocated by the compiler for the work datasets. Specifying BUF(32760) gives the best performance.

```
CMPR2        Options: CMPR2, NOCMPR2
             Abbreviations: None
```

This option provides compatibility with COBOL II, Release 2. Note: That version of COBOL II is not covered in this book. The Release 2 implementation of COBOL II was a subset of ANSI 85, and there are some incompatibilities. NOCMPR2 should be the option you use to take full advantage of the features of COBOL II in this book. If you have earlier COBOL II programs, use CMPR2 and the FLAGMIG compile option to identify potential incompatibilities, if any. CICS and SQL/DS applications must specify NOCMPR2. Refer to *VS COBOL II Application Programming Guide* (Chapter 9) for more guidance.

```
COMPILE      Options: COMPILE, NOCOMPILE, NOCOMPILE(n)
             Abbreviations: C, NOC, NOC(n)

             where n = W for level 4 errors  (Warning)
                       E for level 8 errors  (Error)
                       S for level 12 errors (Severe)
```

This option specifies whether a compile is to generate object code after detecting an error. COMPILE means to generate object code anyway. NOCOMPILE means to generate no object code, regardless. NOCOMPILE(n) means to stop generating object code if an error of that severity occurs. For example, NOCOMPILE(E) would mean to stop generating object code after the appearance of the first level 8 error message. Syntax checking of the program is not affected.

```
DATA         Options: DATA(24), DATA(31)
             Abbreviations: None
```

This option is ignored for VSE applications. This option is provided for upward compatibility with MVS applications. DATA specifies whether DATA

Option	Performance	Documentation	Structure	Standards	Test-debug	Runtime Effect?
ADV	R					X
APOST		X				
AWO	R					
BUFSIZE	C					
CMPR2*				X		
COMPILE	C			X		
DATA (N/A)	R		X			X
DBCS						X
DECK (N/A)	O					
DUMP					C	
DYNAM*	R		X			X
EXIT	C	X		X		
FASTSRT	R					
FDUMP	R				X	
FLAG		X				
FLAGMIG				X		
FLAGSAA				X		
FLAGSTD				X		
LANGUAGE		X				
LIB	O	X				
LINECOUNT		X				
LIST		X				
MAP		X				
NAME	O		X	X		
NUMBER		X				
NUMPROC	R					X
OBJECT (N/A)	O					
OFFSET		X				
OPTIMIZE	R					
OUTDD (N/A)						X
RENT*	R		X	X		X
RESIDENT*	R		X	X		X
SEQUENCE		X				
SIZE	C					

Figure 3.3. COBOL II compile options. * = CICS-sensitive. *Items marked with N/A are not processed by the Compiler.*

Option	Performance	Documentation	Structure	Standards	Test-debug	Runtime Effect?
SOURCE		X				
SPACE		X				
SSRANGE	R				X	X
TERM	O					
TEST	R				X	
TRUNC	R					X
VBREF		X				
WORD		X		X		
XREF		X				
ZWB						X

Figure 3.3. *(Continued)*

DIVISION entries are to be allocated below or above the 16-megabyte address in an MVS/XA or MVS/ESA environment. DATA(31) provides optimum flexibility. The primary use of DATA(24) is to maintain compatibility with older, non-COBOL II programs. The DATA option is ignored for MVS if NORENT is specified.

```
DBCS        Options:  DBCS, NODBCS
            Abbreviations:  None
```

This option provides support for the Double Byte Character Set (DBCS), allowing use of non-English characters if the 256 EBCDIC character set is insufficient. There is no further reference to this option in this book. Most applications will specify NODBCS.

```
DECK        Options:  DECK, NODECK
            Abbreviations:  D, NOD
```

If desired, specify DECK via JCL OPTION statement (i.e., ignored if specified via COBOL II PROCESS statement or JCL PARM). This option specifies that object code is to be written to SYSPCH in 80-byte records. This option is also dependent on your use of the NAME option. See also the OBJECT option.

```
DUMP        Options:  DUMP, NODUMP
              Abbreviations:  DU, NODU
```

This option is not for application debugging. Instead, it is for use by your systems programmers when a compiler error is occurring and they are diagnosing it. It should normally be NODUMP. If desired, the JCL OPTION statement must include DUMP or PARTDUMP.

```
DYNAM       Options:  DYNAM, NODYNAM
              Abbreviations:  DYN, NODYN
```

This option specifies whether CALL 'literal' statements are to generate static CALLS (resolved by the Linkage Editor) or dynamic CALLs (resolved at run-time). For more information, see the topic Static versus Dynamic Calls. For CICS, this must be NODYNAM. DYNAM may not be used with NORES.

```
EXIT        Options:  NOEXIT, EXIT(options)
```

The various options are not shown here because, if needed, your installation must specify what they are. EXIT is specified where an installation has one or more of the following:

1. A user-written routine that intercepts all reads from SYSIPT (COBOL source), providing them through the user routine.
2. A user-written routine that intercepts all COPY statements, providing the source statements through the routine instead of from the LIBDEF SOURCE file.
3. A user-written routine that intercepts all output to SYSLST and reformats or otherwise processes it.

These are powerful features, allowing a company to (1) "read" all source statements or COPY statements prior to being processed by the compiler, (2) provide direct access to a source program management system internally instead of through JCL, or (3) provide reformatted or duplicate compiler output listings. For most installations, this is NOEXIT.

```
FASTSRT     Options:  FASTSRT, NOFASTSRT
              Abbreviations:  FSRT, NOFSRT
```

This option specifies whether you want SORT/MERGE II to optimize processing for a COBOL SORT application. FASTSRT can improve processing for any

SORT statement that has either a USING or GIVING statement or both (i.e, a SORT... INPUT PROCEDURE...OUTPUT PROCEDURE would not be optimized). When FASTSRT is specified, COBOL II ignores it if the feature cannot improve your program performance. IF NOFASTSRT is specified, COBOL II will still produce information messages if optimization could have been realized.

```
FDUMP       Options:  FDUMP, NOFDUMP
            Abbreviations:  FDU, NOFDU
```

This option specifies that a formatted dump is to be produced at run-time in case of an ABEND. A SYSLST data set is required. For CICS, the dump is written to the CEBRxxxx temporary storage queue (which can be suppressed by the EXEC CICS HANDLE ABEND command). The formatted dump is not produced if TEST was also specified as a compile option. For more information, see Chapter 4 ("Debugging Techniques").

```
FLAG        Options:  FLAG(x,y), NOFLAG
            Abbreviations:  F(x,y), NOF

            where x and y =  I for Informational messages
                             W for level 4 errors   (Warning)
                             E for level 8 errors   (Error)
                             S for level 12 errors (Severe)
```

This option specifies whether error messages are to appear imbedded in the source listing (new with COBOL II). The "x" value specifies what error level (and above) messages appear at the end of the listing. The "y" value specifies what error level (and above) messages appear within the listing. The "y" value must not be lower than the "x" value. For example, FLAG(I,E) means all messages appear at the end, but only level 8 errors and above appear within the listing. NOFLAG specifies no error messages.

```
FLAGMIG     Options:  FLAGMIG, NOFLAGMIG
            Abbreviations:  None
```

This option flags migration errors for incompatibility between COBOL II Release 3.0 and previous levels. See CMPR2 for more information. Normally this is NOFLAGMIG.

```
FLAGSAA     Options:  FLAGSAA, NOFLAGSAA
            Abbreviations:  None
```

This option flags statements that are incompatible with IBM's Systems Application Architecture (SAA). If your company has standardized on SAA, it should be FLAGSAA. Otherwise, it should be NOFLAGSAA. For more information on SAA, see Chapter 9 ("Related Publications").

```
FLAGSTD    Options:  FLAGSTD(options), NOFLAGSTD
```

This option flags statements that do not conform to the ANSI standard and specified subsets. The options are not listed here; they are specific to your installation. If your shop enforces a level of ANSI 85 or a Federal Information Processing Standard, your shop will be using FLAGSTD with some options specified. Otherwise, use NOFLAGSTD.

```
LANGUAGE   Options:  LANGUAGE(n)
           Abbreviations:  LANG(n)

           where n = EN  for mixed-case English
                     UE  for upper-case English only
                     JA or JP for the Japanese language
```

This option specifies the language to use to print the compile listing. This includes diagnostic messages, page headers, and compilation summary information. A special Japanese Language Feature must be installed to use options JA or JP. To print output in mixed-case English, specify LANG(EN).

```
LIB        Options:  LIB, NOLIB
           Abbreviations:  None
```

This option specifies whether COPY, BASIS, or REPLACE statements can be used. Since most shops use COPY statements, it should be set to LIB. There is no further reference to BASIS or REPLACE statements in this book. When used, there must be an IJSYS05 file in JCL and a LIBDEF SOURCE statement defining the COPY sublibrary.

```
LINECOUNT  Options:  LINECOUNT(n)
           Abbreviations:  LC

           where n = number of lines to print per page
```

This option specifies the number of lines to print per page on SYSLST during compilation. Specifying 0 causes no page ejects. Since the compiler uses three lines for titles, there will be three fewer COBOL statements per page than the specified line count.

```
LIST       Options:  LIST, NOLIST
           Abbreviations:  None
```

This option specifies whether a listing of generated assembler code for the compiled program should be produced to SYSLST. It is mutually exclusive with the OFFSET option. If both are used, OFFSET receives preference. For information on using this listing, see Chapter 4 ("Debugging Techniques"). The LIST option may also be specified as LISTX, through the JCL OPTION statement.

```
MAP        Options:  MAP, NOMAP
              Abbreviations:  None
```

This option specifies whether a DATA DIVISION map for the compiled program is to be produced to SYSLST. The MAP option may also be specified as SYM, through the JCL OPTION statement.

```
NAME       Options:  NAME, NAME(ALIAS), NAME(NOALIAS), NONAME,
              Abbreviations:  None
```

This option is used in conjunction with the JCL OPTION statement and your choice of DECK or OBJECT. When used with OBJECT, and either LINK or CATAL is on the JCL OPTION statement, it inserts a Linkage Editor PHASE control statement immediately preceding the first object statement for each program being compiled. The PHASE statement will use the PROGRAM-ID to construct the phase name (PHASE phasename,*).

When DECK is specified, and DECK is on the JCL OPTION statement, it inserts a VSE Librarian CATALOG statement immediately preceding the first object statement for each program compiled (CATALOG programid.OBJ,REPLACE=YES).

These actions occur if any NAME option other than NONAME is coded, [i.e., coding NAME(ALIAS), NAME(NOALIAS), or NAME causes the same result]. For an example of where this is useful, see the section JCL Requirements in this chapter. Usually, the default for this is NONAME.

```
NUMBER     Options:  NUMBER, NONUMBER
              Abbreviations:  NUM, NONUM
```

This option specifies whether the compiler should use sequence numbers from your program in columns 1–6. If so, they are sequence-checked. To me, this was important when programs were on punched cards. Now, with most people using DASD to store source programs, I suggest using NONUMBER. With NONUMBER, the compiler generates numbers for the compilation and all diagnostics refer to those generated numbers.

```
NUMPROC    Options:  NUMPROC(n)
              Abbreviations:  None

              where n = MIG   for migration support
                        PFD   for preferred sign support
                        NOPFD for no preferred sign support
```

This option specifies how signs in data fields are to be handled by generated code. This topic is explored under the section Defining, Initializing, and Using Data Areas. Your shop probably has a companywide standard on this option. If, after reading the mentioned topic, you feel your application should use a different option, I suggest you test the application and discuss it with others at your shop. I say this because a book can never address the many possibilities that may exist. If in doubt, NUMPROC(NOPFD) works, but at the cost of efficiency. The most efficient option is NUMPROC(PFD).

```
OBJECT     Options:  OBJECT, NOOBJECT
           Abbreviations:  OBJ, NOOBJ
```

To use this option, specify LINK or CATAL on the JCL OPTION statement (i.e., ignored if specified via COBOL II PROCESS statement or JCL PARM). Specifies whether the object module is to be written to SYSLNK in 80-byte records. OBJECT is required if the TEST option is also specified. This option is also dependent on your use of the NAME option. See also DECK. To generate object code, either OBJECT or DECK must be set on.

```
OFFSET     Options:  OFFSET, NOOFFSET
           Abbreviations:  OFF, NOOFF
```

This option specifies whether a condensed listing of generated code will be produced to SYSLST. This listing shows the beginning offset location of each procedural statement. See also LIST. If used in conjunction with LIST, LIST will be ignored. For information on using this listing, see Chapter 4 ("Debugging Techniques").

```
OPTIMIZE   Options:  OPTIMIZE, NOOPTIMIZE
           Abbreviations:  OPT, NOOPT
```

This option specifies whether optimized code is to be generated for the compiled program. This is enhanced from the optimizing facility in DOS/VS COBOL. When OPTIMIZE is specified, it not only seeks to optimize individual statements, but also to combine statements if possible. In addition, it will attempt to create inline PERFORMs when possible and to bypass any code that will not be executed. Because the generated code is often quite different on a statement-by-statement basis, you may want to specify NOOPTIMIZE during initial testing. NOOPTIMIZE also reduces costs if you do many compiles before putting a program in productional use.

```
OUTDD      Options:  OUTDD(ddname)
           Abbreviations:  OUT(ddname)
```

This option is ignored for VSE. This specifies what ddname will be used for DISPLAY messages at run-time in MVS systems. The option normally specified is OUTDD(SYSOUT).

```
RENT        Options:  RENT, NORENT
            Abbreviations:  None
```

This option specifies that the compiled program is to be generated with reentrant code. It also allows the program to be executed in the SVA. RENT programs may not be mixed with NORENT programs. RENT is required for CICS programs. Unless you have special considerations, I suggest specifying RENT to take advantage of the extended memory accessibility. See RESIDENT for related information. Also, see the Linkage Editor PHASE statement (the SVA option) and the topic, RESIDENT and REENTRANT Options, in the previous section, Creating a Phase.

```
RESIDENT    Options:  RESIDENT, NORESIDENT
            Abbreviations:  RES, NORES
```

This option specifies that CALLs to COBOL II run-time modules will be resolved at run-time, not during the link-edit process. This produces smaller phases that access the most current version of the COBOL II modules. RES is required for CICS programs. See RENT for more information.

```
SEQUENCE    Options:  SEQUENCE, NOSEQUENCE
            Abbreviations:  SEQ, NOSEQ
```

This option specifies whether the source statement sequence numbers are to be validated. Unless your program is on punched cards, which could be dropped, NOSEQ is more efficient and prevents irrelevant error messages.

```
SIZE        Options:  SIZE(nnnn) or SIZE(MAX) or SIZE(nnnK)
            Abbreviations:  SZ(...)

            where n = memory requirements
```

This option specifies how much GETVIS memory is to be used by the compiler. To a degree, the compiler is more efficient if more memory is specified. The number specified must be at least 180K if the compiler is using the SVA, and at least 600K if not using the SVA. My suggestion (for performance) is to set it to a number that works well in your environment, and at least 1000K. Setting SIZE(MAX) causes the compiler to use all memory in the partition, which causes problems under ICCF.

```
SOURCE       Options:  SOURCE, NOSOURCE
             Abbreviations:  S, NOS
```

This option specifies whether the source listing is to be produced to SYSLST. See the following section on JCL for tips on managing this listing. This option may also be specified by coding LIST on a JCL OPTION statement.

```
SPACE        Options:  SPACE(1), SPACE(2) or SPACE(3)
             Abbreviations:  None
```

This option specifies single, double, or triple spacing of the SOURCE listing from the compile.

```
SSRANGE      Options:  SSRANGE, NOSSRANGE
             Abbreviations:  SSR, NOSSR
```

This option specifies whether the debug code for subscript and index range checking is to be included in the object module. The debug code is also included to check reference modification. This can increase cpu use during running. Output from this option is written to SYSLOG or to the CICS CEBRxxxx queue. The program will be terminated upon occurrence of any detected error. This option can be affected by the matching run-time option, following.

```
TERMINAL     Options:  TERMINAL, NOTERMINAL
             Abbreviations:  TERM, NOTERM
```

This option requests that compile-time messages and diagnostics be sent to SYSLOG.

```
TEST         Options:  TEST, NOTEST
             Abbreviations:  TES, NOTES
```

This option requests that object code be produced to run with the COBOL II Debug facility, COBTEST. This option forces these additional options: RES, NOFDUMP, NOOPTIMIZE, OBJECT. Information on COBTEST is contained in Chapter 4.

```
TRUNC        Options:  TRUNC(n)
             Abbreviations:  None

             where n = BIN    allow full binary value
                       OPT    optimize object code
                       STD    conforms to American National
                              Standard
```

This option determines how binary (COMP) data will be truncated in your application. Binary data is stored as 2-byte or 4-byte values, regardless of the PIC clause. Your choice of TRUNC specifies whether the maximum binary value should be allowed, TRUNC(BIN); the American National Standard should be used, TRUNC(STD); or optimized code based on an assessment of the PIC clause and the field size, TRUNC(OPT). This option is discussed at length in an earlier section on data efficiency. IBM suggests that you use BIN if your program uses CICS or SQL/DS. Because of the performance implications, you may want to test other settings for your application.

BIN allows the maximum value, regardless of the PIC clause. STD uses a generic approach, using only the PIC clause. OPT assesses the field size (2 or 4 bytes) and the PIC clause to generate the most efficient code.

There is no one-to-one correspondence with the TRUNC options of earlier COBOL compilers.

```
VBREF       Options:  VBREF, NOVBREF
            Abbreviations:  None
```

This option generates a listing at compile-time of the different verbs used and how many times each verb is used. It can be useful to assess whether a program uses verbs that are unfamiliar to you or that do not follow your shop standards. NOVBREF causes a more efficient compilation.

```
WORD        Options:  WORD(xxxx) or NOWORD
            Abbreviations:  WD, NOWD

            where xxxx = 4-character name of a word table
            developed by your installation
```

This option allows a company to develop a table of verbs that are to be checked during compilation. For example, if ALTER or GO TO are not allowed, they could be placed in this table, and at compile-time could generate a warning message developed by your shop.

```
XREF        Options:  XREF, XREF(SHORT), XREF(FULL) or NOXREF
            Abbreviations:  X, NOX
```

This option specifies whether a cross-reference list is to be produced by the compiler. The cross-reference list is at the end of the source listing, and if SOURCE is specified also appended at the right of related source statements. XREF and XREF(FULL) generate a list of all names. XREF(SHORT) generates a list of referenced names. This option may also be specified with a JCL OPTION statement, specifying XREF for the XREF(FULL) option and SXREF for the XREF(SHORT) option.

```
ZWB          Options:  ZWB, NOZWB
                  Abbreviations:  None
```

ZWB causes a compare of a signed numeric item with an alphanumeric item to have the sign stripped prior to the compare, e.g., a +5 (hex C5) would be equal to 5 (hex F5). Although I don't recommend it, NOZWB could be used if you compare numeric items to SPACES.

COBOL II run-time options.

These options may be different for different environments (e.g., CICS and non-CICS). These options are usually set for an entire shop. They are presented here so you may modify (some of) them at run-time. You may need to contact your technical staff for assistance in their selection and use. Figure 3.4 lists them by some general categories. Several run-time options appear in more than one column. The categories are

Performance: These are options that affect resource usage.

Documentation: These are options that affect the messages from COBOL II run-time modules.

Structure: These are options that affect the module-to-module structure, and the residency and addressing facilities of the run-time module.

Standards: These options provide opportunities your company may wish to use to monitor or enforce standards.

Test-debug: These options provide debugging capabilities, but at the expense of extra resource usage.

How to specify: These two columns specify whether your company defaults may be overridden and how. For information on how to do this, see the topics Specifying Options at Run-time, and Specifying Options via Preassembled Modules.

Before reviewing these, you may want to get a list of your company defaults. That may be accomplished by submitting a COBOL II program for a compile, link, and execute. If you have no program, this one works fine:

```
ID DIVISION.
PROGRAM-ID.  EXAMPLE.
PROCEDURE DIVISION.
1.  STOP RUN.
```

Option	Performance	Documentation	Structure	Standards	Test-debug	How to specify	
						Use IGZEOPT	Use JCL
AIXBLD	X			X		X	X
DEBUG*	X				X	X	X
LANGUAGE		X					
LIBKEEP*	X		X	X			
MIXRES*	X		X			X	
RTEREUS*	X		X			X	
SIMVRD*	X					X	X
SPOUT		X			X	X	X
SSRANGE	X				X	X	X
STAE	X		X	X	X	X	X
UPSI			X			X	X
WSCLEAR	X			X			

Figure 3.4. COBOL II run-time options. * Option ignored for CICS

The run-time EXEC statement for the linked program needs this format:

```
//  EXEC  programname,PARM='/ SPOUT'
```

Output is written to SYSLOG. Options listed will be those for the batch environment. For a CICS environment, ask your systems programmer. Normally, you won't need to override or even know about most of these options, other than some of those for debugging purposes. Here is an example of the output:

```
+IGZ025I   Run-time options in effect: 'SYSTYPE(OS), LANGUAGE(UE),
+          NOAIXBLD, NODEBUG, LIBKEEP, NOMIXRES, RTEREUS, NOSIMVRD, SPOUT,
+          NOSSRANGE, STAE, NOWSCLEAR, UPSI(00000000)'
+          Default options overidden: 'NOSPOUT'
```

The option *SYSTYPE(OS)* is not an error. This is how the systems programmer specifies that the options are not for CICS (i.e., SYSTYPE(CICS) is used to specify CICS).

AIXBLD   Options: AIXBLD, NOAIXBLD

If the option is specified, the system checks for empty VSAM indexes at OPEN and invokes Access Method Services to build alternate indexes. This affects performance and also requires that a SYSLST statement be included for Access Method Services messages. NOAIXBLD means that VSAM indexes are already defined.

DEBUG   Options: DEBUG, NODEBUG

This option is effective when WITH DEBUGGING MODE is specified in the source program. This is the only reference to WITH DEBUGGING MODE in this book.

LANGUAGE   Options:

See this option previously under Compile-time options.

LIBKEEP   Options: LIBKEEP, NOLIBKEEP

This option causes all COBOL II run-time modules to be retained in memory during a run unit. This can increase performance, especially if COBOL modules are CALLed by non-COBOL main programs. In most cases, LIBKEEP should be specified.

MIXRES   Options: MIXRES, NOMIXRES

This option is specified when RES and NORES programs are combined within a single run unit. This is primarily for migration assistance to COBOL II, where NORES was the previous default. This should be used only if needed and not used as an ongoing standard. Considerations on using MIXRES are in the topic COBOL II to DOS/VS COBOL, in the section Module Structures.

RTEREUS   Options: RTEREUS, NORTEREUS

This option was discussed earlier, in the section Module Structures. RTEREUS initializes the run-time environment for reusability. This option does not apply to CICS. It affects program structure and may or may not be set at your installation.

SIMVRD   Options: SIMVRD, NOSIMVRD

When processing a variable length relative dataset, this option uses a VSAM KSDS to simulate that data organization. For more assistance, see *COBOL II Application Programming Guide* (Chapter 9, "Related Publications").

SPOUT   Options: SPOUT, NOSPOUT

This option issues a message indicating the amount of storage allocated and the selected run-time options in effect. This uses the WTP (Write-to-programmer) facility. In CICS, the message goes to the CEBRxxxx queue.

SSRANGE   Options: SSRANGE, NOSSRANGE

This option activates SSRANGE object code, if any, generated during the compile. This feature allows you to compile with SSRANGE, yet control its use at run-time. Using NOSSRANGE at run-time can reduce cpu usage somewhat, and eliminates the need to recompile to activate SSRANGE. Many shops set the default to NOSSRANGE to prevent inadvertent use of SSRANGE in productional applications.

STAE   Options: STAE, NOSTAE

STAE causes COBOL II to intercept ABENDs and clean-up the run-time environment in addition to producing a formatted dump (if FDUMP was specified). STAE is the normal setting and is recommended for CICS applications as well as batch applications. Batch requires a SYSLST assignment. (Note: The word *STAE* is an MVS word, being the name of the facility to allow interception to occur. The proper VSE term is *STXIT*, in case you need to discuss this with a systems programmer.)

UPSI   Options: UPSI(nnnnnnnn)

            where n = digit from 0 to 7

There are 8 UPSI switches. They are provided for backward compatibility when a shop is dependent on their use. These switches cannot be referenced if the option NOCMPR2 is set. Since NOCMPR2 is the preferred option to take advantage of the newest COBOL II features, the UPSI feature is meaningless at most shops. Also, COBOL II ignores the JCL UPSI statement.

WSCLEAR   Options: WSCLEAR, NOWSCLEAR

This option causes all external data records and working storage areas acquired by a RENT program to be set to binary zeros (other than fields with VALUE clauses). This can reduce performance. Another approach is to write initialization code in your program or use more VALUE statements.

Additional COBOL II options.

There are other options that you cannot use, but that affect COBOL II. They are listed in case some of the information I've given you in other sections appears to conflict with what is happening to your code. These options are used at the time COBOL II is installed or modified by your systems programmers. If you believe the options are incorrect at your installation, you will need to see your systems programmers to determine the settings.

ALOWCBL(YES) This option specifies whether PROCESS or CONTROL statements may be imbedded in the source program. The default is YES. It is required for CICS. (You will want to use these statements, as they allow programmers to control the SOURCE output.)

DBCSXREF(NO) The default is NO. This specifies some cross-reference options for DBCS (the double byte facility for languages with extensive alphabets). If you specify YES, you must order more software. If your installation needs DBCS, this option must be set to YES.

INEXIT, LIBEXIT, PRTEXIT These are the three components that make up the EXIT facility. If your company uses one or more of these, they can be set to be the default by your systems programmer.

LVLINFO This is a Systems Engineering option to specify what level is used at your company. If specified, up to 4 characters may follow the IBM Release number. It is a means of keeping track of different releases in your shop's terms, if desired. Default is to just print the IBM level number.

NUMCLS (PRIM) This is the technical side of NUMPROC. This setting determines what signs NUMPROC will accept. NUMPROC(PRIM) is the assumption used in this book, as that supports signs that are either C, D, or F.

3.11.2. Specifying COBOL II Options via JCL at Compile-Time

The options you need to specify are those other than the installation defaults. All options may be coded this way except for those identified in the previous topic that were invoked by the JCL OPTION statement (e.g., DECK, OBJECT). They may be coded as follows:

```
//  EXEC IGYCRCTL,PARM='option-1,option-2,...'

Example:  //  EXEC IGYCRCTL,PARM='SOURCE,OFFSET,OPTIMIZE'
```

3.11.3. Specifying COBOL II Options Within the Source Program

There will be times when you want to keep a program's compile options with the source code. That can be done with PROCESS statements. A PROCESS statement may be anywhere between columns 1 and 66. There may be no spaces between options. You may use more than one PROCESS statement. The format is

```
PROCESS  option-a,option-b,...

Example:  PROCESS   SOURCE,OFFSET,VBREF
          PROCESS   XREF,OPTIMIZE
                    ID DIVISION.
                       .
                       .
```

Other than for installation options that have been defined as not eligible for override, the PROCESS options take precedence over any in the JCL and those of the installation defaults. You may code CBL in place of PROCESS, if desired. (Don't confuse it with *CBL statements, covered in the section JCL Requirements.)

3.11.4. Specifying COBOL II Options at Run-Time via JCL

As noted above, the run-time options may be specified (1) via JCL at run-time or (2) via a module called IGZEOPT. This topic addresses the JCL approach. The JCL option may be used if your program is capable of accepting a PARM at run-time (e.g., CICS programs cannot). The syntax is to code the PARM statement with the selected run-time option(s) preceded by a slash. Any PARM the application program is to receive must be to the left of the slash mark.

The following example executes a program called MYPROG, and sets SSRANGE on (assuming the program was compiled with SSRANGE). The second example has two logical PARMs, one for the application and one for the COBOL II run-time options. The first PARM is WEEKLY and is made available to the program through the PROCEDURE DIVISION USING statement. The second PARM is SSRANGE,MIXRES and is processed by the COBOL II run-time environment.

```
//   EXEC MYPROG,PARM='/SSRANGE'
```

    or

```
//   EXEC MYPROG,PARM='WEEKLY/SSRANGE,MIXRES'
```

3.11.5. Specifying COBOL II Run-Time Options in Preassembled Modules

There will be times when you need to specify run-time options and can't use JCL (e.g., CICS) or you want to specify options that cannot be specified via JCL (see Figure 3.4). In those cases, your installation must establish a module called

IGZEOPT for each combination of desired options. (IBM provides a facility that your technical staff can use to create this module.) You can include the module into your program during link-edit processing. You use normal INCLUDE processing (see the previous section, Creating a Phase) to accomplish this. The reason it works is that COBOL II inserts a weak external reference (WXTRN) into your program for IGZEOPT. The module is never required, but if it is present at run-time, the COBOL II modules use it to establish options for the run unit. Note: If COBOL II is new at your shop, the needed IGZEOPT modules may not have been created. Your systems programmers need to be told all possibilities that may be needed, so they can create them. At a minimum, this is usually at least one version with the setting for SSRANGE opposite the shop default (e.g., if the default is NOSSRANGE, a version is needed with SSRANGE to support testing).

3.12. JCL REQUIREMENTS: COMPILE, LINK, AND EXECUTE

Your installation will probably use JCL differently from that shown here. This information may be useful, however, to assist you in improving performance or in understanding some of the processing steps. While you may have other facilities at your shop, such as on-line compile and test facilities, this section deals with the batch facility. It is a common format across most installations and usually is the least expensive.

3.12.1. JCL for Compilation

In many installations, JCL procedures (PROCs) will be used for the compile, since there is so much JCL to specify. An example of using the IBM-supplied PROC follows:

```
// JOB    jobid
// EXEC  PROC= COB2UC
PROCESS SOURCE,OFFSET,FDUMP
      ID DIVISION.
         .
         .
         .
/*
/&
```

In many cases, you may want more flexibility and will use your own JCL. See Figure 3.5 for an example of the JCL for VSE.

While the JCL at your shop may be different, let's review the sample VSE compile JCL in Figure 3.5.

```
 1.  //  JOB    jobid
 2.  //  LIBDEF  PHASE,SEARCH=(cob2.sublibrary)
 3.  //  LIBDEF  SOURCE,SEARCH=(copy.sublibrary)
 4.  //  ASSGN  SYS001,DISK,VOL=volume-serial,SHR
     //  DLBL   IJSYS01,'file id',0,SD
     //  EXTENT  SYS001,volume-serial,...
     //  ASSGN  SYS002,DISK,VOL-volume-serial,SHR
     //  DLBL   IJSYS02,'file id',0,SD
     //  EXTENT  SYS002,volume-serial,...
     //  ASSGN  SYS003,DISK,VOL=volume-serial,SHR
     //  DLBL   IJSYS03,'file id',0,SD
     //  EXTENT  SYS003,volume-serial,...
     //  ASSGN  SYS004,DISK,VOL=volume-serial,SHR
     //  DLBL   IJSYS04,'file id',0,SD
     //  EXTENT  SYS004,volume-serial,...
 5.  //  ASSGN  SYS005,DISK,VOL=volume-serial,SHR
     //  DLBL   IJSYS05,'file id',0,SD
     //  EXTENT  SYS005,volume-serial,...
     //  ASSGN  SYS006,DISK,VOL=volume-serial,SHR
     //  DLBL   IJSYS06,'file id',0,SD
     //  EXTENT  SYS006,volume-serial,...
     //  ASSGN  SYS007,DISK,VOL=volume-serial,SHR
     //  DLBL   IJSYS07,'file id',0,SD
     //  EXTENT  SYS007,volume-serial,...
 6.  //  ASSGN  SYSLNK,DISK,VOL=volume-serial,SHR
     //  DLBL   IJSYSLN,'file id',0,SD
     //  EXTENT  SYSLNK,volume-serial,...
 7.  //  ASSIGN  SYSLST,device
 8.  //  OPTION  LIST,LISTX,LINK
 9.  //  EXEC   IGYCRCTL,SIZE=IGYCRCTL,PARM='XREF'
10.  PROCESS  VBREF
            IDENTIFICATION DIVISION.
               .
               .

     /*
     /&
```

Figure 3.5. Sample COBOL II compile JCL for VSE.

- Statement 1 specifies the JOB statement for accounting.
- Statement 2 specifies the sublibrary where the COBOL II compiler resides (not needed if COBOL II is accessed via system libraries).
- Statement 3 identifies the name of the sublibrary for locating COPY statements (LIB option must be specified).
- Statement number 4 (SYS001 through SYS007) are compiler work files. Your choice of BUFSIZE controls what block size is used for these (a larger BUFSIZE will reduce I/O and improve performance). Note: These files are normally predefined by systems programmers and need not be specified.
- Statement number 5 is only needed when LIB is specified, although it is easier to leave it in place if there is sufficient DASD space available. Note: Specifying NOLIB when COPY statements are not used will improve compiler performance, as an extra pass of the source code is avoided.
- Statement number 6 identifies a dataset for the object module (see OBJECT and DECK compile options) for use later as input to the Linkage Editor. In the example, SYSLNK is used because LINK was specified on the // OPTION statement. If DECK is specified on the // OPTION statement instead of LINK (or CATAL), the statements should be:

```
//   ASSGN   SYSPCH,DISK,VOL=volume-serial,SHR
//   DLBL    IJSYSPH,'file id',0,SD
//   EXTENT  SYSPCH,volume-serial,...
```

- Statement number 7 specifies the system-file for the compiler listing, SYSLST. Usually, this statement is not necessary if system defaults are acceptable.
- Statement number 8 is the JCL OPTION statement, specifying these COBOL II options: SOURCE (LIST), LIST (LISTX), and OBJECT (LINK). This could also have been done by using the PARM or PROCESS statements. (Exception: The OBJECT compiler option is ignored in VSE, requiring use of the // OPTION LINK statement when desired.)
- Statement number 9 invokes the COBOL II compiler, passing a PARM of XREF.
- Statement number 10 is an example of a PROCESS statement.
- In this example, the source program is part of the job-stream (SYSIPT). If the program is in a dataset, the following JCL could be inserted before the EXEC statement, replacing the PROCESS statement and in-stream source program. The EXEC must be followed by the CLOSE statement to reassign SYSIPT:

```
//   ASSGN   SYSIPT,DISK,VOL=volume-serial,SHR
//   DLBL    IJSYSIN,'file id',0,SD
//   EXTENT  SYSIPT,volume-serial,...
```

```
// EXEC   IGYCRCTL,SIZE=IGYCRCTL,PARM='XREF'
// CLOSE  SYSIPT,SYSRDR
```

- Efficiency is increased if the dataset has a large block size, especially for big programs (by large block size, I mean 12,000 or more).

MULTIPLE COMPILES. There are two ways to do multiple compiles. One is used when you want to compile a main program and one or more CALLed subprograms in one step and plan to link them into one phase. The other is used when you want to compile multiple programs that are to each be linked as separate run units. Let's take them separately:

Compiling a main module and subprogram(s): Insert "END PROGRAM program-id." as the last statement in each program. This lets the compiler tell the various programs apart. The second step is to arrange the sequence of source programs in the order you want the object modules to be created. Then, one execution of the compiler creates all the object modules in the specified sequence, such as,

```
// JOB
// LIBDEF  SOURCE,SEARCH=(copy.sublibrary)
// OPTION  LINK
// EXEC IGYCRCTL,SIZE=IGYCRCTL
     ID DIVISION.
     PROGRAM-ID.  MAINA.
          .
          .
          .
     END PROGRAM MAINA.
     ID DIVISION.
     PROGRAM-ID.  SUBPROGB.
          .
          .
          .
     END PROGRAM SUBPROGB.
/*
// EXEC LNKEDT
          .
          .
```

This generates the object code first for MAINA, and then for SUBPROGB. From the information in the previous section, Creating a Phase, you know that this minimizes or eliminates the need to code Linkage Editor control statements (e.g., LIBDEF OBJ and INCLUDE statements).

Compiling several independent modules. Insert "END PROGRAM program-id." as in the previous example, as the last statement in each program. This lets the compiler tell the various programs apart. The second step is to specify the

NAME option (along with any other desired options) on the EXEC statement, and specify DECK on the JCL OPTION statement. Then, one execution of the compiler creates all the object modules with VSE Librarian CATALOG statements preceding each object module.

This example generates the object code for PROGA, and PROGB and places a CATALOG statement before each one. This allows the compiler to create separate object modules from only one invocation of the compiler. A following step executes the VSE Librarian program to catalog the separate modules.

```
//   JOB   jobid
//   LIBDEF   SOURCE,SEARCH=(copy.sublibrary)
//   ASSGN   SYSPCH,DISK,VOL=volume-serial,SHR
//   DLBL   IJSYSPH,'object.code',0,SD
//   EXTENT   SYSPCH,volume-serial,...
//   OPTION   DECK
//   EXEC IGYCRCTL,SIZE=IGYCRCTL,PARM='NAME'
         ID DIVISION.
         PROGRAM-ID. PROGA.
                .
                .
                .
         END PROGRAM PROGA.
         ID DIVISION.
         PROGRAM-ID. PROGB.
                .
                .
                .
         END PROGRAM PROGB.
/*
//   IF $RC>4 THEN
//   GOTO   $EOJ
//   CLOSE   SYSPCH,device
//   ASSGN   SYSIPT,DISK,VOL=volume-serial,SHR
//   DLBL   IJSYSIN,'object.code',0,SD
//   EXTENT   SYSIPT,volume-serial,...
//   EXEC   LIBR,PARM='ACCESS SUBLIB=obj.sublibrary'
/*
//   CLOSE   SYSIPT,SYSRDR
/&
```

Warning: Do not specify the NAME option with the OBJECT option for this purpose. That combination causes PHASE statements to precede each object module, which the VSE Linkage Editor cannot process separately. Use that combination only when compiling a single module.

LIMITING PRINTED OUTPUT with *CBL. You can control the printing of SOURCE statements, generated assembler statements (LIST option), and data maps (the MAP option). This could be useful (and save some trees) when you have a large program, have changed a few statements, and need to see the output from one or more of those three options (SOURCE, LIST, MAP). Here is how it is done.

1. Specify appropriate compile options using the JCL OPTION statement, a PARM, or PROCESS statements (or some combination). These must include those which you want to control. In our example of controlling source and assembler statements, we would specify SOURCE and LIST with one of these three choices (if not already the installation default). This causes the compile to begin with the options set on. That is mandatory. If the options are set to NOSOURCE, NOLIST, or NOMAP, the next steps cannot take effect.

2. Include a statement in your source program that is similar to the PROCESS statement. This is a *CBL statement (also known as a CONTROL statement—CONTROL may be specified instead of *CBL, if desired). The *CBL statement is similar to PROCESS, but can only specify SOURCE or NOSOURCE, MAP or NOMAP, LIST or NOLIST, or some combination of the three. When encountered by the compiler, the compiler adjusts the compile options according to the *CBL options specified. The *CBL statement may begin in any column, starting with column 7. As with PROCESS, no spaces may appear between options. A reason to code the *CBL immediately is to negate any listings until we reach the part of our program we want to list. For our example, we would specify:

```
*CBL   NOSOURCE,NOLIST
```

3. Then, immediately preceding the code you want a listing of, insert another *CBL statement, such as:

```
*CBL   SOURCE,LIST
```

4. Finally, at the end of the code you want listed, insert another *CBL statement, identical to that in step 2, above.

Let's put it all that together in an example using PROCESS statements. Assume that SOURCE and LIST are set to NOSOURCE and NOLIST as installation defaults.

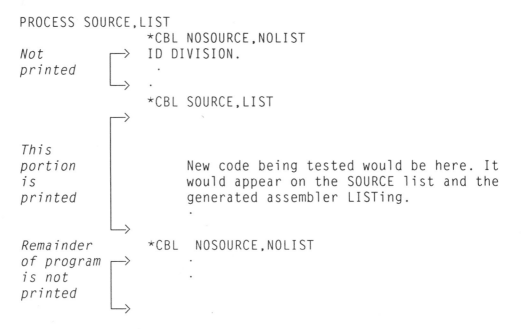

```
PROCESS SOURCE,LIST
                    *CBL NOSOURCE,NOLIST
                    ID DIVISION.
                     .
                     .
                    *CBL SOURCE,LIST


                        New code being tested would be here. It
                        would appear on the SOURCE list and the
                        generated assembler LISTing.
                         .

                    *CBL  NOSOURCE,NOLIST
                     .
                     .
```

Not printed

This portion is printed

Remainder of program is not printed

Using *CBL statements takes practice and adds work to the compile process, but this feature puts the ability to reduce paper usage in the programmer's hands. Prior to COBOL II, it was an all-or-nothing situation.

3.12.2. JCL for Link-edit Processing

The processing of the Linkage Editor was covered under the section Creating a Phase. This topic deals with the JCL requirements and how the control statements are processed.

JCL for the Linkage Editor.

There are several system assignments needed for the Linkage Editor, but some (the work files) are set up by your systems programmer. In this book, I will focus on the ones that you normally control. Here is a brief definition of each.

```
// OPTION  LINK  or  OPTION  CATAL
```

This JCL OPTION statement signals to VSE that a link-edit is to be performed in this job. Any assignment (ASSGN) of SYSLNK following this statement nullifies the option.

```
// LIBDEF OBJ,SEARCH=(sublibraryname,...)
```

This statement must precede the EXEC LNKEDT. It identifies the sublibraries that should be searched to locate INCLUDEd modules or to resolve

CALL statements. The search list should include the name of the COBOL II sublibrary.

```
// LIBDEF PHASE,CATALOG=(phase.sublibrary)
```

This statement must also precede the EXEC LNKEDT statement. It identifies the sublibrary where a phase will be stored. This statement is needed only when CATAL is specified on the // OPTION statement. (A PHASE control statement is also required.)

```
SYSLNK
```

SYSLNK is the input dataset to the Linkage Editor. If not explicitly assigned (ASSGN) in the job-stream, VSE provides a temporary one for the job.

Processing Control statements.

The control statements, defined in the section, Creating a Phase, may be defined in a dataset assigned to SYSLNK or, more commonly, in the input job-stream. In this book, all examples use the job-stream. The job-stream approach requires that LINK or CATAL be specified on the JCL OPTION statement. When one of those options is specified, VSE writes all Linkage Editor control statements to SYSLNK, based on order of appearance within the job-stream. This is why control statements for the Linkage Editor always appear in the job-stream before the EXEC LNKEDT statement. This allows situations such as the following to appear:

```
// OPTION LINK
   PHASE TRANSA,*
   INCLUDE DFHECI
// EXEC IGYCRCTL,SIZE=IGYCRCTL
      ID DIVISION.
         .
         .
         .
/*
   INCLUDE  PROGB
// EXEC LNKEDT
      .
```

In the above example, the PHASE statement and the INCLUDE DFHECI statement will be written to SYSLNK by VSE. The compiler (also because of option LINK) places the object code for the compiled program into SYSLNK. Finally, VSE encounters the next INCLUDE statement and writes it into SYSLNK. Then, when the Linkage Editor starts, it will read the INCLUDE DFHECI statement before encountering the object code from the compile, placing DFHECI at the beginning of the phase. Next, it will read the object module from the compile, placing it behind DFHECI. Finally, it will read the INCLUDE statement and search for the module PROGB, and place it last in the phase.

Here is an example of VSE link-edit JCL to use with the previous VSE example for compiling:

```
1.  // JOB    jobid
2.  // LIBDEF  OBJ,SEARCH=(obj.sublib,cobolii.sublib)
3.  // LIBDEF  PHASE,CATALOG=prod.sublibrary
4.  // OPTION  CATAL
5.     ACTION   MAP,SMAP
6.     PHASE    MAINA,*,,SVA
7.     INCLUDE  PROGA
8.     INCLUDE  PROGB
9.  // EXEC    LNKEDT
    /&
```

Figure 3.6. Sample link-edit JCL for VSE.

To review the VSE link-edit JCL:

- Statement 1 is the JOB statement for accounting.
- Statement 2 specifies the sublibrary that will be searched to resolve any INCLUDE statements or CALLs.
- Statement 3 identifies the sublibrary in which the newly linked phase will be catalogued (not needed for "link & go" job-streams).
- Statement 4 specifies that the output from the link will be catalogued (relates to statement 3).
- Statements 5 through 8 are the input to the Linkage Editor. ACTION must always be first, if used. PHASE specifies the phase name and also identifies that this phase is eligible to be loaded into the SVA (requires RENT compile option). PHASE must precede any object code or IN-CLUDE statements. The two INCLUDE statements tell the Linkage Editor what modules of object code to include in the phase. Since PROGA precedes PROGB and there is no ENTRY statement, the logical entry to the program will be the first executable statement in PROGA.

Selecting Link-edit options.

Options to the Linkage Editor are specified in the ACTION statement. When used, the ACTION statement must be the first record processed by the Linkage

Editor. The format is the same as for Linkage Editor control statements (documented in a previous topic).

ACTION [MAP or NOMAP] [,NOAUTO] [,CANCEL] [,SMAP]

MAP produces a listing to SYSLST of the CSECTs in the phase and their relative offsets

NOAUTO specifies that the AUTOLINK feature (whereby the Linkage Editor automatically searches available libraries for missing modules) is not to be done for this execution. This can be useful when a CALLed module is not needed for planned execution of the phase (e.g., testing specific logic paths).

CANCEL specifies that the link step is to be canceled if serious messages occur.

SMAP specifies that a sorted list of the CSECTs is to be produced to SYSLST. This is useful when a phase contains a large number of CSECTs.

Summary of Linkage Editor control statement order.

The control statements to the Linkage Editor must appear in the following certain order:

ACTION If used, it must appear first. Only one ACTION statement is allowed.

PHASE If used, it must appear here, before any object code or other control statements. Only one PHASE statement is allowed (for COBOL II phases).

INCLUDE If used, any number may appear before the ENTRY statement.

ENTRY If used, it must appear last. Only one ENTRY statement is allowed.

Linkage Editor Listing.

The Linkage Editor Listing may include weak external references (WXTRN), depicted as

```
UNRESOLVED EXTERNAL REFERENCES          WXTRN   IGZETUN
```

If the prefix of the module is IGZ, this is normal and does not require that you attempt to correct it. Also, AUTOLINK does not attempt to resolve WXTRN references.

3.12.3. JCL for Batch Execution

In executing a program, you need to consider these JCL requirements that are imposed on you by COBOL II. They are in addition to other JCL statements your application may require.

JCL assignment statements.

To execute your program, you may need one or more of these statements:

LIBDEF PHASE To identify to VSE where phase sublibraries are for the phases to be executed in this job. This may need to include the name of the COBOL II run-time library. Check with your systems programmers.

```
LIBDEF PHASE,SEARCH=(phase.sublibrary,...)
```

SYSLST To list COBOL II ABEND intercept information (STAE option), FDUMP output, COBTEST output, or application output generated by the DISPLAY statement.

```
//  ASSGN  SYSLST,device
```

SYSIPT To process any input from an ACCEPT statement or for use of COBTEST.

```
//  ASSGN  SYSIPT,appropriate parameters
```

If your run-unit has dynamically CALLed modules or the modules were compiled with RES, you may want to identify specific memory requirements on the EXEC statement (via SIZE). COBOL II modules use the GETVIS area of the partition for dynamically CALLed modules and COBOL II run-time modules (RES compile option) that are loaded specifically for this application. You can specify this on the EXEC statement by coding SIZE=phasename. This specifies that all memory in the partition beyond that needed for the phase may be allocated for GETVIS use.

Write After Advancing & ADV option.

When writing reports, you probably use the WRITE AFTER ADVANCING statement. Remember the ADV option, which allows you to not include a byte in the 01-level record for the ASA control character. For example, if you are writing a report that is to be 115 characters wide (they don't have to be 120 or 132 as some people believe), you would code it differently, depending on the setting of ADV.

With ADV

```
FD  FD-REPORT-FILE
    RECORD CONTAINS 115 CHARACTERS
    RECORDING MODE IS F.
01  FD-REPORT-RECORD   PIC X(115).
     ↑
     |_____|

    MOVE field-name TO FD-REPORT-RECORD
    WRITE FD-REPORT-RECORD AFTER ADVANCING 1
```

With NOADV

```
FD  FD-REPORT-FILE
    RECORD CONTAINS 116 CHARACTERS
    RECORDING MODE IS F.
01  FD-REPORT-RECORD.
    05              PIC X.        <— Not referenced
    05 FD-DATA-AREA PIC X(115).
             ↑
             |_____|

    MOVE field-name TO FD-DATA-AREA
    WRITE FD-REPORT-RECORD AFTER ADVANCING 1
```

In the first example, notice that the FD and 01-level specify the actual size of the report, freeing the programmer from being concerned with machine dependencies. This still requires the JCL to acknowledge the real record and block size of 116 (record size plus ASA control character).

The second example, using NOADV, has the same size on FD, 01-level, and JCL. It requires different coding, however. The first byte of the 01-level must not be referenced and no MOVEs may be made to the 01-level name. I recommend ADV, as I don't want to be concerned with accidentally modifying an ASA control character.

Sample Execution JCL

This is an example of a simple JCL stream to execute a program with one input file and a report file:

```
// JOB jobid
// LIBDEF  PHASE,SEARCH=(prod.sublibrary)
// ASSGN   ←⎤
// DLBL           ⎤        <—— Program file assignments
// EXTENT  ←⎦
// ASSIGN  SYSLST,device           <— Printer
// OPTION  PARTDUMP
// EXEC    PROGA,SIZE=PROGA
/&
```

3.12.4. SORT JCL Considerations

In preparing JCL for a sort, you need to consider the memory requirements and the amount of DASD needed for a sort. Calculating DASD space is beyond this book and that information is probably with your technical staff. Instead, let's review the memory use of COBOL II modules and SORT/MERGE II.

As mentioned previously, compiled COBOL II modules use the GETVIS area of a partition for certain COBOL II run-time modules (RES compile option) and for modules loaded dynamically (DYNAM option or CALL data-name technique). SORT/MERGE II, on the other hand, uses no GETVIS areas, requiring that all dynamic memory be in the remainder of the partition. This requires that you explicitly specify (through the SIZE parameter on the EXEC statement) how memory is to be allocated. For example, assuming a partition of 1500K, where 400K is needed for GETVIS and the phase is approximately 300K, the EXEC statement might be:

```
// EXEC phasename,SIZE=(phasename,800K)
```

This EXEC statement would allocate the partition as follows:

```
┌─────────────────────────────────┐
│                                 │
│  phase loaded here (300K)       │
│                                 │
├─────────────────────────────────┤
│  For SORT/MERGE II              │
│     (800K)                      │
│                                 │
│                                 │
├─────────────────────────────────┤
│                                 │
│  GETVIS area (400K)             │
│                                 │
└─────────────────────────────────┘
```

This is an example in which a COBOL SORT program has a USING statement and an OUTPUT PROCEDURE statement. The OMIT and INREC statements (see next section for information on SORT control statements) provide the logic needed to omit certain records from processing and to reformat the record to contain only the needed data fields for the OUTPUT processing. There are no COBOL changes required to use the OMIT process, but the INREC requires that the SD 01-level reflect the new data positions. For this example, the COBOL II program would need the statement, MOVE 'SYSIPT' TO SORT-CONTROL, because the control statements are in the job-stream. You will need to know the name of the sublibrary that contains the sort run-time modules so the LIBDEF PHASE statement can be coded.

```
// LIBDEF  PHASE,SEARCH=(lib.sublib,sort.sublib)
// ASSIGN  SYS002,DISK,VOL=volume-serial,SHR
// DLBL    SORTWK1,'sort work 1 id',0,SD
// EXTENT  SYS002,volume-serial,...
//    ·
//    ·                   <- other assignments as needed
//    ·
// EXEC phasename,SIZE=(phasename,800K)
   OMIT    COND=(26,2,CH,EQ,C'25')
   INREC   FIELDS=(1,5,6,20,26,2,28,2,47,2)
/*
```

The above example is not intended to be a complete JCL example for sorting. Your shop probably has certain standards or conventions. The intent is to demonstrate how control statements may be part of the job-stream.

3.12.5. SORT/MERGE II Control Statements

This topic appears in several places. See section 3.5, Making a Program More Efficient, and SORT Techniques, section 3.8, for more information on using sort control statements. This topic contains the control statements you would most likely use in a SORT application.

GENERAL Syntax. All the following statements are coded as part of the SYSIPT dataset, and specified via the SORT-CONTROL special register. All statements must leave column one blank and must not exceed column 71. Statements may be continued to a following line by ending a parameter with a comma, coding any character in column 72, and then coding the next parameter on the next line, beginning between column 2 and 16. This book does not show all options for these statements, as some options would rarely apply.

Warning: When using control statements, remember the sequence in which they are processed (see the SORT Techniques section). For example, an INCLUDE statement would reference the field locations as they appear in the input file, as would the INREC statement. However, statements processed after the INREC statement would need to reference the fields as they were realigned.

INCLUDE and OMIT syntax. (Use one or the other, not both.)

```
┌INCLUDE COND=(st,len,ty,cond,┌st,len,ty┐ [,AND or  OR]...)
│OMIT                         │C'xxxx'  │
└                            │X'xxxx'  │
                             │+number  │
                             └-number  ┘
```

```
Where: st      = first position of field
       len     = length of the field in bytes
       ty      = type of data, i.e., CH (DISPLAY), FI (COMP),
                 ZD (numeric DISPLAY), PD (COMP-3)
       cond    = EQ,GT,LT,GE,LE,NE
```

Including records where positions 25–28 equal 'LIFE':

```
INCLUDE  COND=(25,4,CH,EQ,C'LIFE')
```

Omitting records where positions 25–28 equal 'LIFE' or positions 25–30 equal 'HEALTH':

```
OMIT  COND=(25,4,CH,EQ,C'LIFE',OR,25,6,CH,EQ,C'HEALTH')
```

INREC Syntax. (only specified fields will be in sort record):

```
INREC  FIELDS=([pad,] start,length, [al,] [pad,] start,length,...)
               |_____|              |_____|
                   1st field                   2nd field  etc.
```

```
Where
pad      = indicator for padding of blanks or binary zeros,
             plus length of padding. coded as 'nX' for blanks
             and 'nZ' for binary zeros.
start    = 1st byte of field to relocate
length   = length of field to relocate
al       = alignment (H for half-word, F for full-word,
             D for double-word)
```

Extract fields in positions 35–40 and 61–90, creating a sort input record of 36 bytes. (SORT is faster with shorter records.) Reminder: SD 01-level must show that these two fields are now in positions 1–6 and 7–36. While the new record length is now 36, the SD 01-level should continue to reflect the original length.

```
INREC FIELDS=(35,6,61,30)
```

Above example, but with two blanks between the fields and five blanks following last field:

```
INREC FIELDS=(35,6,2X,61,30,5X)
```

SUM Syntax

```
SUM  FIELDS=(start,length,type,...)
```

Fields must be FI, PD, or ZD. This summarizes data based on sort keys used. Fields being summarized must not be sort key fields.

OUTREC Syntax (same as INREC)

Reformat output from above to include 30 blanks, making the output record 66 bytes long:

```
OUTREC FIELDS=(1,36,30X)     <- inserts 30 blank bytes

OUTREC FIELDS=(1,36,30Z)     <- inserts 30 bytes of binary
                                zeros
```

Reformat output from above to begin with 10 blanks, followed by first 30 bytes of data, followed by 2 blanks, followed by the last 5 bytes from input record, creating a 47-byte record:

```
OUTREC FIELDS=(10X,1,30,2X,31,5)
```

SUMMARY

This chapter covers a lot of material, all of which is designed to help you be a better, more knowledgeable, more efficient programmer. Some techniques may appear not to work correctly in your shop. If this happens, first review the material to ensure you have followed the guidelines carefully. Many of these techniques are not routinely used and you may encounter people who swear the techniques will never work. For many years, many of us have viewed COBOL as just a black box and had no understanding of it. You won't master all these techniques by reading. Keep the book nearby and try something new on your next program.

4

Debugging Techniques
with COBOL II

This chapter will not teach you how to debug specific problems. Instead, the goal of this chapter is to ensure that you know what information is available and how it may be used. As a professional programmer, your interest is in developing a foundation of knowledge on which to build, not to learn tricks for specific situations. Despite that statement, the first section in this chapter is a tutorial, presenting concepts to readers with limited background. If you need special information about COBOL II dumps beyond what is covered in this section, see Chapter 9 ("Related Publications").

Unfortunately, many programmers think debugging means reading dumps. Not true. Reading a dump is a last resort and should be postponed as long as possible. Additionally, with several proprietary dump interpretation software products on the market, the pain from reading system dumps is a memory. (Note: If your shop still reads raw dumps from the system, I suggest you encourage your management to investigate the dump interpretation software products available. They save a mountain of paper, reduce costly training time, and isolate most problems, often including a statement in plain language of the problem and how to solve it.)

COBOL II provides several aids to assist you in solving problems, including options for compile output, object code generation, and error interception. In fact, some problems that caused an ABEND in earlier versions of COBOL cause only an error message and termination today. You will also notice that COBOL II provides facilities to let you be proactive in anticipating and resolving ABENDs.

Because the focus of this book is on helping you develop efficient applications with COBOL, and not on teaching various work practices to solve problems, the debugging environment (called COBTEST) provided by COBOL II is not covered in depth. Another reason is that COBTEST is a separate product that may not be at your installation. For specifics on the compile options that support debugging, see the section Specifying COBOL II Options in Chapter 3.

4.1. REMOVING THE MYSTERY FROM DUMPS

This section is a tutorial, taking some license with the actual specifics that occur. If you are comfortable with dumps and using compiler output to resolve them, you will find little new information here. You may even disagree with some of the details as I present them. The goal of this section is to ensure there is no mystery surrounding dumps for people with little experience. So long as a topic is mysterious, you cannot learn techniques to deal with it.

With many debug courses oriented around specific problems (e.g., "How to solve an 0C7," "How to solve multi-module problems"), junior programmers often view dumps as a mystery. Let's tackle that first. With a grasp of how the elements fit together, it is easier to develop a strategy for a variety of application problems.

4.1.1. Why Is the Dump in Hex, Anyway?

Contrary to a popular belief, the computer does not do hexadecimal arithmetic. (Yes, you can buy one of many handheld calculators that do hex arithmetic, but the mainframe cannot.) Instead, the mainframe does binary arithmetic for memory management and certain other functions, yet uses hexadecimal as a shorthand format when printing memory contents. (If a dump were nothing but 1s and 0s, life would be tough, indeed.) Also, the operating system has no idea whether the data components of your program were EBCDIC, binary, packed-decimal, or floating point. The common format for all formats is the bit configuration they use, so that is what you get—in hexadecimal format. The operating system correctly assumes that the compiler with which you compiled your program will provide documentation to assist in locating your program and data elements. The operating system further assumes, also correctly, that the Linkage Editor listing will provide assistance in determining which program was involved in the ABEND. I'll cover that information shortly.

Do you need to be good at hex arithmetic? Although I may incur the wrath of many senior programmers, my answer is no. For most of us, we have a sufficient knowledge of hex if we can

- Write our name in hex,
- Count from 1 to 20 in hex,
- Write our age in binary, in hex, and in packed-decimal, and
- Using our fingers, subtract numbers such as 4A minus 3C.

The above items aren't difficult and emphasize that what we need is the ability to recognize patterns. For example,

- C4C1E5C5 is a pattern of EBCDIC characters ("DAVE").
- F2F5, 19, and 025C are patterns of the decimal value 25 in EBCDIC, hex, and packed-decimal. (No, I'm not 25, but it was a nice age when I was.)
- In the subtraction example, I know that 4A is greater than 3C. This also means I know that 3D through 49 are numbers that occur between those two. With my fingers, I can do whatever is needed there.

In most cases, the information you have from the compiler and Linkage Editor are hex numbers. Usually, all you need to do is search high/low and match values. You'll see that later. If, for your application, you consistently do arithmetic such as

```
3A2CD4 - 2FC19A
```

or

```
4C9A0F + 19CDF0
```

you should consider buying one of the many calculators on the market that do this for you. Why? They aren't expensive (around $20) and their use removes a lot of drudgery. The need to do it once with a dump is okay; doing it several times is painful. For a person to be a superior programmer, there are many skills to master that are more important than hex arithmetic, so why waste the time? I stopped teaching the details of hex arithmetic years ago and have no regrets.

Other questions you may have are, "Do I need to be able to convert decimal numbers to hex and hex numbers to decimal?" and "Do I need to be able to read negative hex numbers (i.e., master the technique of two's-complement notation)?" Unfortunately, these two techniques are in many textbooks and can be frightening. Instead of answering those questions, let's turn them around. A better question is, "How do I eliminate the need to convert hex to decimal and cope with two's-complement notation?" The answer is simple. Just don't use the COMP format. That's all there is to it. Yes, you may still have to add or subtract hex numbers to locate programs or statements or data elements, but you never need to convert those answers to decimal and you won't be dealing with negative numbers.

From the above, you may wonder why some programmers use COMP. One, they were probably taught it was more efficient (see Chapter 3 for more information) and, two, it is still true for limited use. One of the reasons many programmers use packed-decimal (COMP-3) is that it requires no hex conversion in a dump. That, in itself, improves your productivity. If you would like to learn more about hexadecimal values, see Chapter 7.

4.1.2. Identifying Where Information Is Located

Earlier, I mentioned that the operating system assumed information was available to assist you in reading a dump. Using Figure 4.1, let's look at how that information is constructed. For our example, assume a batch program, PROGA, has an ADD statement on line 23 of the program and that it will ABEND because of a bad data field. (In our example, it also CALLs PROGB, but that is incidental to the problem.) Here are the steps:

1. The first step, the compile, produces two important pieces of information. One, the SOURCE option shows that the ADD statement is on line 23. Two, the OFFSET option shows that it is in the range 2FC through 305. (Remember my comment, about knowing ranges. ABENDS never point to where a failing instruction begins, but to where the next instruction begins.) Those two items from SOURCE and OFFSET will be important in the event of an ABEND. The purpose of the compiler-produced information is to locate which statement or data element within a specific program caused the ABEND.

2. Next, the Linkage Editor prints a listing of how the phase is constructed (MAP on the Linkage Editor ACTION statement). It shows that PROGA is at the beginning, with an offset into the phase of 0. You may also note that PROGA occupies addresses 0 through 4CEF and that PROGB occupies addresses 4CF0 through 52BF. The purpose of the Linkage Editor listing when debugging is to locate which program within a phase caused the ABEND (although this information is rarely needed when using compiler-produced debugging aids, such as FDUMP or STAE).

3. Third, when the program ABENDs, VSE has two outputs. One is a series of messages, normally available via SYSLOG or SYSLST for batch applications. (The COBOL II run-time error intercept routines also put messages here.) The second output is the dump itself. The dump is produced only if there is an appropriate assignment, such as SYSLST, and you specified DUMP or PARTDUMP on the JCL OPTION statement. Information from VSE confirms in which phase the ABEND occurred.

Now, let's follow that flow in reverse, going from VSE to the Linkage Editor to the COBOL II listing. By following these steps as a standard routine, you will solve most of the ABENDs you will encounter. Remember that much of this is conceptual. We're still on basics in this section.

From VSE. On ABEND, VSE prints that the ABEND was an 0C7. The dump shows the actual memory location, 32D2A2, and the entry point, 32CFA0. Locating location 32D2A2 in the dump will be a waste of time because it will be all in hex—so don't do it. Instead, compute the instruction's offset. This is done by subtracting 32CFA0 from 32D2A2, giving a result of 302. This is the offset of

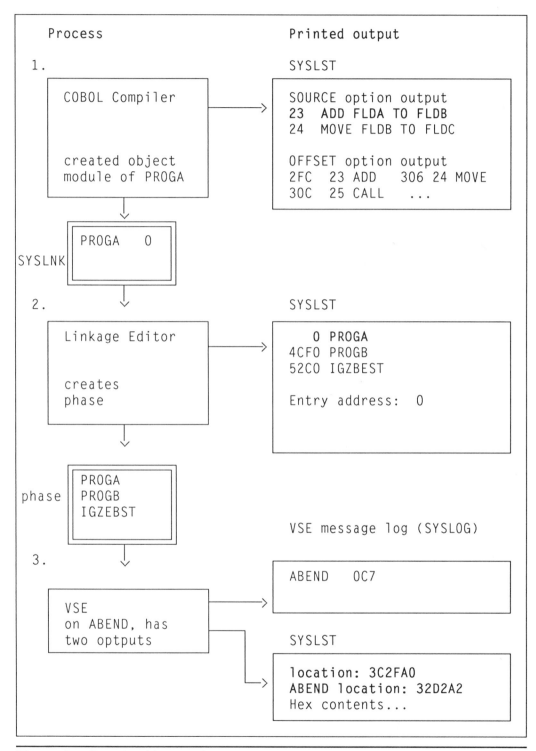

Figure 4.1. Sample of information to analyze a dump.

the instruction beyond the logical beginning point of the phase. To confirm which program it is in, look at the Linkage Editor listing. Reminder: VSE always shows the next sequential instruction's address, not the address of the offending instruction. When you locate the correct offset in the correct program, you will be looking at the instruction just beyond the one that caused the ABEND.

From the Linkage Editor. From this listing, you want to confirm the location of the ABEND from the physical beginning, not the logical beginning of the phase. Since the physical beginning (always 0) matches the logical beginning (entry address) in the example, you know the offset of 302 needs no further adjustment. (Note: If the entry address (logical beginning) was other than 0, you would need to ADD it to the number from VSE to get an address relative to the Linkage Editor listing.)

Since the Linkage Editor listing shows us that instructions between relative location 0 and 4CEF are in the program PROGA, you now know in which program to search for the problem. When you are using facilities from COBOL II, you usually do not need to reference the Linkage Editor listing, since the STAE error message will include the name of the offending program.

From the compiler listing. Here is where planning helps. If you compiled the program and specified none of the possible options to help in debugging, you should stop pursuing the problem until you recompile the program with some debugging options (see Chapter 3). Assuming you specified SOURCE (to list all source code and sequence numbers) and OFFSET (to show at what offset the instructions begin), you can continue with this problem. In our example, the OFFSET listing in Figure 4.1 shows that location 302 occurs somewhere between the beginning of an ADD statement on line 23 and a MOVE statement on line 24. Again, notice that no hex arithmetic has been needed. This confirms that the ABEND was caused by the ADD statement on line 23.

A reminder about an OFFSET listing: Earlier, I mentioned that VSE always points not to the instruction causing the error, but to the next sequential instruction. For example, if the offset address had been 306 (the address of the MOVE instruction), it would still confirm the ADD instruction as the one causing the ABEND. Likewise, had the offset address been 2FC, it would confirm whatever instruction preceded this ADD statement. With the specific instruction confirmed, it is usually a small matter of determining whether it was FLDA or FLDB in the example that caused the 0C7. (Note: When the OFFSET listing is insufficient, you may prefer the listing produced by the LIST option, since it lists all generated instructions. An example is in the next section.)

Review. To review that flow again, all programs must go through three steps in their life. One, they must be compiled into machine code. Two, they must be transformed into executable code as a phase. Three, they must be loaded into memory and executed. On an ABEND, VSE indicates which phase, the Linkage Editor listing shows which program, and the compiler listing shows which statement.

Bypassing any of these three steps can cause confusion in solving the problem. These steps are needed whenever VSE or the COBOL II run-time modules cannot identify the problem—but sometimes they can. Examples will follow.

My suggested steps in solving a dump follow:

1. At the risk of offending programmers everywhere, I suggest not reading the system dump when testing a program unless other approaches fail. In most cases, it isn't needed. From my experience, programmers tend to read (or keep) everything the computer prints for a testing error. If this is true at your shop, you will get a productivity gain by not even seeing the unnecessary dump, other than to retrieve the entry point address and the ABEND address. For example, I once got an ABEND dump for misspelling a file name. One of the system messages was "filename not found" (or words to that effect). With that message, I corrected the situation in minutes. Despite this, VSE still produced a dump for me to throw away. When I discussed this with several other programmers, many felt I should have read (or kept) the dump anyway. Why? Because it was there. Let's get out of that trap.

2. Read the system messages first. This may solve the problem. For example, if you meant to execute a phase called GLOP, but coded EXEC FLOP on the JCL statement, VSE produces an ABEND message, stating that the phase called FLOP could not be located. The problem is solved. Reading the dump is unnecessary.

3. Even if the system messages do not produce any clear solution, check them anyway for ABEND messages that may give you a clue. For example, once I got an ABEND of 0C9 (divide by zero). Since I had just added a group of statements to the program, one of which was a COMPUTE statement with the divide operator, I knew where to look for the problem.

4. You can now usually go to the source listing and locate the offending statement.

Most of the time, these steps will do it for you. If they solve 90 percent of your problems, you will be viewed as a technical genius and you can then afford to seek additional assistance beyond that. Our goal in this topic was to remove the magic, not to make you an expert. In the following topics, you will see additional information to assist you. If you desire to master every facet of dump reading, you may want to get the appropriate IBM manuals (Chapter 9, "Related Publications").

4.2. READING THE SYSTEM MESSAGES

Earlier, I suggested that you check the system messages first. Let's get a feel for that here. One of the most difficult challenges is being patient as you read the many messages logged during your job. Some are useful; some are not. One of your challenges is to weed out the irrelevant material. Since VSE never knows the true cause of a problem, it gives you every shred of information it has, leaving it to you to discard most of it.

Earlier, I mentioned a couple of conceptual messages that VSE gives. Here is an example of a specific message, provided by the COBOL II run-time modules. What would once have been a difficult ABEND to solve is now a simple error message. The ABEND occurred when the program attempted to READ the file. Again, an example of an error in which no DUMP or PARTDUMP options are needed. This gives the program name, so the Linkage Editor listing also isn't needed. With the offset of 0516 from the message, the OPEN causing the error can be found from an OFFSET or LIST option.

```
+IGZ035I There was an unsuccessful OPEN or CLOSE of file 'PAY102' in
+        program 'DKA10200' at relative location X'0516'.  Neither FILE
+        STATUS nor an ERROR declarative were specified.  The I-O status
+        code was '39'.
```

While this is only one example, I believe it represents the type of messages that COBOL II generates, so you may adjust your debugging technique accordingly. Our goal here is to work smarter, not harder. For information and detailed explanations of the run-time messages (all COBOL II messages have the prefix of IGZ), see *VS COBOL II Application Program Debugging* (Chapter 9, "Related Publications"). Note: If the message has a prefix of C1, it will be from the DOS/VS COBOL run-time library, indicating a non-COBOL II component of your run unit.

4.3. READING THE OFFSET AND LIST OUTPUT
FROM A COMPILE

OFFSET and LIST are mutually exclusive. If both are selected, OFFSET gets priority. I recommend that OFFSET, as a minimum, be specified for every compile in which you anticipate executing the module. Without one of the two, you will be unable to identify a specific COBOL statement in case of an ABEND, and OFFSET uses less paper.

Here is an example, showing both the OFFSET list for part of a program and the LIST for that part of the program. In this example, the LIST option is needed due to the complexity of the ABENDing statement. The statement causing the error is the ADD statement on line 76. With so many data-names represented, the OFFSET listing is, by itself, insufficient to locate the problem. The LIST, because it shows every instruction, helps us identify the data field at the added expense of producing more paper at compile-time. The example ABEND was caused by an 0C7 ABEND at offset 464 (derived from VSE messages).

The SOURCE listing from COBOL II. The numbers to the right of the listing are produced by the XREF option and show the line numbers on which the data elements are defined. The number 1, to the left of the COBOL statements in lines 75 through 78, shows the depth of nested statements.

```
000071
000072     2000-PROCESS.
000073         PERFORM 2100-READ-DATA                               80
000074         IF NOT END-OF-FILE                                   49
000075  1          MOVE FD2-EMP-NAME TO WS2-EMP-NAME                34 53
000076  1          ADD FD2-DED1 FD2-DED2 FD2-DED3 FD2-DED4 TO WS1-ACCUM  35 36 37 38 45
000077  1          MOVE WS1-ACCUM TO WS2-TOTAL-DED                  45 55
000078  1          WRITE FD1-OUT-REC FROM WS2-OUT-REC.              27 51
```

The OFFSET listing from COBOL II. Notice how many statements can be identified in so little space. The OFFSET listing has the line number, the hex offset, and the verb. The OFFSET listing should be read from left to right, not from top to bottom. In our example, the offset of 464 occurs between lines 76 and 77, confirming the ADD statement. Because this ADD statement contains so many data-names, more information will be needed. See the LIST output for a comparison.

```
LINE #  HEXLOC  VERB         LINE #  HEXLOC  VERB           LINE #  HEXLOC  VERB
000062  00035A  PERFORM      000063  000376  PERFORM        000064  00039A  PERFORM
000065  0003B2  STOP         000068  0003C6  INITIALIZE     000069  0003E6  OPEN
000073  000428  PERFORM      000074  000440  IF             000075  00044C  MOVE
000076  000452  ADD          000077  000488  MOVE           000078  0004AA  WRITE
000081  0004E8  READ         000083  000532  MOVE           000085  00053A  ADD
000089  00054C  MOVE         000090  000558  WRITE          000091  000590  CLOSE
```

The LIST output from COBOL II. The LIST option is mutually exclusive with OFFSET. If you specify both, OFFSET takes effect. You do not need to know assembler language to use the LIST option, even though it lists the machine instructions generated for COBOL statements. To the right of each instruction are some abbreviated words and codes to assist you in deciphering what data elements are involved. It takes practice and an occasional leap of faith to interpret them, but it isn't difficult to survive here.

Since you know the address of the next sequential instruction is 464, you can determine that the offending instruction was at location 45E, the preceding instruction. That instruction, AP (for ADD Packed-decimal data) is adding the contents of temporary storage area # 2 (TS2-n) to the contents of temporary storage area # 1 (TS1-n). You know this from reading the comments at the right. (Note: Temporary storage areas are just intermediate work areas the compiler added to our program to accomplish various functions. The numbers of the storage areas used have no special meaning.)

If you look at the preceding instructions that are affiliated with the ADD statement, you find two statements, one at location 452 and one at location 458. Both are PACK instructions (a PACK instruction converts EBCDIC DISPLAY data to COMP-3 format data and moves the result to a receiving field). The first PACK instruction moves a data field called FD2-DED2 to TS1 and the second PACK instruction moves the data field FD2-DED1 to TS2.

Now things are beginning to take shape. The two PACK instructions moved FD2-DED1 and FD2-DED2 to the two temporary fields, TS1 and TS2. The AP instruction that ABENDed was adding those two fields. Therefore, of all the data fields specified in the ADD instruction, the error was either FD2-DED1 or FD2-DED2. The other fields on the ADD statement on line 76 may also cause errors, but the program never got that far. At this point, you can look at those two areas in the dump. One of them probably has a blank in it.

```
    00043A                  GN=12EQU   *
    00043A  D203 D17C D18C   MVC  380(4,13),396(13)       VN=5            PSV=4
000074  IF
    000440  95E8 900A        CLI  10(9),X'E8'             WS1-EOF-SW
    000444  58B0 C020        L    11,32(0,12)             PBL=1
    000448  4780 B22E        BC   8,558(0,11)             GN=3(0004E2)
000075  MOVE
    00044C  D213 9012 8000   MVC  18(20,9),0(8)           WS2-EMP-NAME    FD2-EMP-NAME
000076  ADD
    000452  F274 D1B0 8019   PACK 432(8,13),25(5,8)       TS1=0           FD2-DED2
    000458  F224 D1BD 8014   PACK 445(3,13),20(5,8)       TS2=5           FD2-DED1
    00045E  FA32 D1B4 D1BD   AP   436(4,13),445(3,13)     TS1=4           TS2=5
    000464  F224 D1BD 801E   PACK 445(3,13),30(5,8)       TS2=5           FD2-DED3
    00046A  FA32 D1B4 D1BD   AP   436(4,13),445(3,13)     TS1=4           TS2=5
    000470  F224 D1BD 8023   PACK 445(3,13),35(5,8)       TS2=5           FD2-DED4
    000476  FA42 D1B3 D1BD   AP   435(5,13),445(3,13)     TS1=3           TS2=5
    00047C  FA34 9002 D1B3   AP   2(4,9),435(5,13)        WS1-ACCUM       TS1=3
    000482  F833 9002 9002   ZAP  2(4,9),2(4,9)           WS1-ACCUM       WS1-ACCUM
000077  MOVE
    000488  D209 D1BE A063   MVC  446(10,13),99(10)       TS2=6           PGMLIT AT +79
    00048E  D203 D1CC 9002   MVC  460(4,13),2(9)          TS2=20          WS1-ACCUM
```

That wasn't so hard, was it? Usually, the LIST option isn't needed, but it's nice to know it is available. If you sometimes find it difficult to locate the source statement with LIST, it may be because the program was compiled with OPTI-MIZE. While OPTIMIZE is recommended for productional use, its ability to restructure the program at the machine code level can make it difficult to match instructions to source statements. In such a situation, recompile with NOOPTIMIZE and rerun the test.

4.4. USING FDUMP, STAE, AND SSRANGE

4.4.1. STAE

The SYSLST statement, although not required for STAE, is used to record elementary information in case of an ABEND (for CICS, this information goes to the CEBRxxxx queue). The STAE option must be set for this to take effect. (STAE causes the COBOL II run-time error intercept code to take control in the event of an ABEND.) The purpose of using output from STAE is to determine the program name that caused the ABEND, including the date compiled. For me, that is all I get from it. Here is an example:

```
- VS COBOL II ABEND Information -
Program = 'PRTFILE' compiled on '04/17/91' at '12:35:37'    <- Useful
    TGT = '04303028'
Contents of base locators for files are:
    0-00007FD8        1-0004C300
Contents of base locators for working storage are:
    0-00045210
Contents of base locators for the linkage section are:
    0-00000000
No variably located areas were used in this program.
No EXTERNAL data was used in this program.
No indexes were used in this program.                   <- Possibly useful
- End of VS COBOL II ABEND Information -
```

As you see, this shows you the PROGRAM-ID, the date compiled, and some other bits and pieces. For most of us, the STAE information is only to confirm the name of the offending program. Since STAE is the default at most installations (see compiler run-time options for more information), you may want to have this information. This information does not override other information sources, such as FDUMP.

4.4.2. FDUMP

FDUMP is a compile option that produces a formatted dump when an ABEND occurs if the STAE run-time option is set. This option increases the size of your phase and the amount of virtual memory used, so should be reset off (NOFDUMP) after testing applications that need high performance. If the application is volatile, new, or not performance-sensitive, you may decide to leave FDUMP set even when used in production. (See the next topic, A Proactive Approach to Problem Resolution, for more information.) Use of FDUMP is not dependent on the DUMP or PARTDUMP JCL options.

FDUMP requires SYSLST for non-CICS applications and uses the CEBRxxxx queue for CICS applications. If you specify FDUMP and use the DUMP or PARTDUMP JCL options, you will get both dumps. In most cases, you will find you don't need two dumps, as the FDUMP will usually be more than sufficient (and saves trees).

FDUMP presents you with a format of the DATA DIVISION, using names from the source code, with the data converted for readability, if needed. Additionally, it presents you with the line number and statement number of the verb that caused the ABEND if NOOPTIMIZE was specified, and the hex offset of the verb (remember the OFFSET and LIST features?) if OPTIMIZE was specified. This eliminates virtually all hex arithmetic when reading dumps, the need to review the Linkage Editor listing to determine what program caused the ABEND, and the need to review the dump to determine the value of various data fields.

Here is an FDUMP example, produced with the same ABEND that caused the earlier STAE information:

```
VS COBOL II Formatted Dump at ABEND —
Program = 'PRTFILE'
Completion code = 'S0C7'
PSW at ABEND = '078D1000843005CC'
Line number or verb number being executed: '0000076'/'1'   <— line number in
The GP registers at entry to ABEND were                          source program
    Regs   0 - 3  - '00000001 0004C300 043005A2 00045090'
    Regs   4 - 7  - '00045090 84300674 007C5FF8 00007FD8'
    Regs   8 - 11 - '0004C300 00045210 0430020C 0430041C'
    Regs  12 - 15 - '043001E8 04303028 500323EC 800323FC'
Data Division dump of 'PRTFILE'
000023 FD PRTFILE.FD1-REPORT FD
FILE SPECIFIED AS:
   ORGANIZATION=SEQUENTIAL   ACCESS MODE=SEQUENTIAL
   RECFM=FIXED BLOCKED
CURRENT STATUS OF FILE IS:
   OPEN STATUS=EXTEND
   QSAM STATUS CODE=00                        <—File status information
000027 01 PRTFILE.FD1-OUT-REC X(37)
      DISP    ===> JOHN E. DOE              213.35
000029 FD PRTFILE.FD2-INPUT FD
FILE SPECIFIED AS:
   ORGANIZATION=SEQUENTIAL ACCESS MODE=SEQUENTIAL
   RECFM=FIXED BLOCKED
CURRENT STATUS OF FILE IS:
   OPEN STATUS=INPUT
   QSAM STATUS CODE=00
000033 01 PRTFILE.FD2-INP-REC AN-GR
```

```
000034 02 PRTFILE.FD2-EMP-NAME X(20)
     DISP   ===>JANE S. DOE
000035 02 PRTFILE.FD2-DED1 S999V99
                                                    INVALID SIGN

       DISP   ===>+000.00
              HEX> FFF FF
                   000 00
000036 02 PRTFILE.FD2-DED2 S999V99
                                          INVALID DATA FOR THIS DATA TYPE

       DISP    HEX> 44444
                                          <— This field has blanks (hex 40)

                   00000
000037 02 PRTFILE.FD2-DED3 S999V99
                                                    INVALID SIGN

       DISP   ===>+020.00
              HEX> FFF FF
                   020 00
000038 02 PRTFILE.FD2-DED4 S999V99
                                                    INVALID SIGN

       DISP    ===>+030.00
               HEX> FFF FF
                    030 00
000039 02 PRTFILE.FILLER X(40)
       DISP     ===>04000
  .
  .
  .
```

— End of VS COBOL II Formatted Dump at ABEND —

In reviewing the sample FDUMP output, you noticed that it states the error was caused on line 76, the first (and only) verb on that line. If the program had been compiled with OPTIMIZE, the statement would have shown the hex offset instead. Here is that verb and the 01-level entry it was referencing:

```
000033        01 FD2-INP-REC.
000034            05  FD2-EMP-NAME    PIC X(20).
000035            05  FD2-DED1        PIC S999V99.
000036            05  FD2-DED2        PIC S999V99.
000037            05  FD2-DED3        PIC S999V99.
000038            05  FD2-DED4        PIC S999V99.
000039            05                  PIC X(40).

000076            ADD FD2-DED1 FD2-DED2 . . .
```

Since the ABEND was an 0C7, you know that FD2-DED1 or FD2-DED2 probably contained blanks. By looking at the FDUMP, you can confirm it. Also notice how FDUMP points out incorrect signs—acceptable, but incorrect for this choice of the NUMPROC option. This could be useful information if the program logic had IF NUMERIC statements.

4.4.3. SSRANGE

SSRANGE is an excellent aid when testing a program that has subscripts, indexes, or uses reference modification. (Chapter 2 explains reference modification, and subscripting and indexing are described in Chapter 3). Also, SSRANGE is not dependent on SYSLST or FDUMP, although it may be combined with FDUMP or TEST, and it appears as a compile-time option and as a run-time option. This provides you with the opportunity to control its impact on performance. Here are your choices:

Compile option	Run-time option	
• SSRANGE	SSRANGE	Debugging is activated, with some impact on performance.
• SSRANGE	NOSSRANGE	No SSRANGE monitoring, but run unit may be activated by changing run-time option.
• NOSSRANGE	SSRANGE	No SSRANGE monitoring. Program must be recompiled with SSRANGE before monitoring takes effect.
• NOSSRANGE	NOSSRANGE	No SSRANGE monitoring.

Many companies have the run-time option default set to NOSSRANGE to prevent inadvertent productional running of programs with SSRANGE specified at compile-time. If you are unsure about your shop's default setting, see the section Specifying COBOL II Options in Chapter 3 for instruction on how to determine them. That topic also specifies how to turn run-time options on or off. (There is an example of this in the next topic, but the example assumes you are familiar with the mechanics from Chapter 3.)

SSRANGE should normally be part of your proactive debug technique, covered in the next topic. Testing programs with untested subscripts, indexes, or reference modification without specifying SSRANGE is not professional.

4.5. A PROACTIVE APPROACH TO PROBLEM RESOLUTION

Usually, problem solving is done when a program is being tested, when you have time to use a variety of techniques to solve a problem. Sometimes, however, you are trying to debug productional applications and can't afford the luxury of extensive use of DISPLAY statements or other code modifications. Here are a couple of tips to use when the program won't cooperate. These tips work for all environments.

Approach # 1.

First, compile the suspected (or untested) module with FDUMP and NOOPTIMIZE. Yes, this will affect performance, but if the program is having problems you are not getting the desired performance anyway. I recommend NOOPTIMIZE because FDUMP, OFFSET, and LIST output from COBOL II are easier to use than when OPTIMIZE is specified. FDUMP, as explained earlier, does increase phase size (due to the tables—not extra code) and also increases use of virtual memory. While you normally do not have debug code in productional applications, doing so will position you to get maximum usable information at the time of an ABEND.

Second, if subscripts, indexes, or reference modification code are suspect, include SSRANGE in the compile-time options specified. If you do not anticipate one of these problems, specify NOSSRANGE at run-time to minimize performance degradation. (See previous chapter under the section Specifying COBOL II Options for information on setting options.) Now run the program. If it ABENDs, you will have the FDUMP output. If the problem appears to be one of the types that SSRANGE handles (and you specified NOSSRANGE at run-time), all you need to do is

1. If the module is executed by the JCL EXEC statement, change the PARM to '/SSRANGE' and reexecute.
2. If you were not running from the JCL EXEC (e.g., CICS), then relink the module with a copy of IGZEOPT that includes the SSRANGE option and rerun the application to (I hope) solve the application. Since the phase now contains IGZEOPT with SSRANGE, you must remove it to restore processing efficiency, either by creating a new phase directly from compiles or by relinking with the OBJ files (See section, Creating a Phase, in prior chapter).

Step 2 assumed the installation default for the run-time option was NOSSRANGE. If the installation default had been SSRANGE, you could have left it as is, running with degraded performance until the problem surfaced or linked a version of IGZEOPT with NOSSRANGE until the problem surfaced and then relinked to remove IGZEOPT to reactivate SSRANGE. The important item to remember is that IGZEOPT is an alternate to the installation defaults. Once placed into a phase, IGZEOPT must be removed by relinking if its options are no longer desired.

Approach # 2.

This approach is more long-term than the previous one. If you have an application that isn't sensitive to performance concerns, you might want to use FDUMP all the time. This can be useful if an application is volatile or is being maintained by a less experienced programmer. With FDUMP, less experienced programmers build confidence more rapidly than if they continually face a hex dump, and problems are generally resolved more quickly. Unless the run unit is complex, I suggest omitting the OPTION PARTDUMP or DUMP also, relying solely on FDUMP. While some of you will dismiss the thought out of hand (because you've always used hex dumps), I encourage you to consider the option.

4.6.   USING THE COBTEST FACILITY

COBTEST is a separate product from IBM and may not be installed at your shop. There was a similar (but not identical) product with DOS/VS COBOL called TESTCOB. The COBTEST facility is embedded within your object module(s) by using the compile option TEST. COBTEST runs with these options, even if not specified: TRUNC(STD), NOZWB, NUMPROC(NOPFD). I want you to be aware of COBTEST, but it is not the focus of this book. I find it useful for the professional who uses test scripts and I have included some examples. For more information on work practices with COBTEST, or for a complete list of all commands and syntax, see *VS COBOL II Application Program Debugging* (Chapter 9).

4.6.1.   COBTEST Debug Environment

One of the reasons some companies don't use COBTEST (or don't use it extensively) is that COBTEST does not support all VSE environments. This is unfortunate because COBTEST is a much-improved testing tool with COBOL II and has much to recommend it.

With VSE, COBTEST runs only in batch mode (under MVS/XA, COBTEST can also run in full-screen and line mode from on-line terminals, although all features are not supported in all modes).

Batch mode is available for batch programs and for CICS applications (see next section for CICS considerations). Instead of specifying the name of your program on the EXEC statement, specify COBDBG. For example, assume a program was compiled with the TEST option and linked into a phase sublibrary called TESTRUN.PHASE, with a phasename of DAVEMOD. The PROGRAM-ID of the COBOL II program is DAVEPROG. To test in batch mode, my JCL might look something like Figure 4.2.

While the JCL in Figure 4.2 is relatively simple, explaining the function of each and briefly describing the control statements will help you get a feeling for the power of COBTEST in batch mode. The commands are read from SYSIPT. The numbers were added for clarity.

```
 1. // JOB  jobid
 2. // LIBDEF PHASE,SEARCH=(TESTRUN.PHASE)
 3. // ASSGN SYSLST,...
 4. // ASSGN ...     ←─────┐
 5. // DLBL  ...           ├ application files
 6. // EXTENT ...    ←─────┘
 7. // EXEC COBDBG,SIZE=(COBDBG,500K)
 8. COBTEST DAVEMOD
 9. RECORD
10. QUALIFY DAVEPROG
11. SET WS3-TASK-CODE = '01'
12. TRACE PARA PRINT
13. FLOW ON
14. AT DAVEPROG.36 (IF (WS3-TASK-CODE NE '01'),
    (LIST WS3-TASK-CODE))
15. ONABEND (FLOW(25))
    /*
    /&
```

Figure 4.2. Sample COBTEST in batch.

Statement 2 defines the phase sublibrary.

Statement 3 assigns SYSLST (normally not needed if predefined for your partition—the SYSLST file is required for printed output from COBTEST).

Statements 4 through 6 are examples of assignments for application-specific files.

Statement 7 executes COBTEST. Note that the SIZE parameter is needed to ensure adequate memory for COBDBG to load the application phase DAVEMOD. Any dynamically CALLed subprograms will be loaded into the GETVIS area. Note: Any PARM needed by the application should be coded on the EXEC statement. (This contrasts with how PARMs are made available via COBTEST on MVS systems.)

The debug script file (SYSIPT) begins with statement 8. While I haven't explained these statements (and will not, extensively, in this book), let's review them here.

COBTEST DAVEMOD tells COBTEST the name of the phase to load for this execution.

RECORD tells COBTEST to create a log on SYSLST of all commands.

QUALIFY DAVEPROG tells COBTEST the name of the PROGRAM-ID to which the following statements apply.

SET WS3-TASK-CODE = '01' forces an initial value into a WORKING-STORAGE field.

TRACE PARA PRINT specifies that a trace (similar to TRACE ON in DOS/VS COBOL) of paragraph names is to be printed (default is to SYSLST).

FLOW ON specifies that a log of paragraphs executed is to be kept by COBTEST (later referenced by line 13).

AT DAVEPROG.36 ... specifies that an IF statement is to be executed when the statement on line 36 is executed, in this case printing out the value of WS3-TASK-CODE whenever it is not equal to '01'. (The commands inside the parentheses, IF and LIST, are also COBTEST commands.)

ONABEND (FLOW(25)) specifies that, if an ABEND occurs, the most recent 25 paragraphs executed are to be printed out (similar to the FLOW option from DOS/VS COBOL).

You would normally not want both a TRACE and a FLOW, as those two options overlap. A restriction of batch mode is that all commands are processed immediately, preventing any interaction. This limits your set of commands, but batch mode has much to offer, as you'll see.

I like to keep things simple because there are so many skills a professional programmer needs to have. I use standard batch facilities whenever I suspect a potential problem and that relieves me from mastering all the various commands. By setting up a test script of basic debug commands, I have a tool that can be reused with minor changes with many programs. I'll cover the use of test scripts in the next topic.

This book's focus is on program development techniques, not work practices, so I avoid doing more than make you aware of the tool and present some techniques for packaging standard commands. For a thorough reference to COBTEST, see *VS COBOL II Application Program Debugging* (Chapter 9, "Related Publications"). You will need that manual since it includes all the error messages for COBTEST.

4.6.2. Sample Batch Mode Scripts

Here are my suggestions for some common COBTEST statements that you can use with most applications when you need simple, canned scripts. While the examples use batch JCL, the commands could also be used for CICS applications (see section 4.7, CICS Debug Considerations). With each example, you must replace the name of the phase on the COBTEST statement and the name of the PROGRAM-ID on the QUALIFY statement.

Simple Trace.

Unlike DOS/VS COBOL, where READY TRACE printed the name of every paragraph executed, this prints only the names where logic flow changed.

```
// LIBDEF PHASE,SEARCH=(phase.sublibrary)
//    ...
//    ...
//    ...
// EXEC COBDBG,SIZE=(COBDBG,500K)
COBTEST phasename
RECORD
QUALIFY program-id
TRACE PARA PRINT
/*
/&
```

Sample Flow Trace.

This is useful if you are getting an ABEND, but do not know how the logic flow is creating it. This example produces a list of the 25 most recently executed paragraphs that caused a change in the logic flow prior to the ABEND.

```
// LIBDEF PHASE,SEARCH=(phase.sublibrary)
//    ...
//    ...
//    ...
// EXEC COBDBG,SIZE=(COBDBG,500K)
COBTEST phasename
RECORD
QUALIFY program-id
FLOW ON
ONABEND (FLOW(25))
/*
/&
```

Sample subroutine test.

This is useful if you are testing a CALLed subprogram and have no module to initiate the CALL or you want to test how it performs with certain variables. With this script, a subprogram with PROCEDURE DIVISION USING can be tested alone. In this example, the subprogram is a variation of one of the examples in Chapter 8, DKA101BN. Part of that program is

```
LINKAGE SECTION.

01  LS1-RECORD.
    05  LS1-JOB-CODE              PIC XX.
    05  LS1-SICK-DAYS             PIC 99.
    05  LS1-VACATION-DAYS         PIC 99.
    05  LS1-ERROR-SW              PIC X.
            .
            .
    PROCEDURE DIVISION USING LS1-RECORD.
```

Here are sample control statements to test it with a value of LS1-JOB-CODE equal to '05'. (I continue to use the FLOW and ONABEND statement because, being proactive, I don't want an ABEND to leave me wondering what happened.)

```
// LIBDEF PHASE,SEARCH=(phase.sublibrary)
//     ...
//     ...
//     ...
// EXEC COBDBG,SIZE=(COBDBG,500K)
COBTEST phasename
RECORD
QUALIFY program-id
LINK (LS1-RECORD)
SET LS1-JOB-CODE = '05'
TRACE PARA PRINT
WHEN TST1 (LS1-ERROR-SW = 'Y') (LIST ALL)
FLOW ON
ONABEND (FLOW(25))
/*
/&
```

This example introduced a new statement, LINK. You may have already figured out what it does. LINK establishes addressability for an 01-level entry in the LINKAGE SECTION. In practice, it simulates a CALL statement. LINK can be followed (not preceded) by a SET statement to initialize the field. In effect, the program is "CALLed," passing a value of '05' to it. Once you have developed such canned statements, you will find it is easier to use them than to locate the parent CALLing program and set it up to CALL the subprogram.

The WHEN statement is testing a switch in the program. Whenever the named data element has a value of 'Y', this statement will list the entire DATA DIVISION. Since that is a small program, it was easier to code than naming the fields in which I was concerned. Also, "LIST ALL" fits better with my philosophy of having several canned tools in my arsenal for program testing. (Note: While the command summary below may indicate that IF and WHEN are equivalent, they are not. IF takes place immediately, which is inappropriate for batch. WHEN tests constantly throughout the run.) Here is sample output from the above script, as written to SYSLST:

```
                  ┌──> RECORD
Printed by        │   QUALIFY DKA101BN
RECORD            │   LINK (LS1-RECORD)
statement         │   SET LS1-JOB-CODE = '05'
                  │   TRACE PARA PRINT
                  │   WHEN TST1 (LS1-ERROR-SW = 'Y') (LIST ALL)
                  │   FLOW ON
                  └──> ONABEND (FLOW (25))
                      IGZ100I PP - 5668-958 VS COBOL II DEBUG FACILITY - REL 3.2
                      IGZ100I (C) COPYRIGHT IBM CORPORATION
                      IGZ102I DKA101BN.000035.1
                  ┌──> IGZ106I TRACING DKA101BN
Program TRACE     │   IGZ109I 000040.1
                  └──> IGZ109I 000051.1
                  ┌──> IGZ103I WHEN TST1 DKA101BN.000037.1
Output from       │   000025 01 DKA101BN.LS1-RECORD AN-GR
WHEN statement    │   000026 02 DKA101BN.LS1-JOB-CODE XX
condition         │          DISP    ===>05
being set         │   000027 02 DKA101BN.LS1-SICK-DAYS 99
                  │          DISP    ===>00
                  │   000028 02 DKA101BN.LS1-VACATION-DAYS 99
                  └──>        DISP    ===>00
                      IGZ129I PROGRAM UNDER COBTEST ENDED NORMALLY
                      IGZ350I ******** END OF COBTEST ********
```

In the previous example, the program was to set LS1-ERROR-SW if passed an invalid value. If you browsed through the program listing in Chapter 8, you noticed that only values of 01, 02, or 03 were valid in LS1-JOB-CODE. By asking for a listing only if the error switch was set, I confirmed that the program worked correctly for this set of test data. The commands were also listed because I included a RECORD statement.

4.6.3. The Debug Language—summary

This includes rudimentary syntax of some of the commands I've shown you, so you can experiment with test scripts. I also include a brief description (no syntax) of the other COBTEST commands (batch only), so you will have access to them within one book. Complete descriptions are in *IBM VS COBOL II Application Programming Debugging* (Chapter 9).

AT	This command establishes breakpoints in the program. It is helpful when you want to pause at a statement (not in batch) or execute other commands at a given statement. This is a major command for scripts.
COBTEST	This command specifies the name of phase.

```
— COBTEST — phase name ——————————————————————————————————><
```

COMMENT	This command inserts comments in your scripts and in your debugging output.
DROP	This command deletes symbols established with EQUATE.
DUMP	This command terminates a debug session and prints a SNAP dump of storage areas. It prints to SYSLST (non-CICS) or to the CICS dump dataset.
EQUATE	This command allows you to use a shorthand technique to assign names for various parts of the debug session. If you will be developing complex scripts, this is a must.
FLOW	This command turns on (or off) an internal trace of program flow. The flow is printed by a second execution of the statement with different options. See example.

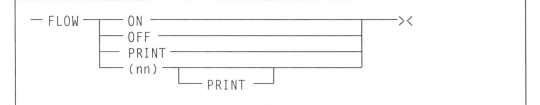

```
— FLOW ——— ON ——————————————————————><
         —— OFF ———
         —— PRINT ———
         —— (nn) ——
               —— PRINT ——
```

FREQ	This command tallies how many times verbs were executed.
GO	This command starts or resumes execution of a program.
IF	A powerful debug command, it provides logic capability to your debug script. See example.

```
————————IF —(expression)————(command list) ——————————————><
```

LINK

This command is useful for debugging CALLed subprograms when you are testing them without the CALLing program. It sets up the LINKAGE SECTION addressability. It must be followed by the SET command to initialize the values of the variables. See example.

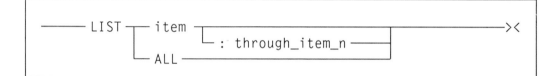

```
——— LINK ——— (01_level_name ┬─────────────────────────┬ ) ———><
                             └─ additional 01_items ─┘
```

LIST

This command displays or prints data areas from the program.

```
——— LIST ┬─ item ┬─────────────────────────┬ ———><
         └─ ALL ─┴─ : through_item_n ─┘
```

LISTBRKS

This command is useful when you've set many breakpoints with AT, NEXT, or WHEN commands and need a refresher on what is still set. It is helpful when you are in a debug session and want to determine the next step to take.

LISTEQ

Similar to LISTBRKS, this command lists all active EQUATEs in your program. It is useful if you didn't write them down.

LISTFREQ

This command lists the number of times verbs were executed for all programs for which FREQ was specified. It may be useful if seeing the count of verbs gives you information on what was or was not properly executed.

NEXT

This command sets a temporary breakpoint at the next verb. It is useful when you want a breakpoint set from the current position in the program for one iteration.

OFF

This command resets breakpoints that were set with AT.

OFFWN

This command resets breakpoints that were set with WHEN.

ONABEND   This command specifies a list of commands to
                            execute if the program ABENDs. It is very useful
                            if you want information listed or other processes to
                            occur only at ABEND.

```
——————— ONABEND ———————(command list) ————————————————>< 
```

PROC   A powerful command, PROC allows you to inter-
                            cept CALLs to an existing (or nonexisting) subpro-
                            gram. From this, you can specify SET commands
                            that dictate what values to return to the CALLing
                            program.
QUALIFY   This command does double duty. It identifies the
                            name of the PROGRAM-ID to which following
                            commands apply. It also can qualify data names
                            (e.g., where the same name exists in two or more
                            programs being tested together).

```
——————— QUALIFY———————programid ┬———————————————————>< 
                                └—.—nested_program_id —┘
```

QUIT   This command terminates the session.
RECORD   This command starts (or stops) recording of the
                            debug session. It is useful for reviewing what hap-
                            pened during a debug session. It records to SYSLST.
RESTART   This command deletes and reloads a program,
                            making it available in its initial state. It does not
                            apply to CICS.
RUN   This command causes the program to ignore all
                            breakpoints and begin/continue execution. If the
                            program does not ABEND, it will cause it to ex-
                            ecute to STOP RUN or GOBACK.
SET   This command sets a variable to a value. It is
                            useful when initializing areas or, at a breakpoint,
                            changing them to monitor program logic.

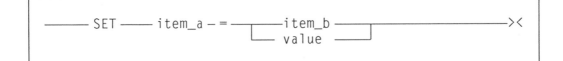

TRACE   This command displays a flow of program or para-
                               graph execution. See examples.

```
      ———— TRACE ——————————————————————————————————————————>|<
                  |—— PARA ——————|    |—— PRINT ——|
                  |—— ENTRY ——————|
```

WHEN   This command is excellent for scripts. It continu-
                               ously tests a condition while the program is ex-
                               ecuting. It also establishes a name for the condi-
                               tion for reference. See example.

```
   —WHEN  when_name ———— (expression)  (command list) ———>|<
```

4.7. CICS DEBUG CONSIDERATIONS

This section assumes you are familiar with the earlier topics in this chapter; this
section presents only those details that are unique for these environments.

Most of the specifics for CICS were covered earlier, including the following:

- Output from STAE or FDUMP or SSRANGE goes to the CEBRxxxx
  queue instead of to SYSLST (where "xxxx" is the terminal-id of the
  transaction). If the CEBR queue has not yet been established at your
  shop, see your technical staff.
- All commands must be prepared prior to running the CICS transaction.
  The commands must be stored in the CSCOxxxx queue. Commands
  follow the same syntax as shown in prior topics and follow the same
  order, e.g.:

```
COBTEST  phasename
RECORD
QUALIFY program-id-name
   .
   .
```

- Changes to run-time options must be made through the IGZEOPT
  module.

A programming item to consider is that the EXEC CICS HANDLE ABEND
command will bypass the COBOL II debug facilities.

SUMMARY

In writing this book, I was torn between whether or not to include this chapter. Debugging is not a skill for building better productional systems. By following the guidelines in Chapter 5 ("Program Design"), problems will diminish. I finally decided to include this chapter because FDUMP and SSRANGE can help. I use COBTEST only for packaging scripts.

While I attempted to be as thorough as possible in other chapters, I've avoided it here. IBM's COBOL II debugging manual covers it thoroughly (over 300 pages) and you will need that manual anyway; that is where the error messages are located. Still, I hope you picked up a few tricks here that will help you be proactive in your approach to resolving problems.

The best programmers often do poorly at debugging or reading dumps. The better the code, the less opportunity there is to engage in debugging practices. Writing errorfree code is possible. Believe it and you will write it, but first you must believe.

COBOL Program Design Guidelines

Unlike the previous chapters that focused on exploiting COBOL II, this chapter focuses on program design. This chapter is presented because some shops have no design guidelines at all, other shops have design guidelines that are so outdated that no one uses them, and still other shops have design standards that use terminology that prevents direct translation to the programming process. Effort has been placed on simplicity and clarity instead of more rigorous definitions of the design process. Emphasis has been placed on structure and style components, using COBOL II facilities when they enhance the issues. Some awareness of structured design and structured programming is necessary to use these guidelines. This chapter relates to the next chapter, "COBOL Coding Guidelines." Both are presented to assist you in evaluating and establishing your own program design and coding guidelines.

In reading this chapter, you may find areas in which this book conflicts with your shop's standards. Since your shop has its own circumstances, this is to be expected. I hope that this will cause active dialogue to occur about why the differences exist and why your company standards are the way they are. At too many companies, the standards manuals were developed with little awareness of the restrictions of earlier versions of COBOL. This is an effort to remove those restrictions. Too often, the programmer is criticized for poor program structure, when the real culprit was a design so convoluted that the programmer had to patch it together.

5.1. STRUCTURE VERSUS STYLE

Quality finds its way into a program by two routes: structure and style. Good structure ensures the application does exactly what is required and also minimizes debug efforts. Style is a contribution by the programmer to ensure clarity in the structure.

5.1.1. Structure

Structure is an end product, not a process or a technique. Good structure is evidenced by balance and consistent decomposition of a program's components. Common examples of structure within the code are verbs such as CALL, PER-FORM, EVALUATE, INITIALIZE. Their appearance alone is not, however, proof of good structure. A program gets its structure during the program design phase of application development.

5.1.2. Style

Style is the approach taken by the programmer to achieve clarity, consistency, maintainability, and portability. Good style is simple, using as few syntax elements as possible to represent the solution. This is apparent in the coding by a uniform format with predictable and recurrent placement of both data and procedural items. A programmer will be able to absorb the structure and processes of a program designed with good style using a minimum number of eye movements. A program gets its style during the coding phase of application development. Most style aspects are addressed in the section, Program Layout Guidelines.

5.2. ACHIEVING GOOD STRUCTURE

These are practical tips to assist the programmer in developing good structure. Reasonable effort has been made to ensure these steps do not conflict with the majority of design processes being used.

5.2.1. Use Top-Down Development

This initial step is where you should do the JCL for batch processes and ensure that all screen-to-screen interactions for on-line applications are complete. By doing this now, before getting into the details of each program, you ensure the structure is complete from the top down. For example, in doing the JCL you will complete all external names (e.g., system-names, PROGRAM-IDs) required and may discover that some processes, such as the use of various utilities (e.g., IDCAMS, SORT/MERGE II), were overlooked. This step should also confirm what processes should be daily, weekly, on-line, batch, etc.

A side benefit of this step is that it allows a programming team to start dividing the work effort, with senior programmers beginning program design, while junior programmers begin coding JCL or statements for utility programs.

If documentation specialists are on the team, they can begin structuring the documentation for the system.

Note: If the application will use VSAM, DL/1, or SQL/DS, ensure the data design has been properly done. See the topic, Data Structures and System Environments in Chapter 3 for more information.

5.2.2. Design Each Program from the Top Down

This is a major factor for success. Here are some techniques to assist you.

Decompose each box on structure chart into subordinate boxes. Decomposition allows you to focus on the solution and not on the mechanics. Decomposition begins with a high-level statement of what is to be done. If you can state it in one sentence, you can depict it as a box on a chart. For example, decomposing a box called "Do final processes" might create these subordinate processes: "Print totals," "Update audit file," "Close files." Each description begins with a verb. Together, they represent the processing described by the parent box. Descriptions such as "Error routine," "Handle I/O" are invalid, since they can't be decomposed and reflect an incomplete decomposition. Where possible, the subordinate boxes should be shown from left to right in their anticipated processing sequence.

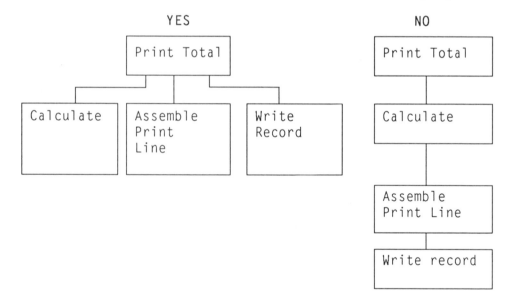

Represent one COBOL paragraph or CALLed subprogram per box. This ensures decomposition occurs and that too many functions aren't attempted within a single module. This can be easily tested. You should be able to fully code any module above the lowest level (e.g., after coding the third level of a structure chart, you should be able to code the first and second levels). GO TO statements that are required during the coding phase are evidence that the decomposition was incomplete or incorrect.

Place control higher and action lower. By placing control (e.g., IF) in upper-level modules and action (e.g., COMPUTE) in lower-level modules, you contain the scope of each module. Moving action to a lower level is the management equivalent of delegation, whereas moving control to a lower level is the management equivalent of abdication. Not following this guideline is a major reason that lower level modules must abort or GO TO another module to correct an error in the structure or resolve an issue caused by a higher module's abdication. Note: The authority to terminate the program (STOP RUN or GOBACK) should never be delegated to a lower-level module. This verb should appear only in the highest module.

Be sensitive to cohesion and coupling aspects. Here are basic definitions.

> **COUPLING.** The degree that two modules are dependent on each other. This should be low.
> **COHESION.** The degree that all the code within a paragraph or program relates to the purpose of the paragraph or program. This should be high.

For example, a module titled "Initialize work areas" might consist of many MOVE or INITIALIZE statements and even the loading of a data table. All of these processes are setting data areas to initial values before processing and, therefore, this module would have high cohesion (desirable). Here are some tips to increase cohesion and reduce coupling.

1. Isolate functions.   For example, the READ of a file should be alone in one module (paragraph). Other examples might be "Compute withholding tax," "Assemble print line."
2. Separate one-time processes from repetitive processes.   This is often the first decomposition within a program, separating those processes that occur at program initiation, program termination, and those that are repetitive.
3. Avoid setting switches to trigger action in peer-level or lower-level modules.   This is known as pathological coupling, the tying of one module's actions to another's without higher-level modules being involved or aware. This defeats the isolation desired within modules and creates complexity in maintenance when higher level modules are not in control of processes.
4. Avoid defining general-purpose modules.   Modules such as "Do database I/O" are not functional and are difficult to debug. Instead, identify what must occur, (e.g., "Read policy segment," "Add beneficiary segment").

5.2.3. Use structured programming techniques

Structured programming is a process and a technique, not an end product. It is a process of building programs by a rigid discipline, following a technique of combining logically related components. Each of the five possible structures has one entry and one exit (see Figure 5.1). With structured programming, all modules, whether paragraphs or programs, should also have one entry and one exit. Definitions of each term follow:

SEQUENCE: Verbs that manipulate data or cause an event to occur. This includes MOVE, ADD, and WRITE among others.

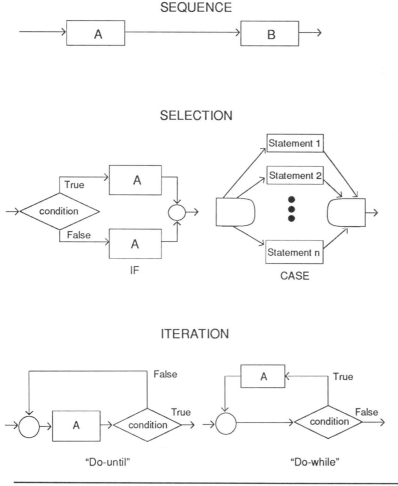

Figure 5.1. Structured programming components.

SELECTION: These are conditional statements that are often dependent on the particular implementation of COBOL to be easily used. These include IF, ON SIZE ERROR, and AT END among others.

DO-WHILE: In COBOL, this is implemented as PERFORM and PERFORM UNTIL. By determining what condition should terminate processing, you prevent abdicating the decision to a lower-level module that must control the process with a GO TO. Repetitive processes should be controlled by the PERFORM UNTIL statement.

DO-UNTIL: Not available before COBOL II, this requires the WITH TEST AFTER clause in the PERFORM statement. Where the DO-WHILE tested a value prior to each repetition, the DO-UNTIL tests the control value after each repetition. The choice is often moot with COBOL, but it does affect the resulting value of any data elements being incremented in the iterations.

CASE: Available only in COBOL II, this is executed with the EVALUATE statement. Because this verb has several different formats, you should be familiar with it; its capabilities may enhance your program design.

Structuring an application cannot be done by simple prose. Check your program design specifications to see if they have an implied GO TO to return to the beginning to repeat the process for the next record, or have imbedded alternate selection logic in the body of the processing specifications. These are two common errors that occur in developing specifications. They are usually avoided only by a conscious view of the entire application as a large DO WHILE or DO UNTIL.

5.2.4. Use CALL and PERFORM to Transfer Control and Delegate Processes

This often begs the question "How big should a program be?" Do not subdivide a program into smaller programs based on some arbitrary limit, such as the number of modules (boxes) or the anticipated number of source statements. A program may stay a single program so long as its primary function is well defined. That consideration, itself, will ensure the program stays small enough to be easily maintained.

5.2.5. Use Structure Charts with Consistent Style and Numbering

Consistency and the ability to readily convert a structure chart into code are key to improving productivity. Also, since the programmer will develop paragraph names from this chart, the naming technique should be predictable. A sample structure should follow these guidelines:

1. Define one uppermost module.
2. Decompose each module in a left-to-right fashion.
3. Define names for each module consisting of one verb followed by at least one word, preferably two.
4. Assign module numbers to each box as follows:
   (1) Level 1 (top)   Set to 0.
   (2) Level 2   Increment by 1000.
   (3) Level 3   Increment by 100.
   (4) Level 4   Increment by 10.
   (5) Level 5   Increment by 1.
   (6) Level 6   Increment by Alphabet (A, B, etc.)
5. Include a horizontal line across the box to depict CALLed subprograms.
6. Draw an angled mark across the upper-right corner to depict modules that are accessed from more than one module.

The benefit of the above numbering scheme is that each module's name contains its origin. For example, a box titled 1100 will be a subset of the box titled 1000. When this numbering scheme is carried into the program's paragraph names, there is a good one-to-one relationship, which is easy to read and walk through.

This represents only one approach to the application. If coded directly from the structure chart, there would be 12 paragraphs (one is a prewritten subprogram and one is PERFORMed from two locations). It also demonstrates the style of the designer, as it depicts where files are OPENed, but leaves it to the programmer to determine where to CLOSE them. (Ideally, there would be a module numbered 3200, named "Close files.") Notice that all paragraphs other than the top one are to be PERFORMed (i.e., no fall through's, no GO TOs).

The style of the programmer may also affect the final structure. For example, the programmer may determine that modules 1100, 1200, and 1300 consist only of one OPEN, one CALL, and a couple of INITIALIZE and MOVE statements. Being only four or five statements, the programmer might decide to put all of them in module 1000. Since this is a style issue, there are no firm rules. If this occurs too frequently in the coding of an application, the structure can be defeated by ending up with a few very large paragraphs that are difficult to decipher and maintain. There should be periodic reviews during the coding process to ensure the structure is intact.

Simple structure chart:

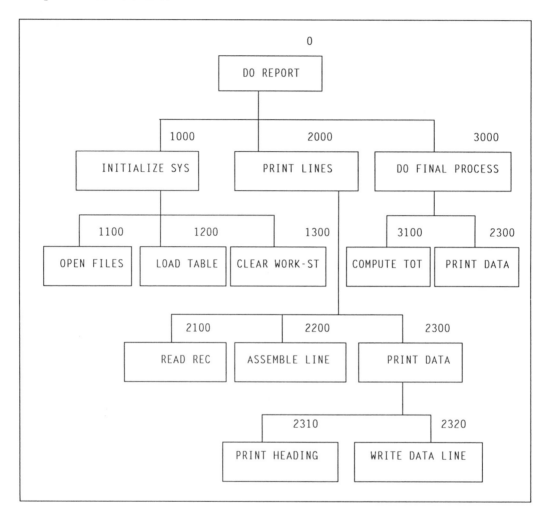

5.3. SORT DESIGN TECHNIQUES

Sorting has unique aspects, since it is a separate program being activated under control of COBOL within the run unit. Here are some considerations to keep in mind whenever specifications indicate a sort is needed.

5.3.1. SORT/MERGE II versus a COBOL SORT

Consider using SORT/MERGE II instead of a COBOL SORT with INPUT/OUTPUT procedures.

SORT/MERGE II is advantageous when the output will be used by more than one application, the volume of records to be sorted is such that restart or recovery processing is not feasible, and the speed of development is primary (SORT/MERGE II statements may be coded more quickly than COBOL SORT statements).

Consider a COBOL SORT when the selection criteria is complex, many of the data fields will not be needed after sorting, the number of records to be sorted will be significantly reduced by using COBOL record selection, and the sorted data is needed by a single application and run-time performance is primary.

5.3.2. SORT/MERGE II Control Statements Versus INPUT or OUTPUT PROCEDURE

Specify that SORT/MERGE II control statements will be provided through SYSIPT (specified in SORT-CONTROL special register) with SORTs whenever selection criteria are simple or the OUTPUT PROCEDURE does not need access to all data fields. This can reduce development and run-time costs. This technique combines the positive features of using SORT/MERGE II alone with the positive features of a COBOL SORT.

5.3.3. SORT Performance Issues

Consider performance issues of sort applications, even though such information is not part of the user's requirements. The volume of records involved in a sort will be the major influence on run-time and cost. This can be reduced by sorting only the records needed and by sorting only the fields necessary for subsequent processing. This can be accomplished by coding control statements through SYSIPT or by an INPUT PROCEDURE.

5.4. SUMMARY OF PROGRAM DESIGN GUIDELINES

While not complete, the following represent highlights to remember in designing programs. Refer to the previous pages for specifics.

1. Do JCL and external processes first.
2. Decompose each program and module.
3. Do control processes first and action processes later.
4. Design each module to be a single paragraph or program.
5. Maintain one entry and one exit for each module.
6. Identify all modules with a verb.
7. Consider management terms such as *span of control*, *delegation*, and *abdication*.

SUMMARY

These design guidelines omitted any COBOL examples and assume the reader is familiar with the terms and techniques defined in Chapters 2 and 3. I would appreciate hearing whether they help you organize the up-front part of your programming.

6

COBOL Coding Guidelines

This chapter complements the previous chapter, providing a framework for program coding. As with Chapter 5, this chapter is provided because many shops either have no guidelines or their guidelines were developed in the 1970s. These guidelines may be used to help you develop your own coding guidelines, or you can use them as they stand. While Chapter 3 showed various ways of using COBOL for specific applications, this chapter focuses only on the mechanics of the coding process. I'm sure these guidelines differ from any your shop may have. Why can I say this? Because most guidelines I have seen emphasize that the programmer should code every entry in a program. The guidelines in this chapter state that

- The fewest number of statements necessary for the application should be coded. (Optional entries keep getting dropped by ANSI, only creating future conversion headaches.)
- Some verbs should never be coded. This includes some verbs that you might consider popular.
- The period (.) is a curse and should be coded only to end paragraphs.

Surprisingly, most of these guidelines (other than new verbs) work fine with earlier versions of COBOL. In fact, the main reason people find it difficult to convert to COBOL II is because they are still coding syntax from ANSI 68, not because they were using the DOS/VS COBOL compiler.

Examples of programs developed using these guidelines are in Chapter 8. You will notice that the examples do not follow these guidelines completely; I believe the programmer must have some latitude in interpreting any guidelines on the programming process.

Notice to DOS/VS COBOL readers: I do not encourage you to change existing programs to use new techniques. Programs that do not follow these guidelines should not be changed except when it will be beneficial. "If it ain't broke, don't fix it" is my motto for program maintenance.

6.1. GENERAL LAYOUT GUIDELINES

This section deals with general guidelines that apply to all divisions. Emphasis is on neatness, and on preventing the program from becoming dense. Having too many statements per page can make an otherwise simple program difficult to read.

6.1.1. Format—White Space and Indentation Guidelines

SPACING. DIVISION statements should be preceded and followed by at least 2 blank lines. SECTION statements should be preceded and followed by at least 1 blank line. Paragraphs, FDs, SDs, and 01-levels should be preceded by at least 1 blank line. Place each statement (this includes ELSE) on a separate line. This does not include clauses that are subordinate to a statement. Place paragraph names on a separate line.

INDENTATION. Margin A entries (FD, SD, DIVISION, SECTION, Paragraph names, 01-level entries) must begin in column 8 and margin B entries (procedural statements, subordinate data definitions) must begin in column 12. Entries that are subordinate (e.g., 05-level data definitions and related clauses) or are components of the same definition (e.g., FD) should be indented 4 columns and aligned in columnar fashion.

6.1.2. Use of Comments

Use comments liberally, making code more meaningful or explaining complicated logic.

1. Use the * in column 7 for comments.
2. At the end of the program, document every project that causes a change to the program. Here is an example:

```
*------------------------------------------------------------------*
*    MAINTENANCE LOG                                               *
* DATE    * WHO       *    DESCRIPTION                             *
*------------------------------------------------------------------*
* 05/26/90* ANNA LIST  *   CC12345 - NEW BILL OPTION              *
* 07/20/91* JOEL FIXIT *   NP23456 - NEW TERM RIDER               *
*------------------------------------------------------------------*
```

3. At the end of the program, place the COBOL II statement "END PRO-GRAM program-id." The END PROGRAM statement begins in column 8 and does not include a hyphen. The program-id must match that coded in the PROGRAM-ID of the IDENTIFICATION DIVISION.
4. Place the TITLE statement at the beginning of the program and at the beginning of all parts of the program that would benefit (e.g., a SORT INPUT PROCEDURE).
5. Write comments as paragraphs, not as single lines interspersed between other statements. See examples in Chapter 8.

6.1.3. COPY Statement Use

Use the COPY statement for record formats and complex procedural processes that are used in several programs. COPY members should carry a comment line showing the last date changed and why, plus a comment line identifying the COPY member's function (e.g., STATE-NAME TABLE).

6.1.4. Resolving Compiler Error Messages

Resolve warning messages before migrating the program to production. If the compiler generates a return code other than zero, you are receiving warning messages that could cause complications later; the compiler routinely is upgraded to change some warning messages to major error messages. Keep your program listings clean.

6.2. IDENTIFICATION DIVISION GUIDELINES

6.2.1. Specific Layout Guidelines

None, other than general guidelines specified previously.

6.2.2. Minimum Entries and PROGRAM-ID Guidelines

1. PROGRAM-ID must be 8 characters long, matching the productional name of the program.
2. Enter one or more comment paragraphs to describe the purpose and functions of the program. These should be in comment format (* in column 7). Avoid generic descriptions such as "SORT FILE AND PRODUCE REPORT."
3. Use comments to provide information on AUTHOR and on DATE WRITTEN.
4. Do NOT use the COBOL elements AUTHOR, DATE-WRITTEN, INSTALLATION, and DATE-COMPILED. They are obsolete elements.

6.3. ENVIRONMENT DIVISION GUIDELINES

6.3.1. Specific Layout Guidelines

None, other than general guidelines specified previously.

6.3.2. Minimum Requirements

1. The ENVIRONMENT DIVISION is not needed if there are no external VSE files to be processed (those processed with OPEN and CLOSE verbs).
2. The CONFIGURATION SECTION is not usually needed and should not be coded.
3. No I-O-CONTROL entries are usually needed.
4. INPUT-OUTPUT SECTION, followed by FILE-CONTROL, followed by SELECT statements are all that are usually necessary in this division (assuming external files are processed).

6.3.3. SELECT Statement Guidelines

1. The ASSIGN clause must specify "AS-system-name" for VSAM sequential files, and just "system-name" for SAM sequential files and VSAM indexed or relative files. Example, where system-name will be MASTIN:

```
SELECT FD-PAYROLL-FILE
    ASSIGN TO MASTIN.      <- For SAM and VSAM indexed or
                             relative files

SELECT FD-PAYROLL-FILE
    ASSIGN TO AS-MASTIN.   <- For VSAM sequential files
```

2. For SORT files, use ASSIGN TO SORTWK.
3. ORGANIZATION should be specified only for nonsequential files.
4. RESERVE clause should not be specified (use JCL if more data buffers are needed).
5. The selection of system-names for the application should not be left to the individual programmer, but it needs to follow a predefined company standard. This becomes critical when multiple programs are combined into a run unit.

6.4. DATA DIVISION GUIDELINES

6.4.1. Specific Layout Guidelines

1. Data-names. Data-names must be sufficient for a knowledgeable reader to understand (e.g., FLDA is unacceptable). Data-names must be hy-

phenated and use a prefix convention that is consistent throughout the division.

- FDs and SDs should have a prefix of FDn- or SDn- and end with the word FILE. (The phrases, LABEL RECORDS ARE and DATA RECORD IS are obsolete and should not be used.) The suffix *n* should reflect the file's relative number within the program. For example,

```
FD1-identifier-FILE
    RECORD CONTAINS nn CHARACTERS
    BLOCK CONTAINS 0 RECORDS
    RECORDING MODE IS F.
```

```
(Note: nn refers to the number of characters in the
record. For variable-length records, use RECORDING MODE
IS V.)
```

```
SD2-identifier-FILE
    RECORD CONTAINS nn CHARACTERS.
```

- 01-level entries for FD and SD should retain the prefix of the file description and end with the term RECORD.
- 01-level entries for WORKING STORAGE should have the prefix WSn- and end with the term RECORD.
- 01-level entries for LINKAGE SECTION should use the prefix LSn- and end with the term RECORD. For example,

```
FILE SECTION:              01 FD1-identifier-RECORD

WORKING-STORAGE SECTION:   01 WS1-identifier-RECORD

LINKAGE SECTION:           01 LS1-identifier-RECORD
```

2. **Format for subordinate levels.** Subordinate entries are indented 4 columns to the right of their parent entry. If the entry is an elementary item, the PIC and VALUE clauses may appear on the same line. Subordinate entries should begin at level 05 and increment by 5. Their data-name should bear the same prefix as the 01-level entry.

3. **Categories for 01-level entries in WORKING STORAGE.** Group like items together, such as 01-level entries that contain various switches and counters, 01-level entries that are used to store data records during processing, 01-level entries that are used to format print records, or 01-level entries that are used in CALL statements.

4. **Definition of data types.** Specify data fields as either alphanumeric or numeric. Follow these techniques to minimize inefficiencies.

- Use PIC X for all items that are not used in arithmetic or are not intrinsically numeric (e.g., a person's age is intrinsically numeric, whereas a part number is a coding mechanism that could become nonnumeric).
- Define COMP-3 (packed) items as an odd number of digits, plus a sign, to ensure optimum code is generated.
- Define COMP items that will contain a number of 9,999 or less as PIC S9(4) for optimum memory use.
- Define COMP items that will contain a value between 10,000 and 999,999,999 as PIC S9(9) for the same reason.

5. Definition of switches. Define switches as PIC X and show a value of 'Y' if true and 'N' if not true. The name of the switch must specify a readily understood condition, with 88-level entries also provided. For example,

```
05 WS3-FD1-PAYROLL-FILE-EOF    PIC   X   VALUE 'N'.
    88  WS3-FD1-PAYROLL-AT-END          VALUE 'Y'.
    88  WS3-FD1-PAYROLL-NOT-AT-END      VALUE 'N'.
```

6. Use of 88-level entries. The 88-level removes literals from the PROCEDURE DIVISION, improving readability of the procedural code and simplifying conditional statements. Use them wherever they accomplish this. Use a meaningful name that will be appropriate in the procedural code.

6.4.2. Minimum Requirements and Restrictions

1. Use SECTION names only when there are entries within them (e.g., the FILE SECTION is not required if there are no FDs or SDs to be processed).
2. Do NOT use the 77 level or 66 level entries. Instead, combine what would be 77 entries into a common 01-level. Common data types (e.g., counters, switches) are easier for maintenance than 77 level entries. Likewise, a REDEFINES entry is clearer and more readily understood than 66 level entries.
3. Do not use the word USAGE, and abbreviate PICTURE and COMPUTATIONAL. For example,

```
05 WS2-PAGE-COUNTER   PIC S9(5)   COMP-3.
```

6.4.3. Performance Considerations

To improve performance of programs, follow these guidelines:

1. Define tables with indexes and, where possible, in ascending order. This supports binary search techniques (SEARCH ALL), and it is more efficient than using subscripts. Note: As a general rule, subscripts are no less efficient than indexes when the subscript data element is changed for each use. In all other cases, indexes are more efficient. For example,

```
IF WS-PREM-AMT (WS-APP-AGE) = WS-APP-PAID
    PERFORM 2300-PROCESS-FULL-PREM
ELSE
    IF WS-PREM-AMT (WS-APP-AGE) > WS-APP-PAID
        PERFORM 2400-PROCESS-OVERPMT
```

could cause the location within the table of WS-PREM-AMT to be calculated twice. With indexes, this additional calculation would not happen.

2. Use S in PIC for numeric items (e.g., PIC S999) if a sign is present. This reduces object code generated that resets the sign after each operation.

3. Use COMP-3 or COMP for data elements that are involved in arithmetic operations.

   - Use COMP-3 for application data elements and accumulators used to assist the programmer. COMP-3 is more efficient than DISPLAY and more readable in a dump than COMP. For example, the number 123456789 would require this storage and would appear this way in a dump:

```
Data      Bytes
Type      required      As seen in a dump
DISPLAY   9             F1F2F3F4F5F6F7F8F9
COMP-3    5             123456789C
COMP      4             075BCD15
```

   - Use COMP only if specific subprograms or system functions require them. For example, PARM processing requires COMP. Also, use COMP for subscript control elements (i.e., where indexing is not being used).

4. If possible, define arithmetic items that are used in the same computation with the same number of decimal places.

6.5. PROCEDURE DIVISION GUIDELINES

6.5.1. Specific Layout Guidelines

1. Indent conditionally executed statements at least 4 columns beyond invoking statement. For example,

```
IF WS-FD-EOF-SWITCH = 'N'
    PERFORM 3200-PRINT-DETAIL
```

2. Place Scope terminators and ELSE statements in the same column as the prior statement to which it relates. For example,

```
IF WS-SALARY-CODE = 'H'
    PERFORM 2300-COMPUTE-HOURLY-PAY
ELSE
    PERFORM 2400-VALIDATE-SALARY-EMP
END-IF
```

3. Code statements that exceed one line to the next line with a minimum 2-column indentation. For example,

```
MOVE ZEROS TO WS-HOURLY-RATE
              WS-GROSS-PAY
```

4. Develop paragraph names with a structure, such that the name of PERFORMed paragraphs is an extension of the parent paragraph. This should match the structure chart numbering scheme. For example,

```
2000-PRODUCE-FINAL-TOTAL.
    PERFORM 2100-CALCULATE-DATA
    PERFORM 2200-ASSEMBLE-TOTAL-LINE
    PERFORM 2300-WRITE-TOTALS.
```

5. Focus on function. Paragraphs with several functions tend to be large and can become difficult to debug.
6. As a guideline, be conscious of the overuse of literals. They can lead to maintenance headaches. If a literal is used often, consider defining a WORKING-STORAGE data element for it instead.
7. As a guideline, be conscious of the overuse of switches. With good design, fewer switches are needed. Switches are usually misused if a paragraph does not have the authority to take a specific action, but must set a switch to show a condition.
8. Code all paragraphs using structured programming elements such that only one period is used at the end of the paragraph.

6.5.2. Minimum Structural Requirements and Constraints

1. There must be only one STOP RUN (main program) or GOBACK (sub-program). Note: Do **not** use STOP RUN in DL/1 or CICS programs. For CICS, use EXEC CICS RETURN in the highest level module.
2. SECTION entries should not be used.
3. One paragraph, one period.

6.5.3. Program Structure Guidelines

Here is a summary of general considerations to assist you in coding the program.

1. Keep paragraphs small.
2. Code top-to-bottom, left-to-right.
3. Keep balance. Don't string out PERFORMs through a series of serially executed paragraphs.

4. Ensure all paragraphs return control to the PERFORMing paragraph.
5. Place control statements higher and action statements lower.
6. Place I/O processes in separate paragraphs and include a record counter for potential debug assistance.
7. Don't mix several functions in one paragraph. Decompose the paragraph so imbedded functions become new paragraphs that are PERFORMed from the original paragraph.

6.5.4. Use of Control and Action Paragraphs/Subprograms

Ensure PERFORMed action paragraphs return status where outcome is conditional. For example, PERFORMing a paragraph that can have multiple outcomes and then checking results, gives

```
PERFORM 2300-READ-RECORD
IF WS-EOF-SWITCH  = 'N'
    . . . .
```

Making a decision first and then PERFORMing the action paragraph, gives

```
IF VALID-DETAIL-RECORD
    PERFORM 2400-PRINT-DETAIL
    . . . .
```

6.5.5. Preferred COBOL Statements

Appearance of any of the following statements within a program generally indicates that the program is using COBOL II facilities and good structure.

1. **COMPUTE.** Usually more efficient than other arithmetic statements, especially when more than one arithmetic operation takes place.
2. **EVALUATE.** See examples in Chapter 2.
3. **CONTINUE.** See examples in Chapter 2.
4. **INITIALIZE.** Where you have grouped common items together, such as accumulators, the INITIALIZE can reset all entries under a group name, change numeric fields to zero, and change alphanumeric fields to spaces. Examples are included in Chapter 2.
5. **SET.** The SET statement has two formats, SET TO TRUE and SET to adjust indexes or POINTERs. Use SET TO TRUE so they are easier to read in the PROCEDURE DIVISION. (Reminder: When setting indexes, always test that the range of an index is within the table being accessed to prevent causing major program problems.) For example (if a table has 99 entries):

```
IF WS-AGE > 0 AND < 100
    SET WS-PREM-INDEX TO WS-AGE
ELSE
    ...        <- process for invalid age goes here
```

6. **PERFORM and PERFORM UNTIL.** The presence of a PERFORM UNTIL denotes a DO WHILE or a DO UNTIL, both of which show the repetitive portions of a process. See examples in Chapter 2.
7. **SEARCH and SEARCH ALL.** Although not new, many programmers are unaware of their features. You are encouraged to consider their use. See Chapter 3 for more information. Here is an example of a binary search:

Assumed table definition

```
01 WS-STATE-CODE.
    05 WS-STATE OCCURS 50 TIMES ASCENDING KEY STATE-ID
        INDEXED BY ST-INDEX.
        10 STATE-ID       PIC XX.
```

Binary search, indexed

```
SEARCH ALL WS-STATE
  AT END
    PERFORM 2300-RECORD-STATE-ERROR
WHEN STATE-ID (ST-INDEX) = WS-APP-STATE
    PERFORM 2400-RECORD-STATE-VALID
END-SEARCH
```

8. **Nested programs.** Nested programs offer many benefits and their use is encouraged. For more information on nested programs, see the section Module Structures in Chapter 3.

9. **CALL extensions.** Extensions to the CALL statement, including clauses such as BY CONTENT, LENGTH OF, and ADDRESS OF provide opportunities to develop a cleaner module-to-module structure. Their use is not required; in fact, there are many situations in which they serve no purpose.

6.5.6. COBOL Statements That Should Be Used with Caution

While the following statements are useful, consider them carefully before using them. They are listed here to acknowledge that situations may exist where they contribute to structure and clarity.

1. **PERFORM WITH TEST AFTER.** This format works exactly as PERFORM UNTIL except the test of the associated variable occurs after the PERFORM instead of before it. The difficulty is that programmers used to one format may have difficulty rethinking the logic flow for an opposite format.

2. **Inline PERFORM.** While it is no longer necessary to PERFORM outside a paragraph, this statement increases the size of a paragraph, increases the complexity of any paragraph, and increases the possibility of introducing an error into program logic. See example in Chapter 2.

3. **Nested COPY.** The ability to include a COPY statement within another COPY member introduces administrative complexity to maintain the entries.

4. **Hexadecimal literals.** These are machine-dependent, requiring a knowledge of bit configurations. They are coded as X'literal', e.g.,

```
MOVE X'OF' TO WS-PROCESS-ERROR-SWITCH
```

5. **Reference modification.** This feature allows reference to specific bytes within a data element, e.g., MOVE WS-EMP-NAME (3:10) TO WS-EMP-NAME would move ten bytes, beginning with the third byte.

6.5.7. COBOL Statements That Should Not Be Used

These elements violate structured programming techniques. Exceptions: PERFORM THRU, EXIT, and GO TO are sometimes required to construct a meaningful structure with CICS applications. Other than for CICS, these statements should be avoided.

1. **ALTER.** Do not use.
2. **PERFORM THRU.** PERFORM THRU requires a minimum of two paragraphs, encourages the use of GO TO, and violates the concept of decomposition. The format is never required and should be avoided. See exception above for CICS.
3. **EXIT.** The EXIT verb only serves to place a paragraph name. Since it is linked with PERFORM THRU, avoiding use of PERFORM THRU should eliminate this verb, also. See exception above for CICS.
4. **GO TO.** Using GO TO indicates an incomplete or inadequate structure. In DOS/VS COBOL, it was required to function within some restrictions of that compiler (e.g., SORTs), but it no longer has validity. See exception above for CICS.
5. **ENTRY.** The ENTRY statement gives a program more than one entry. Since this is a violation of structured programming, avoid its use. If a subprogram requires multiple entry points, write multiple subprograms instead. It is not required for DL/1 programs.
6. **NEXT SENTENCE** clause. NEXT SENTENCE is an implied GO TO. Use other approaches, such as the CONTINUE statement, or rewrite the statement so NEXT SENTENCE is not required.

6.5.8. Compound Conditions

Conditions are used in IF, EVALUATE, SEARCH, and PERFORM statements. A compound condition is one that combines two or more conditions with AND, OR, or NOT. While these are useful, here are some guidelines to prevent problems:

1. Use arithmetic expressions with caution. They have two potential problems. The first is that if they are used more than once, you lose efficiency and should use a COMPUTE statement to store the result prior to the conditional statement. The second is that the computed value is not truncated into a PICTURE clause, preventing an exact value from being used (e.g., 10 divided by 3 is a never-ending quotient).
2. Use parentheses around conditions to clarify and document what each condition is. For example,

```
IF A > B AND = C OR D   is equivalent to

IF (A > B AND = C) OR
   (A = D)
```

3. Use NOT carefully. When possible use a positive test, not a negative one. Also, remember that NOT, combined with OR, is always true. For example,

IF A NOT EQUAL 1 OR 2. The field A will always be unequal to one of those values; therefore the condition will always be true.

6.6. COBOL SORT TECHNIQUES

Sorting has unique aspects, as it is actually a separate program being activated under control of COBOL. Here are some considerations to take whenever specifications indicate a sort is needed. For performance considerations or to determine whether to use SORT/MERGE II alone or a COBOL SORT, see Chapter 5 (Program Design Guidelines). For usage techniques, see Chapter 3.

Address SORT performance issues. Sort only the records needed, not the entire file. Sort only the fields necessary for subsequent processing, not the entire record.

Use paragraphs, not SECTIONs. The INPUT PROCEDURE and OUTPUT PROCEDURE must specify paragraphs, not SECTIONs. Use a single paragraph for the INPUT and OUTPUT PROCEDURES, i.e., do not specify "paragraph-a THRU paragraph-n."

Validate correct SORT execution. The SORT-RETURN special register will be nonzero if the SORT process terminated prematurely. This field should be tested immediately following the SORT statement.

Terminate a SORT correctly. If a processing discrepancy occurs during an INPUT or OUTPUT PROCEDURE, move 16 to SORT-RETURN, and then issue one more RETURN or RELEASE statement, (i.e, do not immediately issue a STOP RUN, GOBACK, or ABEND). This will terminate the sort and will return control to the statement following the SORT statement, at which time you can test SORT-RETURN and then act accordingly.

Consider using the SORT-CONTROL interface. Using SORT/MERGE II's INCLUDE or OMIT statements via SYSIPT may eliminate the need for an INPUT or OUTPUT PROCEDURE.

In developing a COBOL SORT, here are the basics for the COBOL statements that are used, assuming that both an INPUT and an OUTPUT PROCEDURE are needed. Some portions of the program are omitted. The action taken in this example for a sorting error is an example only.

```
SELECT SD1-sortfile-FILE ASSIGN TO SORTWK.
        .
        .

SD  SD1-sortfile-FILE
```

```
            RECORD CONTAINS nn CHARACTERS.
     01  SD1-sortfile-RECORD.
         05  SD1-sortkey-a  PIC ...
                 .
         05  SD1-sortkey-z  PIC ...
                 .
         SORT SD1-sortfile-FILE
            ASCENDING KEY  SD1-sortkey-a  SD1-sortkey-z
            INPUT PROCEDURE 1000-SELECT-DATA
            OUTPUT PROCEDURE 2000-PRODUCE-REPORT
         IF SORT-RETURN > 0
            DISPLAY ' SORT ERROR OCCURRED'
            STOP RUN
         ELSE
            MOVE 0 TO RETURN-CODE
            STOP RUN
         END-IF.

     1000-SELECT-DATA.
        PERFORM 1010-READ-INPUT
        IF NOT WS-MASTER-EOF
              .
              .       <— Processing to validate or modify data
              .            prior to the sort goes here.
              .
            RELEASE SD-sortfile-RECORD
        END-IF.

     2000-PRODUCE-REPORT.
        RETURN SD-sortfile-FILE
           NOT AT END
              .
              .       <— Processing of data after the sort
              .            goes here.
           END-RETURN.
```

SUMMARY

Admittedly, the format of this chapter was different, rather terse and procedural. As I mentioned at the beginning of this chapter, the focus was on
mechanics, not on logic or design. My goal was to give you a format for assessment. Many times, we don't know what we want to do until we hear someone else
suggest what we clearly do not want to do. If this document helped you determine
how you want to change your programming standards, I'll consider it a success.
Your comments will be appreciated.

Summaries, Tables, and References

7.1. SUGGESTED COBOL COMPILE AND EXECUTION JCL OPTIONS

These options are presented here in summary fashion, and in many cases options for different situations may be combined. For each situation, only the options that normally affect the category are listed (e.g., options such as SOURCE, SEQUENCE, and OBJECT do not appear). You should refer to Chapter 3 for specific options and to Chapter 4 for debugging specifics. You should also know your shop's defaults before using these suggestions.

7.1.1. Options for Syntax Compile

If you're compiling a program to determine if it is coded correctly, but you do not intend to execute it, you incur minimum costs and resource use by coding:

```
NOCOMPILE,XREF,VBREF
```

7.1.2. Options for Routine Tests

Routine testing is for programs that have executed several times and are beyond the unstable phase. These options are proactive (see Chapter 4).

```
OFFSET,FDUMP
```

7.1.3. Options for Minimum Compile Resource Use

This option is for use if you want minimum resource use during the compile (see also, Options for Maximum Compiler Performance below):

```
NOOPTIMIZE
```

7.1.4. Options for Debugging Assistance

These options may be useful for unstable programs or those that have not been tested. SSRANGE increases run-time resource use. Debugging options also require system-name assignments at run-time.

Compile options

```
MAP,XREF(SHORT),OFFSET,SSRANGE,FDUMP
```

Note: If you specify SSRANGE, you must also specify appropriate information at run-time to activate the debugging code for this feature. This can be done in two ways.

1. On the EXEC JCL statement if your program can receive a PARM, the format is

```
// EXEC pgmname,PARM='/SSRANGE'
```

(If your program also expects a PARM value, it must be coded to the left of the / mark.)

2. If your program cannot accept a PARM, or if you prefer not to use that technique, you can include the appropriate code at link edit time. That is done by adding the following Link Edit control statement during the Link-edit step. The desired options must have been previously set in the module named IGZEOPT.

```
INCLUDE IGZEOPT
```

See the section Specifying COBOL II Options in Chapter 3 for more information.

7.1.5. Options for Minimum Run-Time Costs

These options are for programs that are stable and if you want minimum cpu use. You should check Chapter 3 for specifics of each option, as some might affect run-time logic. (Note: NORENT and NORES will reduce run-time costs slightly, but at the cost of lost flexibility. This may be acceptable for certain batch applications.)

```
OPTIMIZE,TRUNC(OPT),NUMPROC(PFD),NOSSRANGE,
NODYNAM,RENT,RES,ADV,AWO,NOTEST
```

7.1.6. Options for Maximum Compiler Performance

These options are my personal suggestion for your shop to use as defaults for maximum performance by the compiler. The partition should be large enough to support the compiler, plus seven times the BUF value, plus 300K (minimum) for internal work areas. I suggest a partition size of at least 1500K. These options should be used with the sample JCL that is in Chapter 3. See the SIZE and BUFSIZE options in Chapter 3 for more information. Before using this suggestion, check with your technical staff for particulars about your installation.

```
SIZE(MAX),BUF(32760)
```

Note: An additional step that should be considered is re-blocking your shop's COPY library (specified by the LIBDEF SOURCE statement) if COPY statements are used frequently. COBOL II allows the block size to be up to 32,767, double the size that DOS/VS COBOL allowed.

7.1.7. Options for CICS

CICS programs need the following options set. You should read the section CICS-DL/1-SQL/DS Issues in Chapter 3 for specifics and additional considerations.

```
RES,RENT,NODYNAM,NOCMPR2,TRUNC(BIN),NODBCS
```

7.1.8. Options for DL/1

DL/1 programs normally use the following options. You should read the section CICS-DL/1-SQL/DS Issues in Chapter 3 for specifics and additional considerations.

```
RES,RENT
```

7.1.9. Options for SQL/DS

SQL/DS programs are not as sensitive as those for CICS, although they benefit from the same options that improve performance flexibility (e.g., RENT, RES). You should read the section CICS-DL/1-SQL/DS Issues in Chapter 3 for specifics.

```
TRUNC(BIN),NOCMPR2
```

7.2.   SUMMARY OF MAJOR COBOL STATEMENTS

This section includes a subset definition of syntax for a subset of the available COBOL statements with emphasis on the new facilities of COBOL II. (You won't find the syntax for the ALTER or GO TO statements here. Nor will you find the more esoteric options of some of the other statements.) Where any clause is omitted, it is noted. Statements that are not new and have no variables (e.g., GOBACK, STOP RUN) are omitted.

Where a loop is evident in the syntax, it represents an optional clause or repetition. Charts should be read from top to bottom, left to right. Each complete statement ends with "—><". Where, due to complexity, I redirected the flow of the syntax from right to left, I inserted arrows (e.g., ——<——<——) to assist you. Statements or clauses that are new with COBOL II are highlighted.

My goal is to provide a ready reference for most of the statements you will encounter, not to provide a reference to every option. For explanations and examples of statements new in COBOL II, see Chapter 2. For complete syntax, see *IBM VS COBOL II Application Programming Language Reference* (Chapter 9).

IDENTIFICATION DIVISION (obsolete clauses omitted).

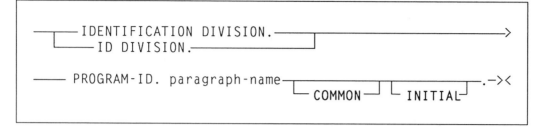

Partial ENVIRONMENT DIVISION (VSAM options and CONFIGURATION SECTION omitted).

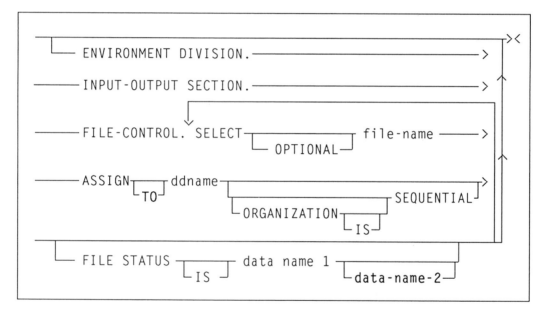

DATA DIVISION.

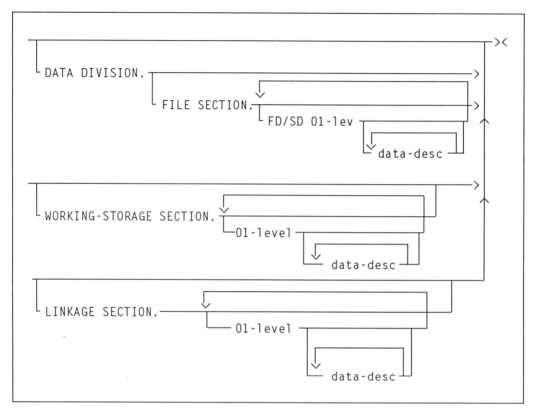

New USAGE and VALUE options.

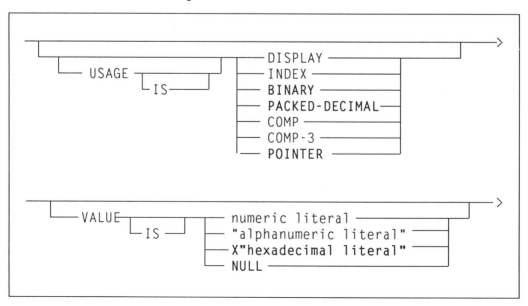

Partial PROCEDURE DIVISION (Declaratives and SECTIONs omitted.)

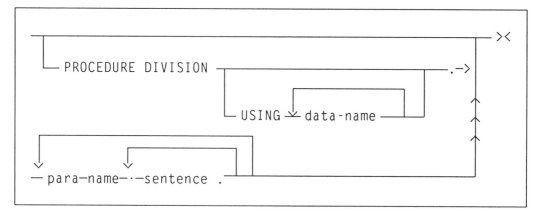

Relational operators.

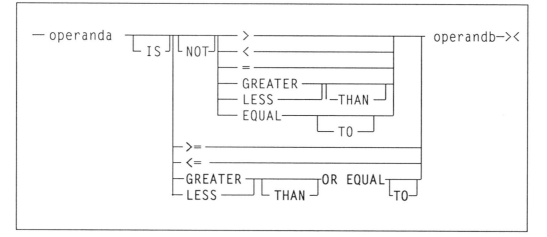

Precedence rules for conditions and arithmetic expressions. Elements are listed in the priority in which they are evaluated.

1. parenthetical elements
2. arithmetic operations
   - 2.a. Unary operator
   - 2.b. exponentiation
   - 2.c. multiplication and division
   - 2.d. addition and subtraction
3. NOT
4. AND
5. OR

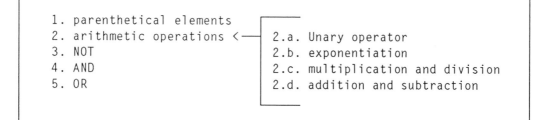

Class condition.

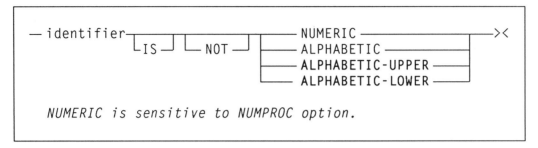

```
— identifier ┬──────┬─┬───────┬─┬── NUMERIC ──────────────┬─ >< 
             └─ IS ─┘ └─ NOT ─┘ ├── ALPHABETIC ───────────┤
                                ├── ALPHABETIC-UPPER ─────┤
                                └── ALPHABETIC-LOWER ─────┘

     NUMERIC is sensitive to NUMPROC option.
```

Sign condition.

```
— identifier ┬──────┬─┬───────┬─┬── POSITIVE ──────┬─ ><
             └─ IS ─┘ └─ NOT ─┘ ├── NEGATIVE ──────┤
                                └── ZERO ───────────┘

     Sign condition is sensitive to NUMPROC option.
```

Reference modification.

```
— data-name ┬──────────────┬─ (leftmost-byte: ┬──────────┬ )><
            ├── subscript ──┤                  └─ length ─┘
            └── index ──────┘

     NOTE: leftmost-byte and length may be numeric literals or
     arithmetic expressions.
```

ACCEPT statement for system transfer.

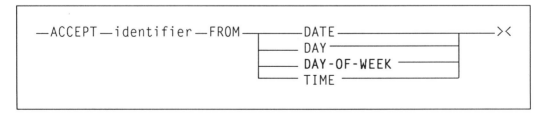

```
— ACCEPT — identifier — FROM ─┬── DATE ─────────┬─ ><
                              ├── DAY ───────────┤
                              ├── DAY-OF-WEEK ───┤
                              └── TIME ──────────┘
```

ADD statement.

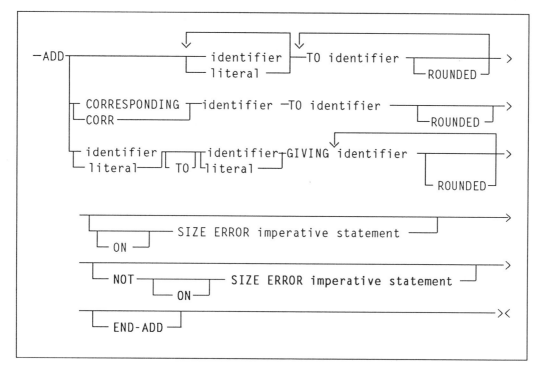

CALL statement.

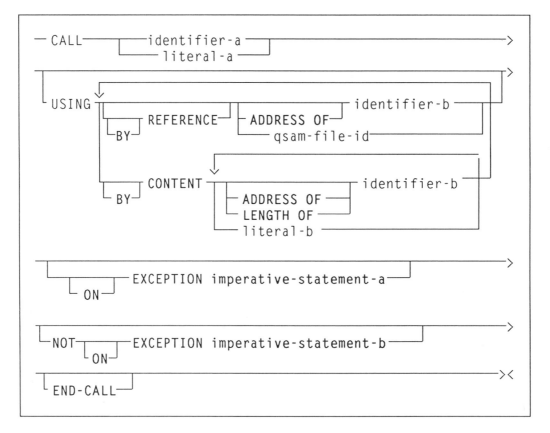

CANCEL statement.

CLOSE statement (tape reel options omitted).

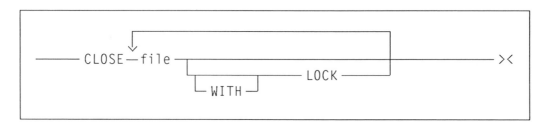

COMPUTE statement.

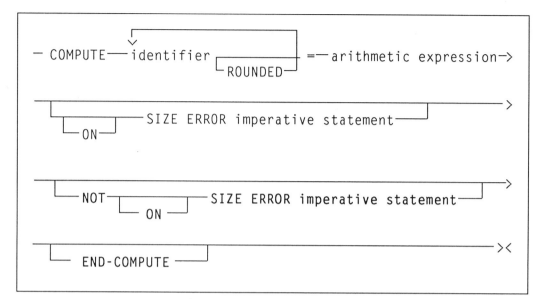

CONTINUE statement.

DELETE statement.

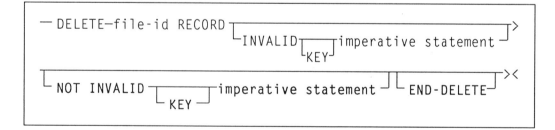

DISPLAY statement, abbreviated.

DIVIDE statement.

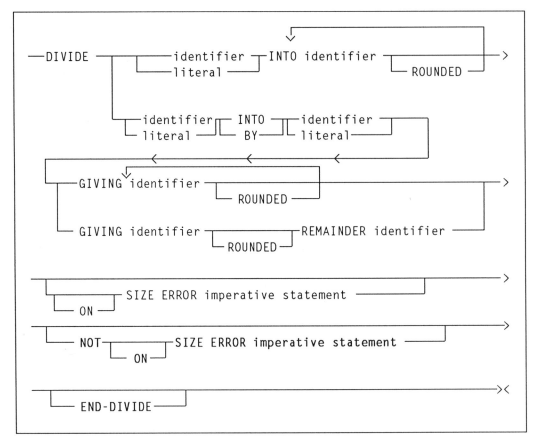

ENTRY statement.

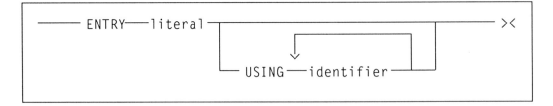

EVALUATE statement.

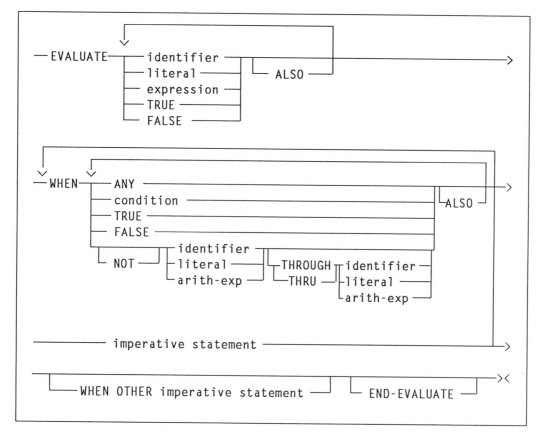

IF statement (NEXT SENTENCE clause omitted).

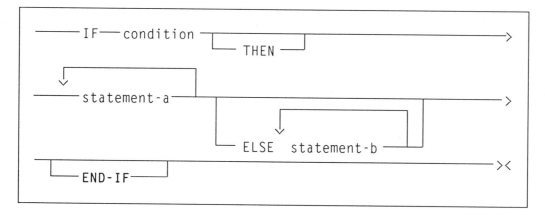

INITIALIZE statement.

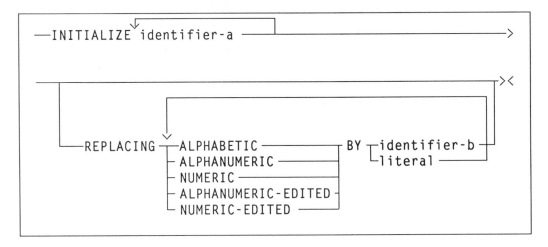

INSPECT statement.

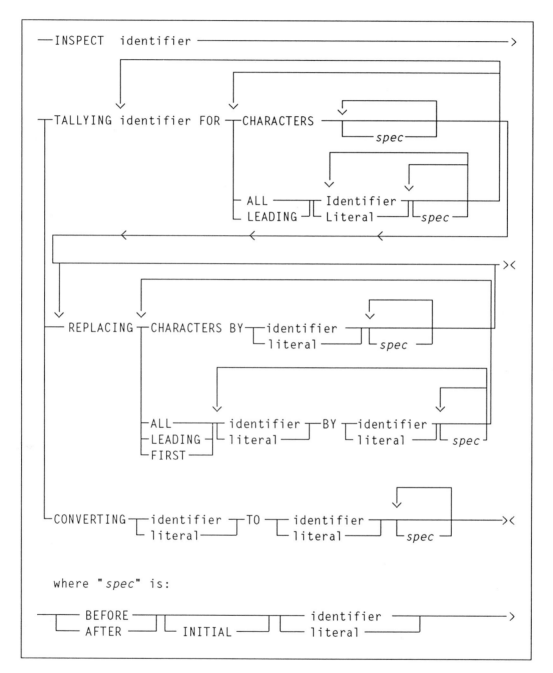

MERGE statement.

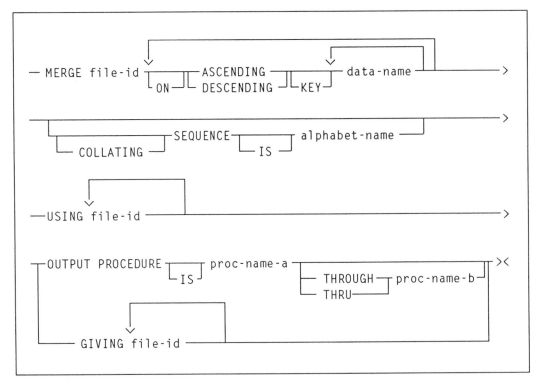

MOVE statement.

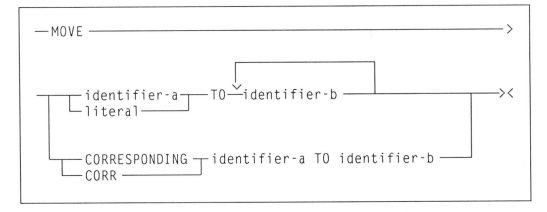

MULTIPLY statement.

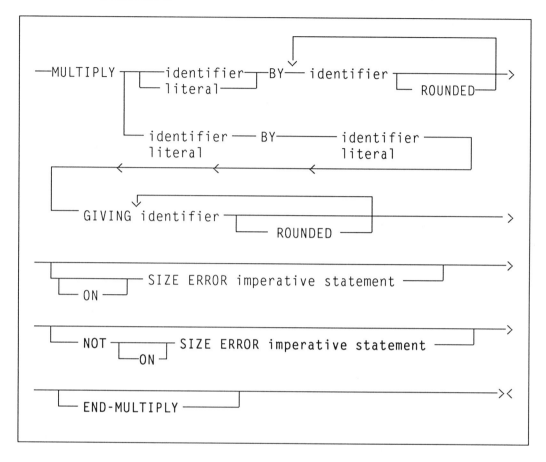

OPEN statement (tape reel options omitted).

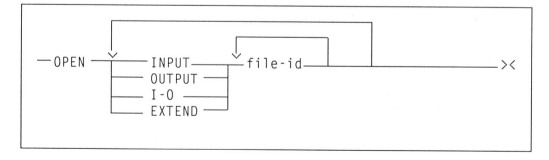

PERFORM statement, except Inline PERFORM.

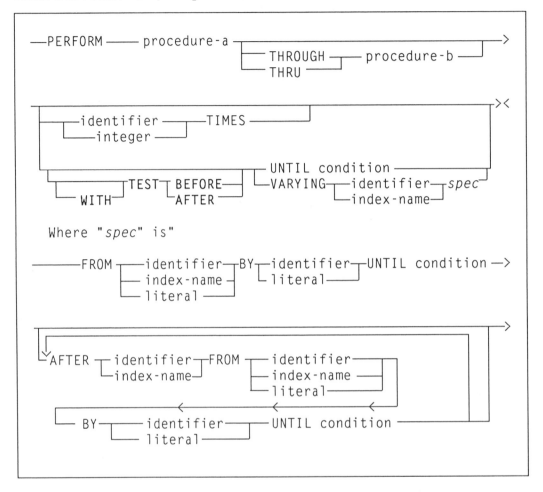

Inline PERFORM.

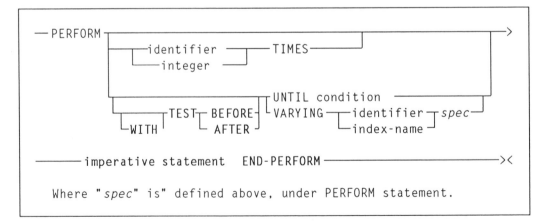

READ statement. AT END/NOT AT END cannot be intermixed with INVALID KEY/NOT INVALID KEY. NEXT has meaning only for VSAM.

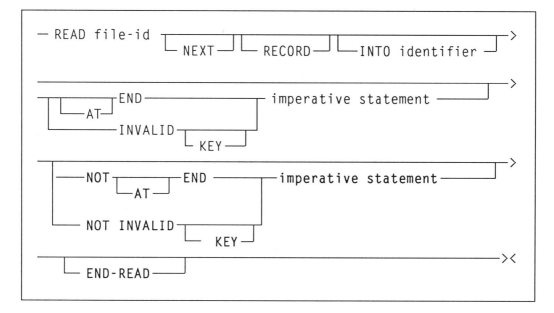

RELEASE statement.

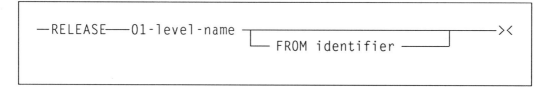

RETURN statement.

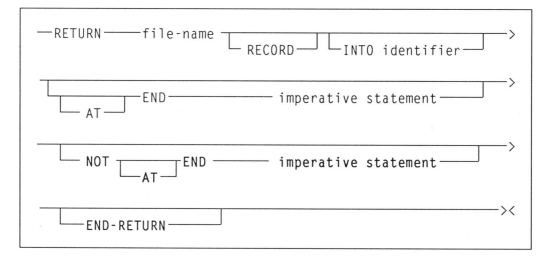

REWRITE statement.

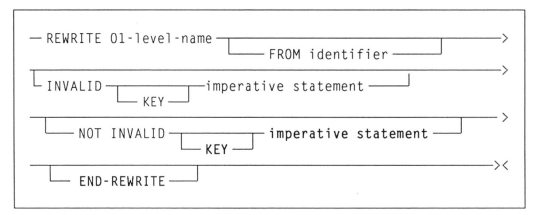

Serial SEARCH statement (NEXT SENTENCE clause omitted).

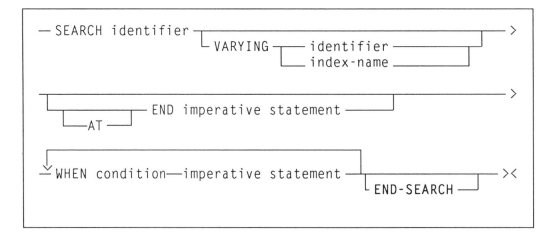

Binary SEARCH ALL statement (IS EQUAL TO omitted).

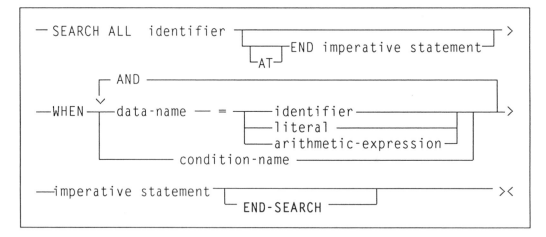

SET statement.

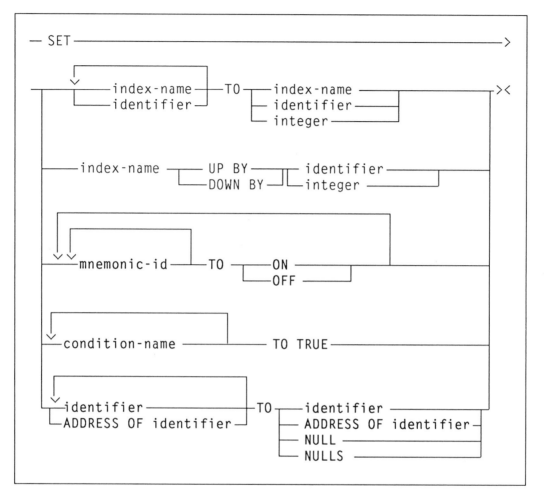

SORT statement.

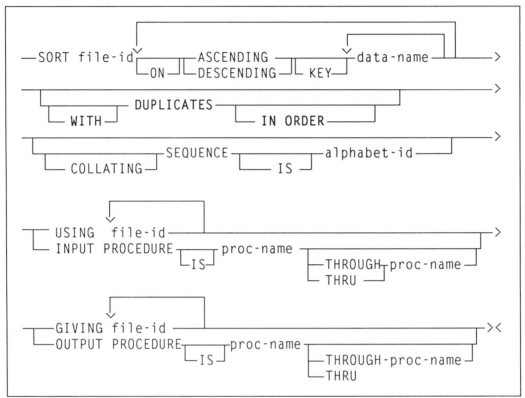

START statement (fully spelled operators, e.g., EQUAL TO, omitted).

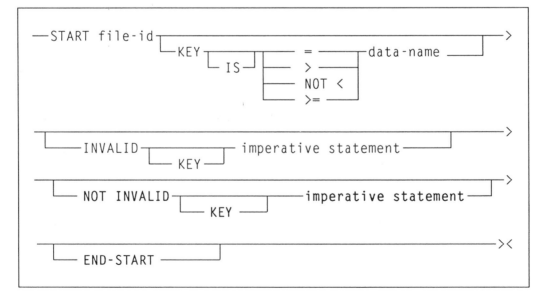

STRING statement.

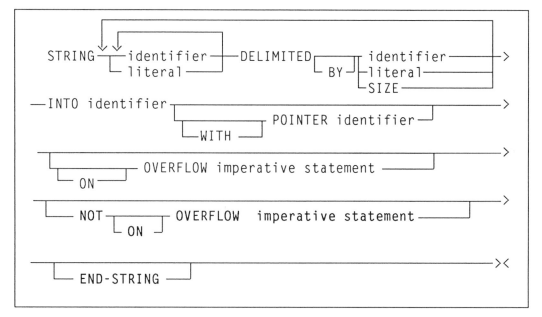

SUBTRACT statement.

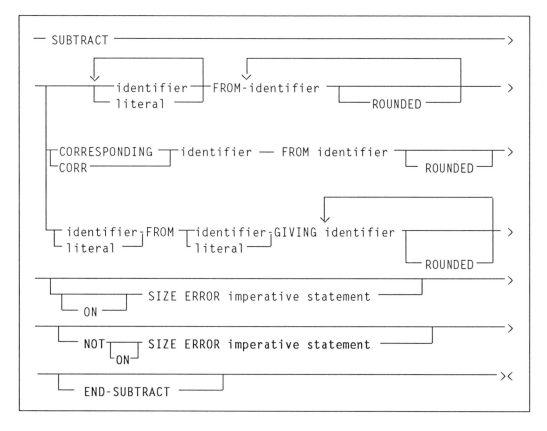

UNSTRING statement.

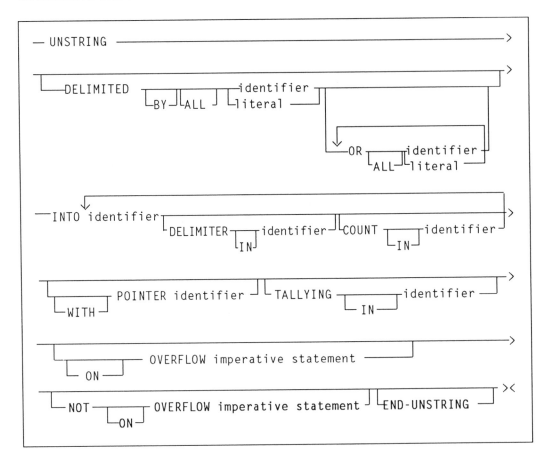

USE statement.

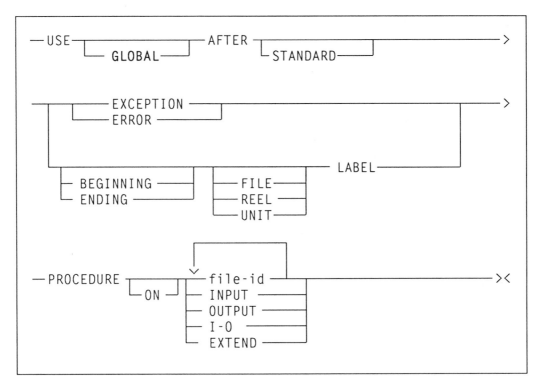

WRITE statement (sequential).

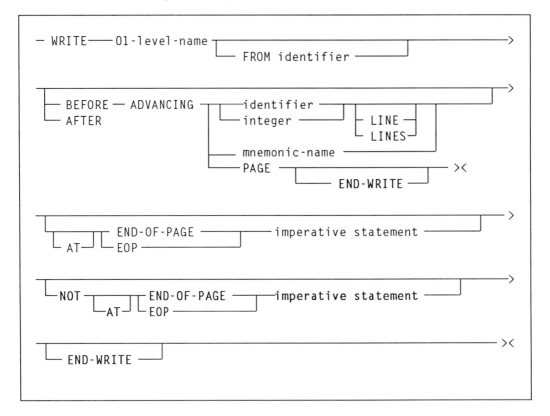

WRITE statement (non-sequential).

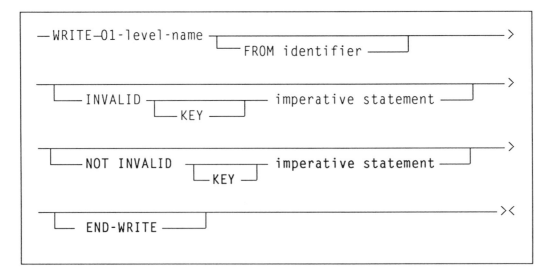

7.3. FILE STATUS CODES

This table of status codes is primarily for quick reference. The keys shown for COBOL II are for use with the NOCMPR2 compile option.

SAM		VSAM		
COBOL II	DOS/VS COBOL	COBOL II	DOS/VS COBOL	
00	00	00	00	Successful completion
N/A	N/A	02	02	Duplicate key
04	N/A	04	00	Wrong length record
05	N/A	05	00	Optional file not present
07	N/A	N/A	N/A	Not a reel-type device, yet was specified
10	10	10	10	End-of-file detected
N/A	N/A	14	N/A	Relative rec # too large—sequential READ
N/A	N/A	20	20	Invalid key
N/A	N/A	21	21	Invalid key, sequence error
N/A	N/A	22	22	Invalid key, duplicate key or not allowed
N/A	N/A	23	23	Invalid key, no record found
N/A	N/A	24	24	Invalid key, attempt to write beyond file limit
30	30	30	30	Permanent error
34	34	N/A	N/A	Permanent error, violation of file boundary
35	93 96	35	93 96	File missing that was not OPTIONAL
37	93	37	90	Device conflict
38	92	N/A	N/A	OPEN error, closed WITH LOCK
39	95	39	95	OPEN fail, conflict of attributes
41	92	41	92	OPEN attempted for open file
42	92	42	92	CLOSE attempted, file not open
43	92	43	92	REWRITE attempted when prior I/O not proper
44	92	N/A	N/A	Attempted REWRITE with different record size

continued on next page

SAM		VSAM		
COBOL II	DOS/VS COBOL	COBOL II	DOS/VS COBOL	
46	92	46	92	READ attempted (sequential), no next record
47	92	47	92	READ attempted when file not OPENed for input
48	92	48	92	WRITE attempted when file not OPENed for output
49	92	49	92	DELETE or REWRITE attempted— OPEN incorrect
90	90	90	90	Undocumented errors
91	91	91	91	VSAM password failed
92	92	N/A	N/A	Logic error
93	93	93	93	VSAM resource not available
94	94	N/A*	94	VSAM file position indicator missing (COBOL II with CMPR2 option)
95	95	95	95	VSAM file information wrong or incomplete
96	96	96	96	NO JCL for VSAM file
N/A	N/A	97	97	OPEN successful—integrity verified

A more thorough review of file status codes is available in *VS COBOL II Language Reference* manual. Sample scenarios are in *DOS/VS COBOL II Application Programming Guide* (Chapter 9).

7.4.   TABLES AND WORKSHEETS

7.4.1. Installation Options

COBOL II Compile-time options.

Use this section to fill in your shop's default options. For information on each option, see the section Specifying COBOL II Options in Chapter 3.

Option	Sample Settings	Your Installation Defaults	
ADV	ADV	_____	
APOST	APOST	_____	
AWO	NOAWO	_____	
BUFSIZE	32760	_____	
CMPR2	NOCMPR2	_____	
COMPILE	NOCOMPILE(E)	_____	
DATA	31	_____	(no meaning for VSE)
DBCS	NODBCS	_____	
DECK	NODECK	_____	(no meaning for VSE)
DUMP	NODUMP	_____	
DYNAM*	NODYNAM	_____	
EXIT	NOEXIT	_____	
FASTSRT	FASTSRT	_____	
FDUMP	NOFDUMP	_____	
FLAG	FLAG(I,W)	_____	
FLAGMIG	NOFLAGMIG	_____	
FLAGSAA	NOFLAGSAA	_____	
FLAGSTD	NOFLAGSTD	_____	
LANGUAGE	UE	_____	
LIB	LIB	_____	
LINECOUNT	60	_____	
LIST	NOLIST	_____	
MAP	NOMAP	_____	

Option	Sample Settings	Your Installation Defaults	
NAME	NONAME	_____	
NUMBER	NONUMBER	_____	
NUMPROC	PFD	_____	
OBJECT	OBJECT	_____	(no meaning for VSE)
OFFSET	NOOFFSET	_____	
OPTIMIZE	NOOPTIMIZE	_____	
OUTDD	n/a	_____	(no meaning for VSE)
RENT*	RENT	_____	
RESIDENT*	RESIDENT	_____	
SEQUENCE	NOSEQUENCE	_____	
SIZE	1500K	_____	
SOURCE	NOSOURCE	_____	
SPACE	1	_____	
SSRANGE	NOSSRANGE	_____	
TERM	NOTERM	_____	
TEST	NOTEST	_____	
TRUNC	BIN	_____	
VBREF	NOVBREF	_____	
WORD	NOWORD	_____	
XREF	NOXREF	_____	
ZWB	ZWB	_____	

* = CICS-sensitive

COBOL II Run-time options.

This may be separate for different environments, e.g., CICS and other. For information on how to determine these settings, see the section Specifying COBOL II Options in Chapter 3. Also, some of these settings cannot be overridden for individual applications.

Option	Sample Settings	Your Installation defaults	
		Other	CICS
NODEBUG	NODEBUG	_____	_____
SSRANGE	NOSSRANGE	_____	_____
STAE	STAE	_____	_____
AIXBLD	NOAIXBLD	_____	_____
SIMVRD*	NOSIMVRD	_____	_____
SPOUT	NOSPOUT	_____	_____
LIBKEEP*	NOLIBKEEP	_____	_____
LANGUAGE	UE	_____	_____
RTEREUS*	NORTEREUS	_____	_____
WSCLEAR	NOWSCLEAR	_____	_____
UPSI	00000000	_____	_____
MIXRES*	NOMIXRES	_____	_____

* Option ignored for CICS

Run-time options may be forced via IGZEOPT assembler module. Global defaults are in IGZEOPD.

7.4.2. Compile Options: COBOL II Versus DOS/VS COBOL

This list is to assist programmers familiar with DOS/VS COBOL compile options who want to locate the similar option for COBOL II. For information on each option, see the section Specifying COBOL II Options in Chapter 3.

COBOL II Option	DOS/VS COBOL Option Settings	Comments
ADV	ADV	
APOST/QUOTE	APOST/QUOTE	
AWO	n/a	
n/a	BATCH	Batch compiles are available by specifying END PROGRAM statement.
BUFSIZE	BUF	For DOS/VS COBOL, this specified the total amount of memory for buffers. For COBOL II, it specifies the maximum per buffer.
CMPR2	n/a	
COMPILE	SYNTAX CSYNTAX SUPMAP	There is no one-to-one relationship, although the function is similar.
n/a	COUNT	This function was moved to COBTEST.
DATA	n/a	DATA has no meaning in VSE.
DBCS	n/a	
DECK	DECK	Provided via JCL OPTION.
DUMP	DUMP	DOS/VS COBOL provided this via JCL OPTION DUMP.
DYNAM	DYNAM	
n/a	ENDJOB	The ENDJOB function is always in effect in COBOL II.
EXIT	n/a	
FASTSRT	n/a	
FDUMP	SYMDMP	
n/a	STATE	COBOL II provides with FDUMP.
FLAG	FLAGW FLAGE	

COBOL II Option	DOS/VS COBOL Option Settings	Comments
FLAGMIG	MIGR	Both compilers use it to monitor migration toward the current release of COBOL II. DOS/VS COBOL only checks for ANSI 74 compatibility.
FLAGSAA	n/a	
FLAGSTD	FIPS	These two have similar goals, but they are different.
n/a	FLOW	This function was moved to COBTEST.
n/a	LANGLVL	COBOL II does not support ANSI 68.
LANGUAGE	n/a	
LIB	LIB	
LINECOUNT	60	
LIST	PMAP	DOS/VS COBOL provided this via OPTION LISTX.
NAME	CATALR	COBOL II provides extended features here.
NUMBER	n/a	
NUMPROC	n/a	
OBJECT	LOAD	
OFFSET	CLIST	
OPTIMIZE	OPTIMIZE	COBOL II does significantly more optimization.
OUTDD	SYS	
RENT	n/a	
RESIDENT	RESIDENT	

COBOL II Option	DOS/VS COBOL Option Settings	Comments
SEQUENCE	SEQ	
SIZE	SIZE	
SOURCE	SOURCE	
SPACE	SPACE	
SSRANGE	n/a	
TERM	TERM	
TEST	TEST	
TRUNC	TRUNC	In DOS/VS COBOL, this was a yes/no option. In COBOL II, it is a more complex issue. See Chapter 3.
VBREF	VBREF VBSUM	
WORD	n/a	
XREF	SXREF	
ZWB	ZWB	

7.4.3. JCL OPTION Statement Versus COBOL II Options

Several COBOL II options may be specified via the JCL OPTION statement. See also the next topic on priority selection.

Feature	COBOL II PARM	JCL OPTION
Source list	SOURCE	LIST
Assembler list	LIST	LISTX
Data Map	MAP	SYM
Object code to SYSPCH	n/a	DECK
Object code to SYSLNK	n/a	CATAL or LINK
Messages to SYSLOG	TERM	TERM
Cross ref - Short	XREF(SHORT)	SXREF
Cross ref - Long	XREF	XREF

7.4.4. Priority of COBOL II Compile Option Selection

COBOL II options may be specified in several ways, requiring that priorities exist to determine which option will apply. Here is the priority scheme:

1. First, any options that are fixed at the time of installation may not be overridden. If done, the option is checked for spelling and ignored. To determine what options, if any, are fixed at your shop, check with your technical staff.
2. Next, the first use of BUFSIZE, LIB, and SIZE will be in effect for all compiles (if more than one) in this step (batched compiles).
3. Options specified on PROCESS statement(s) (also known as CBL statements) are the highest priority the programmer may select. These options apply, following any fixed defaults.
4. Options specified on the EXEC IGYCRCTL statement are accepted next (e.g., PARM='FDUMP,OFFSET').
5. After accepting options on PROCESS statements and the PARM, options from the JCL OPTION statement are processed.
6. Finally, any installation defaults that were not fixed and not specified elsewhere take effect.

You might be wondering what to do with this information. Well, it can be useful if you typically use the same JCL. For example, if two of your shop's defaults are NOSOURCE and NOLIST, you might

1. Set up a JCL OPTION statement for LIST if you usually want the source listing;
2. Use the PARM statement on occasions when NOSOURCE is preferred (thereby overriding the OPTION statement); or
3. Place PROCESS statement with those programs where you always want the generated assembler listing (LIST).

Using combinations such as this can simplify your use of compile options without needing to frequently make changes to existing JCL.

7.4.5. Summary of System Names Used in Compile, Link, Execute

Here is a summary of the system-name file assignments that are normally modified or coded on JCL by programmers during the application development process. For examples, see Chapter 3 and Chapter 4.

Function	SYSIPT	SYSLST	SYSPCH	SYSLNK	LIBDEF SOURCE	LIBDEF OBJ	LIBDEF PHASE
COBOL II							
source-	X						
list-		X					
COPY-					X		
Object code to Librarian-			X				
Object code to Linkage Editor-				X			
Linkage Editor							
input-				X			
INCLUDEs & CALLs-						X	
Phase-							X*
Application							
ACCEPT-	X						
DISPLAY-		X					
COBOL II output-		X					

* The LIBDEF PHASE statement for output from the Linkage Editor is only needed when OPTION LINK or CATAL is specified. The Statement must include the CATALOG parameter.

7.5. HEXADECIMAL CONVERSION CHART

This table represents some hexadecimal and decimal values. Notice that two hex values occupy a byte. The values shown are built from right to left, showing the hex and decimal values that each bit occupies within a binary value.

The techniques shown following the table are simple ways to convert from different numbering systems to others using the table. I apologize to the mathematicians and others who prefer more elegant approaches. I use this approach because, unless hex arithmetic comes easy to you, it is a skill that is rarely needed. As I mentioned in Chapter 4 ("Debugging"), if you need to do hex arithmetic a lot, get a handheld hex calculator.

Finding binary numbers.

The row titled "Binary value of bit within hex number" shows what bits will be on or off for any hex representation. The value will be true for any column, since this represents the bit configuration, not the numeric value. For example, the hex number A will have the binary value 1010, because A (decimal 10) is formed with the 8 and 2 bits on and the 4 and 1 bits off. This lets you determine the binary

Binary value of bit within hex number

Bit position within byte

Hex	Dec	Hex	Dec	Hex	Dec	Hex	Dec	Hex	Dec	Hex	Dec
0	0	0	0	0	0	0	0	0	0	0	0
1	1,048,576	1	65,536	1	4,096	1	256	1	16	1	1
2	2,097,152	2	131,072	2	8,192	2	512	2	32	2	2
3	3,145,728	3	196,608	3	12,288	3	768	3	48	3	3
4	4,194,304	4	262,144	4	16,384	4	1,024	4	64	4	4
5	5,242,880	5	327,680	5	20,480	5	1,280	5	80	5	5
6	6,291,456	6	393,216	6	24,576	6	1,536	6	96	6	6
7	7,340,032	7	458,752	7	28,672	7	1,792	7	112	7	7
8	8,388,608	8	524,288	8	32,768	8	2,048	8	128	8	8
9	9,437,184	9	589,824	9	36,864	9	2,304	9	144	9	9
A	10,485,760	A	655,360	A	40,960	A	2,560	A	160	A	10
B	11,534,336	B	720,896	B	45,056	B	2,816	B	176	B	11
C	12,582,912	C	786,432	C	49,152	C	3,072	C	192	C	12
D	13,631,488	D	851,968	D	53,248	D	3,328	D	208	D	13
E	14,680,064	E	917,504	E	57,344	E	3,584	E	224	E	14
F	15,728,640	F	983,040	F	61,440	F	3,840	F	240	F	15
0 1 2 3		4 5 6 7		0 1 2 3		4 5 6 7		0 1 2 3		4 5 6 7	
8 4 2 1		8 4 2 1		8 4 2 1		8 4 2 1		8 4 2 1		8 4 2 1	
one byte				one byte				one byte			

number directly from a hex number or construct a hex number from a binary one. If you can remember the hex numbers from 0 to 15, you don't even need the table. For example,

To convert E7C to binary, examine each hex number and break it down into the appropriate bit value combination of 8, 4, 2, and 1, using "1" for on and "0" for off.

1. E becomes 1110 because it requires the 8, 4, and 2 bits.
2. 7 becomes 0111 because it requires the 4, 2, and 1 bits.
3. C becomes 1100 because it requires the 8 and 4 bits.
4. Putting the result end to end gives 1110 0111 1100.

To convert 10110110 from binary to hex, first mark the number off in units of 4 bits from right to left.

1. The rightmost 4 bits, 0110, represent 6 (4 and 2 bits).
2. The next 4 bits, 1011, represent B (8, 2 and 1 bits).
3. The hex number, then, is B6.

Converting from hexadecimal to decimal.

To convert a number from hexadecimal to decimal, take the decimal value from each column that corresponds to the hex value and add the decimal values together. For example, to convert 05FA to a decimal value, follow these steps:

1. A in rightmost column has decimal value of   10.
2. F in next column has the decimal value of   240.
3. 5 in next column has the decimal value of   1,280.
4. These numbers add up to   1,530.

Converting from decimal to hexadecimal.

Similarly, to convert a decimal number to hexadecimal, locate the largest decimal number on the chart that is not greater than the decimal number. Subtract it from the decimal number and mark its hex value. Repeat the above until done, finding the largest number on the chart that is less than the remainder, marking its hex value. For example, to convert the decimal number 1,100 to a hex value, follow these steps:

- 1,024 in the third column from right is nearest to 1,100. The hex value from that column is 4. The 4 will then be the hex number that occupies the third position from the right, since it came from that column. The hex value so far is 4xx.
- With a remainder of 76 (1,100 – 1,024), the next decimal number found is 64 in the second column. Using its hex value (4 again) the hex value so far is 44x.
- The final remainder is 12. Taking the hex value C from the rightmost column, the final hex number is 44C.

7.6.   EBCDIC COLLATING SEQUENCE

This is not a complete EBCDIC chart. The focus is on alpha and numeric.

dec	hex	char
0	00	
63	3F	
64	40	SPACE
65	41	
73	49	
74	4A	¢
75	4B	.
76	4C	<
77	4D	(
78	4E	+
79	4F	|
80	50	&
81	51	
89	59	
90	5A	!
91	5B	$
92	5C	*
93	5D	)
94	5E	:
95	5F	¬
96	60	-
97	61	/
98	62	
106	6A	.
107	6B	,
108	6C	%
109	6D	_
110	6E	>
111	6F	?
112	70	
121	79	
122	7A	:
123	7B	#
124	7C	@

dec	hex	char
125	7D	'
126	7E	=
127	7F	"
128	80	**
129	81	A
130	82	b
131	83	c
132	84	d
133	85	e
134	86	f
135	87	g
136	88	h
137	89	i
138	8A	
144	90	
145	91	j
146	92	k
147	93	l
148	94	m
149	95	n
150	96	o
151	97	p
152	98	q
153	99	r
154	9A	
161	A1	
162	A2	s
163	A3	t
164	A4	u
165	A5	v
166	A6	w
167	A7	x
168	A8	y
169	A9	z
170	AA	
192	C0	
193	C1	A
194	C2	B
195	C3	C

dec	hex	char
196	C4	D
197	C5	E
198	C6	F
199	C7	G
200	C8	H
201	C9	I
202	CA	
208	D0	
209	D1	J
210	D2	K
211	D3	L
212	D4	M
213	D5	N
214	D6	O
215	D7	P
216	D8	Q
217	D9	R
218	DA	
225	E1	
226	E2	S
227	E3	T
228	E4	U
229	E5	V
230	E6	W
231	E7	X
232	E8	Y
233	E9	Z
234	EA	
239	EF	
240	F0	0
241	F1	1
242	F2	2
243	F3	3
244	F4	4
245	F5	5
246	F6	6
247	F7	7
248	F8	8
249	F9	9
250	FA	
255	FF	

7.7. COMMON ABEND CODES AND MESSAGES

COBOL run-time module ABENDS.

When an ABEND occurs from the COBOL II run-time modules, there will be a message with the prefix IGZ associated with it. See *COBOL II Application Programming Debugging manual* (Chapter 9) for an explanation of the error. If the run unit includes any DOS/VS COBOL modules, the associated run-time error message will have the prefix C1. ABEND codes from COBOL II will be in the range from 1000 to 1999.

Common application ABENDs.

0C1 Often due to error in OPEN or attempted READ before OPEN. CALLs to nonexisting subprograms may also cause this.

0C4 Usually caused by subscript errors in COBOL. The SSRANGE option will identify this error. Other possibilities include incorrect specification of passed parameters in a CALLing/CALLed structure (e.g., one module passes one parameter and the CALLed module attempts to access two parameters). Other possibilities associated with the LINKAGE SECTION include mishandling of PARMs and failure to SET addresses with POINTER items.

0C7 Bad data in arithmetic operation. The OFFSET or LIST compile option can assist in identifying the offending COBOL statement. Usually caused when spaces are in a numeric field.

0C9 or 0CB Usually caused by a divide by zero.

1037 CICS transaction "fell through" the last statement in the program, causing an implicit EXIT PROGRAM statement to be executed.

7.8. ACRONYMS

This list represents many of the acronyms that a mainframe VSE programmer sees. Some are used in this book; others are not.

ABEND	(ABnormal END)
ALC	(Assembler Language Code)
AMS	(Access Method Services)
ANSI	(American National Standards Institute)
BAL	(see ALC)
BLL	(Base Locator for Linkage Section)
CICS	(Customer Information Control System)

COBOL	(COmmon Business Oriented Language)
DASD	(Direct Access Storage Device)
DBCS	(Double Byte Character Set)
DL/1	(Data Language/One)
EBCDIC	(Extended Binary Coded Decimal Interchange Code)
FIPS	(Federal Information Processing Standard)
HDAM	(Hierarchical Direct Access Method for DL/1)
HIDAM	(Hierarchical Indexed Direct Access Method for DL/1)
ICCF	(Interactive Computing and Control Facility)
ISPF	(Interactive Structured Programming Facility)
JCL	(Job Control Language)
K	(4096 bytes)
Megabyte	(1,048,576 bytes)
MVS/ESA	(Multiple Virtual Storage/Enterprise Systems Architecture)
MVS/SP	(Multiple Virtual Storage/System Product)
MVS/XA	(Multiple Virtual Storage/Extended Architecture)
PL/1	(Programming Language/One)
POWER	(Priority Output Writers, Execution Processors, and Input Readers)
SAA	(Systems Application Architecture)
SAM	(Sequential Access Method)
SORT/MERGE II	(IBM Sort Utility)
SQL	(Structured Query Language)
SQL/DS	(Structured Query Language/Data System)
SQLDA	(SQL Data Area)
TGT	(Task Global Table)
VSAM	(Virtual Storage Access Method)
VSE/ESA	(Virtual Storage Extended/Enterprise Systems Architecture)
VTAM	(Virtual Telecommunications Access Method)

7.9.   REPORT WRITER STRUCTURE

Report Writer is not covered in this book. This is a summary of the basic structure used. See Chapter 9 for the IBM reference manual.

Structure of system-name to FD to RD

```
//  DLBL  system-name, 'file-id',...
                 ↑
                 └──────────────────────────────┐
            SELECT fd-name ASSIGN TO system-name.
                      ↑
                 ┌────┘
            FD  fd-name
                RECORDING MODE IS V
                RECORD CONTAINS 137 CHARACTERS
                BLOCK CONTAINS 0 RECORDS
                REPORT IS report-name.
                                        │
            REPORT SECTION.             │
            RD report-name ←────────────┘
                CONTROL FINAL   major-field  minor-field
                PAGE LIMIT IS 60 LINES
                   HEADING        1
                   FIRST DETAIL   7
                   LAST DETAIL   55
                   FOOTING       57.
```

Structure of data record clauses

```
01  RH          report heading
        PH          page heading
            CH          control heading
                DE          detail line(s)
            CF          control footing
        PF          page footing
    RF          report footing
```

Structure of procedural statements

```
OPEN            done once
    INITIATE        done once
        GENERATE    each detail
    TERMINATE       done once
CLOSE           done once
```

7.10. COMPILER LIMITS AND MACHINE CAPACITIES

Compiler limits.

There are many limits on the compiler, most of which do not interest us. (Do you really care that you can have 999,999 source statements in a program? I hope not, and I sure wouldn't want to have maintenance responsibility for it.) Here are some of the limits that are probably of more use to you in designing applications.

	COBOL II	DOS/VS COBOL
Block size of COPY library:	32,767	16,000

If your shop uses COPY statements extensively, you should consider reblocking your COPY library to reduce I/O.

	COBOL II	DOS/VS COBOL
WORKING-STORAGE total bytes:	127M	1M

With 127 megabytes available, this can change the way you design applications. In some cases, you may find an entire database might fit within WORKING-STORAGE for a batch application, allowing high performance direct retrieval.

	COBOL II	DOS/VS COBOL
Number of data-names:	16M	1M
Number of OCCURS levels:	N/A	3
OCCURS value:	16M	32K

The above three expansions open opportunities to build large multi-dimension tables for complex applications that would have been impossible with DOS/VS COBOL.

	COBOL II	DOS/VS COBOL
LINKAGE SECTION total bytes:	127M	1M

Combined with other options above, this allows sharing of large data areas with other programs.

Machine capacities.

When doing arithmetic, the compiler is aware of the maximum value that can be manipulated in the machine. When the compiler determines that there is the possibility for an intermediate or final value to exceed machine capacity, it invokes a CALL to a COBOL II run-time module to do the arithmetic operation procedurally. This keeps the logic intact and ensures correct numbers, but it could have a major impact on applications with many computations. Naturally, there are situations where you can't prevent it, but an awareness of machine limitations may help you determine when it may be more appropriate to do several smaller calculations instead of one large one.

For packed-decimal, the largest number is 16 bytes, which translates into 31 decimal digits. In multiplication and division, the SUM of the two data fields (multiplicand and multiplier, dividend and divisor) cannot exceed 16 bytes, including the sign.

For binary numbers, the largest value for a half-word field is 32,767, and the largest number for a full-word field is 2,147,483,647. (Whether your program can contain those values is dependent on what TRUNC option you specified.)

From the above, packed-decimal is preferable anytime you are manipulating large numbers. (Yes, the computer could also do floating-point arithmetic, but you rarely encounter the need in business applications.) In fairness to binary arithmetic, its instruction set is faster than the packed-decimal instruction set, but to benefit from it you need to use TRUNC(OPT).

7.11. XA-MODE PORTABILITY CONSIDERATIONS

XA-Mode Portability is important if your shop is planning to migrate to MVS/XA or MVS/ESA. By considering these options now, you can prevent wasted effort later on. The COBOL II compiler encodes many run-time considerations in object modules, some of which are ignored by VSE but have meaning to Extended Architecture systems (MVS/XA and MVS/ESA). If your object modules already have the desired attributes, they may be simply copied to the Extended Architecture system and link-edited for execution. Here is a review of those options, since you may want to specify them for anticipated future use.

DATA In Extended Architecture (XA) systems, this specifies where DATA DIVISION elements will be assigned in memory. For VSCR, this should be DATA(31). This requires that RENT and RES also be specified.

OUTDD This option identifies the system file-name for messages from the application (e.g., DISPLAY statement). At most XA shops, this is set to OUTDD(SYSOUT). Setting this option can prevent extensive JCL conversion efforts or incompatible JCL across applications.

RENT This option has been explained elsewhere in this book and provides VSCR for applications in VSE. RENT provides even more VSCR in XA systems, allowing the applications to run in memory space beyond the 16-megabyte address.

If you plan to migrate to an XA environment and execute previously tested and compiled applications, the object code must be saved (not the phase). Details and JCL examples are in *Application Programming Guide for VSE* (Chapter 9).

EXAMPLES of COBOL Programs

This chapter is unique in this book. It is not a reference chapter and includes no new information. Instead, it contains complete source programs to demonstrate the guidelines presented in Chapters 5 and 6 ("Program Design" and "Program Coding"). Some are COBOL II and some work with both COBOL II and DOS/VS COBOL. The intent of this chapter is not to dazzle you with code, but to demonstrate some of the benefits of structure and decomposition, as well as a few of the new components of COBOL II. The focus is on structure and ways to preserve compatibility, not on using some COBOL II features. For examples of specific COBOL II statements, please refer to earlier chapters.

Importance of style and simplicity.

If you've been writing "GO TO less" code for years, you won't find anything new here. However, if you are accustomed to coding all four divisions and think GO TO is a fact of life, I encourage you to walk through each example. All the programs demonstrate a bit of programmer style; I believe it is important to allow some freedom for the programmer to code less-than-perfect programs.

The style of some of these programs conflicts with several major structured techniques, primarily in the initialization process. Some books suggest that the first record(s) to be processed should be read immediately after OPEN. I don't believe this. After years of teaching new programmers (and reteaching old programmers), I have found that many logic problems occur because of this practice. I have found programs to be simpler to code and to debug by

1. coding one-time housekeeping processes in an initialization routine,
2. coding all repeated processes under the umbrella of a DO-WHILE (PERFORM UNTIL) statement, and
3. coding one-time termination processes in a termination routine.

I included the DL/1 example because, over the years, I have heard complaints from programmers that it is impossible to use structured code with such complex data structure. My approach is to blend the data structure with the program structure. Since DL/1 and structured programming both follow a hierarchical format, the two components can blend well.

Comments and small paragraphs.

I asked several programmers for comments before including these programs in the book. Two frequent comments were "Why are there so many comments in the code?" and "Why are some paragraphs so small?" Since you may have the same questions, let me give my response.

Regarding the many comments, I include comments in code whenever I believe a rookie programmer may not understand the structure or the logic. I want to emphasize to you where I was and where I was not following my approach to structure. Also, while I often see comments in programs that explain a process, I have never seen comments that explain the structure—and this is exactly what most programmers need. Knowing what to do is usually straightforward. Knowing where in the logic flow to do it is sometimes nearly impossible.

Regarding the small paragraphs, I compare programming to architecture. As an industry, we fail in teaching new programmers if we encourage them to use shortcuts for small classroom programs, hoping they will do differently on large, real systems. Consider architects: they follow certain procedures whether they are building a one-story house or a 30-story building. A small building is a big building in miniature. We should do the same for programming: we use specific disciplines regardless of program size. Decomposition is decomposition is decomposition. Novice programmers who are taught to combine many small functions into one paragraph become senior programmers who write indecipherable paragraphs that run several pages.

Knowing that somewhere, for some reason someone will want to eliminate small paragraphs, I redid example 8.1 using COBOL II features (example 8.2), allowing the entire logic of the SORT OUTPUT PROCEDURE to be accomplished in a single paragraph. I don't recommend this type of programming, but the example does display how far COBOL has come.

Aren't the examples too simple?

These programs are indeed simple. I've been asked on occasion to use more complex programs to demonstrate ideas in my programming classes. Unfortunately, 5,000-line programs only confuse students and drown them in the application's logic. These simple structures demonstrate techniques. Where the structure is simple, a program can be easily expanded and retain the simple structure. Also, when a program gets too big to grasp quickly, I break it into several programs. Life is too short to spend it wading through monster programs just to prove you can do it.

8.1. SORT EXAMPLE WITH COBOL II

If you're used to seeing SORT programs with lots of noise, such as SECTION headers, PERFORM THRUs, GO TOs, and EXIT statements, you'll find this to be quite different. The techniques in this program are covered in the section on SORT techniques in both Chapter 5 (design) and Chapter 6 (coding). If the use of SORT-RETURN or the comments about SORT-CONTROL leave you confused, I suggest you review those sections. This program also appears in example 8.2 with extensive use of scope terminators, and in example 8.5 as a nested program.

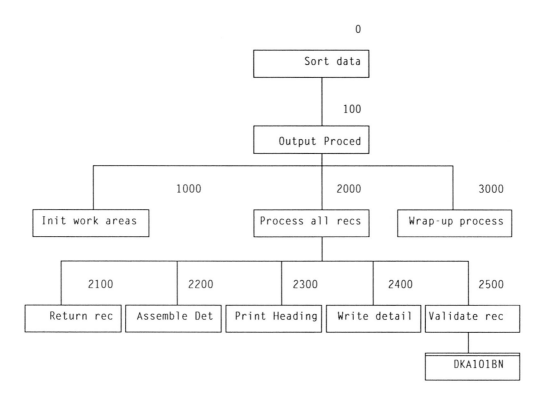

```
TITLE 'SORT Program with external CALL'
IDENTIFICATION DIVISION.

PROGRAM-ID.
    DKA10200.

*AUTHOR.
*    David S. Kirk.
*DATE-WRITTEN.
*    April, 1991.
```

```
***************************************************************
*      SORT Example                                           *
*                                                             *
*  The imbedded comments are tutorial and are not             *
*  meant to indicate you should explain the basics            *
*  of programs you write in this fashion, although            *
*  liberal use of comments is encouraged.                     *
*                                                             *
*  There are several compromises in this example;             *
*  the programmer's style is always a component.              *
*                                                             *
***************************************************************



    ENVIRONMENT DIVISION.

    INPUT-OUTPUT SECTION.

    FILE-CONTROL.

        SELECT FD1-PAYROLL-FILE
            ASSIGN TO PAY102.

        SELECT FD2-PRINT-FILE
            ASSIGN TO REPT102.

        SELECT SD3-SORT-FILE
            ASSIGN TO SORTWK.

    DATA DIVISION.

    FILE SECTION.

    FD  FD1-PAYROLL-FILE
        RECORD CONTAINS 74 CHARACTERS
        BLOCK CONTAINS 0 RECORDS
        RECORDING MODE IS F.

    01  FD1-PAYROLL-REC                       PIC X(74).

    FD  FD2-PRINT-FILE
        RECORD CONTAINS 132 CHARACTERS
        BLOCK CONTAINS 0 RECORDS
        RECORDING MODE IS F.
```

```
* --------------------------------------------
* Notice that the record specifies 132 positions.
* Actually, the record size will be 133 if the compile
* option ADV is used. This keeps the program "machine
* independent," allowing COBOL to insert the ASA control
* character outside the program logic. If compile option
* NOADV were specified, the programmer would need to leave
* the first byte in the record untouched by the program logic.
* --------------------------------------------
 01  FD2-PRINT-REC                         PIC X(132).
 SD  SD3-SORT-FILE
     RECORD CONTAINS 74 CHARACTERS.

 01  SD1-SORT-REC.
     05  SD3-EMP-NO-IN                      PIC X(5).
     05  SD3-EMP-NAME-IN                    PIC X(20).
     05  SD3-TERRITORY-NO-IN                PIC X(2).
     05  SD3-OFFICE-NO-IN                   PIC X(2).
     05  SD3-JOB-CODE-IN                    PIC X(2).
     05                                     PIC X(43).

 WORKING-STORAGE SECTION.

     * --------------------------------------------
     * All counters and switches are combined in the following
     * 01 level.  This simplifies maintenance and saves memory use.
     * --------------------------------------------
 01  WS1-WORK-FIELDS.
     05  WS1-EOF-SW                     PIC X.
         88  ALL-DONE                       VALUE 'Y'.
         88  NOT-EOF                        VALUE 'N'.
     05  WS1-DATE.
         10  WS1-YY                     PIC XX.
         10  WS1-MM                     PIC 99.
         10  WS1-DD                     PIC XX.
     05  WS1-ERROR-MSG                  PIC X(16).
         88  WS4-JOBCODE-ERROR              VALUE 'INVALID JOB CODE'.
         88  WS4-GOOD-JOBCODE               VALUE SPACES.
     05  WS1-INCOUNT                    PIC S9(3)  COMP-3.
     05  WS1-LINE-SPACE                 PIC S9(3)  COMP-3.
     05  WS1-LINECOUNT                  PIC S9(3)  COMP-3.
     05  WS1-PAGENUM                    PIC S9(3)  COMP-3.
     05  WS1-PAGESIZE                   PIC S9(3)  COMP-3
                                            VALUE +50.
```

```
01  WS2-HEADING-LINE1.
    05                              PIC X(40) VALUE SPACES.
    05                              PIC X(17)
                                    VALUE 'EMPLOYEE BENEFITS'.
    05                              PIC X(3)  VALUE SPACES.
    05  WS2-DATE-OUT.
        10  WS2-MM-OUT              PIC Z9.
        10                          PIC X VALUE '/'.
        10  WS2-DD-OUT              PIC XX.
        10                          PIC X VALUE '/'.
        10  WS2-YY-OUT              PIC XX.
    05                              PIC X(5) VALUE SPACES.
    05                              PIC X(5) VALUE 'PAGE '.
    05  WS2-PAGENUM                 PIC ZZ9.

01  WS2-HEADING-LINE2.
    05                              PIC X(10) VALUE SPACES.
    05                              PIC X(3)  VALUE 'JOB'.
    05                              PIC X(10) VALUE SPACES.
    05                              PIC X(8)  VALUE 'EMPLOYEE'.
    05                              PIC X(5)  VALUE SPACES.
    05                              PIC X(8)  VALUE 'EMPLOYEE'.
    05                              PIC X(19) VALUE SPACES.
    05                              PIC X(4)  VALUE 'SICK'.
    05                              PIC X(5)  VALUE SPACES.
    05                              PIC X(8)  VALUE 'VACATION'.

01  WS3-HEADING-LINE3.
    05                              PIC X(5)  VALUE SPACES.
    05                              PIC X(14)
                                    VALUE 'CLASSIFICATION'.
    05                              PIC X(7)  VALUE SPACES.
    05                              PIC X(9)  VALUE 'NO. '.
    05                              PIC X(3)  VALUE SPACES.
    05                              PIC X(4)  VALUE 'NAME'.
    05                              PIC X(21) VALUE SPACES.
    05                              PIC X(4)  VALUE 'DAYS'.
    05                              PIC X(7)  VALUE SPACES.
    05                              PIC X(4)  VALUE 'DAYS'.

01 WS4-DETAIL.
    05                              PIC X(10) VALUE SPACES.
    05  WS4-JOB-CODE-OUT            PIC X(2).
    05                              PIC X(12) VALUE SPACES.
    05  WS4-EMP-NO-OUT              PIC X(5).
    05                              PIC X(9)  VALUE SPACES.
```

```
      05   WS4-EMP-NAME-OUT                PIC X(20).
      05                                   PIC X(6)  VALUE SPACES.
      05   WS4-SICK-DAYS-OUT               PIC Z9.
      05                                   PIC X(9) VALUE SPACES.
      05   WS4-VACA-DAYS-OUT               PIC Z9.
      05                                   PIC X(5) VALUE SPACES.
      05   WS4-ERROR-MSG-OUT               PIC X(16).

  01  WS5-DATA-PASSED.
      05   WS5-JOB-CODE                    PIC XX.
      05   WS5-SICK-DAYS                   PIC 9(2).
      05   WS5-VACA-DAYS                   PIC 9(2).
      05   WS5-ERROR-SWITCH                PIC X     VALUE 'N'.


  PROCEDURE DIVISION.
  * -------------
  * This paragraph is the highest level.
  * While there is no INPUT PROCEDURE, this program
  * can still select which records to sort and can even have
  * the data records reformatted before the sort. This can
  * be accomplished by inserting a SYSIPT JCL statement
  * at run time that contains valid SORT statements.
  * Example:
  *   //IGZSRTCD DD  *
  *      OMIT   COND=(26,2,CH,EQ,C'25')
  *      INREC  FIELDS=(1,5,6,20,26,2,28,2,47,2)
  * -------------
  000-SORT.
      SORT SD3-SORT-FILE
                 ASCENDING   SD3-TERRITORY-NO-IN
                             SD3-OFFICE-NO-IN
                             SD3-EMP-NAME-IN
              USING FD1-PAYROLL-FILE
              OUTPUT PROCEDURE 100-MAIN-MODULE
      IF SORT-RETURN EQUAL ZERO
          MOVE ZERO TO RETURN-CODE
          STOP RUN
      ELSE
          DISPLAY 'SORT ERROR IN DKA10200' UPON CONSOLE
          MOVE 16 TO RETURN-CODE
          STOP RUN.
```

```
* -------------------------------------
* The following paragraph is the SORT OUTPUT PROCEDURE.
* -------------------------------------
 100-MAIN-MODULE.
     PERFORM 1000-INITIALIZE
     PERFORM 2000-PROCESS-ROUTINE UNTIL ALL-DONE
     PERFORM 3000-WRAPUP.


* -------------
* This paragraph does initialization. It is a compromise
* since it does everything in one paragraph. In a larger
* program, it should PERFORM a separate paragraph to OPEN
* files and one to initialize variables.
* The initialization part of a program should do nothing that
* routinely repeats, such as READing files or WRITEing
* headings.
* -------------
 1000-INITIALIZE.
     OPEN OUTPUT FD2-PRINT-FILE
     MOVE ZEROS TO WS1-DATE
                   WS1-INCOUNT
                   WS1-PAGENUM
     MOVE 999 TO WS1-LINECOUNT
     ACCEPT WS1-DATE FROM DATE
     MOVE WS1-YY TO WS2-YY-OUT
     MOVE WS1-MM TO WS2-MM-OUT
     MOVE WS1-DD TO WS2-DD-OUT.


* -------------
* This paragraph controls processing of each detail record.
* Because it follows the same path each time, it is simpler
* to locate problems in page headings or other conditional
* processes. The END-IF is used instead of a period because
* it is more visible and less prone to problems and
* it eliminates need to recode IF NOT ALL-DONE.
* -------------
 2000-PROCESS-ROUTINE.
     PERFORM 2100-RETURN-PAYROLL
     IF NOT ALL-DONE
         IF WS1-LINECOUNT GREATER THAN WS1-PAGESIZE
             PERFORM 2300-PRINT-HEADING
         END-IF
         PERFORM 2500-VALIDATE-JOB-CODE
         PERFORM 2200-ASSEMBLE-DETAIL
         PERFORM 2400-WRITE-DETAIL.
```

```
* -------------
* This paragraph does the only RETURN of the input file.
* The END-RETURN statement isn't needed here, but it minimizes
* problems if additional code is added later.
* -------------
 2100-RETURN-PAYROLL.
     RETURN SD3-SORT-FILE
         AT END
             MOVE 'Y' TO WS1-EOF-SW
         NOT AT END
             ADD 1 TO WS1-INCOUNT
     END-RETURN.


* -------------
* Because this paragraph does all of the assembly of the
* detail line, adding or changing fields is an easier
* process.
* -------------
 2200-ASSEMBLE-DETAIL.
     MOVE WS5-JOB-CODE TO WS4-JOB-CODE-OUT
     MOVE SD3-EMP-NO-IN TO WS4-EMP-NO-OUT
     MOVE SD3-EMP-NAME-IN TO WS4-EMP-NAME-OUT
     MOVE WS5-SICK-DAYS TO WS4-SICK-DAYS-OUT
     MOVE WS5-VACA-DAYS TO WS4-VACA-DAYS-OUT
     MOVE WS1-ERROR-MSG TO WS4-ERROR-MSG-OUT
     MOVE WS4-DETAIL TO FD2-PRINT-REC.


* -------------
* This paragraph prints all page headings, making it
* easy to keep track of page numbers or heading alignment.
* This is a compromise for readability, since it does not
* PERFORM a single WRITE paragraph but repeats the WRITE
* statement for each heading line. In this case,
* the repeated statements make the ADVANCING options
* easier to see.
* -------------
 2300-PRINT-HEADING.
     ADD 1 TO WS1-PAGENUM
     MOVE WS1-PAGENUM TO WS2-PAGENUM
     WRITE FD2-PRINT-REC FROM WS2-HEADING-LINE1
       AFTER ADVANCING PAGE
     WRITE FD2-PRINT-REC FROM WS2-HEADING-LINE2
       AFTER ADVANCING 3 LINES
     WRITE FD2-PRINT-REC FROM WS3-HEADING-LINE3
     MOVE 2 TO WS1-LINE-SPACE
     MOVE ZEROS TO WS1-LINECOUNT.
```

```
* ------------
* This paragraph prints all output except page headings.
* ------------
 2400-WRITE-DETAIL.
     WRITE FD2-PRINT-REC AFTER ADVANCING WS1-LINE-SPACE
     MOVE 1 TO WS1-LINE-SPACE
     ADD 1 TO WS1-LINECOUNT.


* ------------
* This paragraph calls subroutine to validate job code
* and set benefit data. Notice that the paragraph
* handles not only the CALL, but it also does the actions
* that it dictates. If error handling were extensive
* it would be appropriate to PERFORM that portion in
* a separate paragraph.
* ------------
 2500-VALIDATE-JOB-CODE.
     MOVE SD3-JOB-CODE-IN TO WS5-JOB-CODE
     CALL 'DKA101BN' USING WS5-DATA-PASSED
     IF WS5-ERROR-SWITCH EQUAL 'Y'
         SET WS4-JOBCODE-ERROR TO TRUE
     ELSE
         SET WS4-GOOD-JOBCODE TO TRUE
     END-IF.


* ------------
* This paragraph wraps up processing. If there were final
* totals or similar end-of-job processing, those would be
* PERFORMed from here as separate paragraphs.
* ------------
 3000-WRAPUP.
     CLOSE FD2-PRINT-FILE.
 END PROGRAM DKA10200.
```

8.2. THE SORT EXAMPLE WITH OUTPUT PROCEDURE AS ONE PARAGRAPH

This is the previous program, redone by decomposing within a single structure instead of decomposing to subordinate paragraphs. As I mentioned elsewhere, I don't recommend this approach to programming because it is difficult to maintain. It is included to emphasize the power of COBOL II in support of structured programming. Any senior level programmer can read this, but the goal of program design is to develop code that a less skilled programmer can maintain. Managers judge code by the ease of maintenance, not by the purity of style it may exhibit.

I omitted all except the PROCEDURE DIVISION from this listing. The tight structure was accomplished by Scope Terminators (END-IF, END-RETURN, and END-PERFORM), an inline PERFORM, and extensions to the RETURN statement. Periods are used only at the end of the two paragraphs.

```
PROCEDURE DIVISION.

 000-SORT.
     MOVE ' SYSIPT' TO SORT-CONTROL
     SORT SD3-SORT-FILE
             ASCENDING   SD3-TERRITORY-NO-IN
                         SD3-OFFICE-NO-IN
                         SD3-EMP-NAME-IN
           USING FD1-PAYROLL-FILE
           OUTPUT PROCEDURE 100-MAIN-MODULE
     IF SORT-RETURN EQUAL ZERO
         MOVE ZERO TO RETURN-CODE
         STOP RUN
     ELSE
         DISPLAY 'SORT ERROR IN DKA10200' UPON CONSOLE
         MOVE 16 TO RETURN-CODE
         STOP RUN
     END-IF.

 100-MAIN-MODULE.
* Initialization process
     OPEN OUTPUT FD2-PRINT-FILE
     MOVE ZEROS TO WS1-DATE
                   WS1-INCOUNT
                   WS1-PAGENUM
     MOVE 999 TO WS1-LINECOUNT
     ACCEPT WS1-DATE FROM DATEMOVE WS1-YY TO WS2-YY-OUT
     MOVE WS1-MM TO WS2-MM-OUT
     MOVE WS1-DD TO WS2-DD-OUT
* DO-WHILE loop
     PERFORM UNTIL ALL-DONE
         RETURN SD3-SORT-FILE
             AT END
                 MOVE 'Y' TO WS1-EOF-SW
             NOT AT END
                 ADD 1 TO WS1-INCOUNT
                 IF WS1-LINECOUNT GREATER THAN WS1-PAGESIZE
* Page heading routine
                     ADD 1 TO WS1-PAGENUM
                     MOVE WS1-PAGENUM TO WS2-PAGENUM
                     WRITE FD2-PRINT-REC FROM WS2-HEADING-LINE1
```

```
                              AFTER ADVANCING PAGE
                          WRITE FD2-PRINT-REC FROM WS2-HEADING-LINE2
                              AFTER ADVANCING 3 LINES
                          WRITE FD2-PRINT-REC FROM WS3-HEADING-LINE3
                          MOVE 2 TO WS1-LINE-SPACE
                          MOVE ZEROS TO WS1-LINECOUNT
                      END-IF
* Validate job code routine
                      MOVE SD3-JOB-CODE-IN TO WS5-JOB-CODE
                      CALL 'DKA101BN' USING WS5-DATA-PASSED
                      IF WS5-ERROR-SWITCH EQUAL 'Y'
                          SET WS4-JOBCODE-ERROR TO TRUE
                      ELSE
                          SET WS4-GOOD-JOBCODE TO TRUE
                      END-IF
* Assemble detail line routine
                      MOVE WS5-JOB-CODE TO WS4-JOB-CODE-OUT
                      MOVE SD3-EMP-NO-IN TO WS4-EMP-NO-OUT
                      MOVE SD3-EMP-NAME-IN TO WS4-EMP-NAME-OUT
                      MOVE WS5-SICK-DAYS TO WS4-SICK-DAYS-OUT
                      MOVE WS5-VACA-DAYS TO WS4-VACA-DAYS-OUT
                      MOVE WS1-ERROR-MSG TO WS4-ERROR-MSG-OUT
                      MOVE WS4-DETAIL TO FD2-PRINT-REC
* Write detail line routine
                      WRITE FD2-PRINT-REC AFTER
                          ADVANCING WS1-LINE-SPACE
                      MOVE 1 TO WS1-LINE-SPACE
                      ADD 1 TO WS1-LINECOUNT
                  END-RETURN
              END-PERFORM
* Termination routine
          CLOSE FD2-PRINT-FILE.
    END PROGRAM DKA10200.
```

8.3. CALLED SUBPROGRAM EXAMPLE WITH COBOL II

This program is CALLed by DKA10200, the previous program. Notice the missing ENVIRONMENT division and the use of EVALUATE and SET statements. In this example, the SET statement provides clearer documentation than using MOVE statements.

```
IDENTIFICATION DIVISION.

PROGRAM-ID.
    DKA101BN.
*AUTHOR.
*    David S. Kirk.

*DATE-WRITTEN.
*    April 1991.

* -----------------------------------------
* Validates job code and returns appropriate sick and
* vacation days allowed.
* -----------------------------------------

DATA DIVISION.

LINKAGE SECTION.

01  LS1-RECORD.
    05  LS1-JOB-CODE           PIC XX.
    05  LS1-SICK-VAC-DAYS      PIC XXXX.
        88  BEN01                  VALUE '1421'.
        88  BEN02                  VALUE '1014'.
        88  BEN03                  VALUE '2128'.
    05  LS1-ERROR-SW           PIC X.

PROCEDURE DIVISION USING LS1-RECORD.

100-MAIN-MODULE.
    MOVE 'N' TO LS1-ERROR-SW
    PERFORM 200-VALIDATE
    GOBACK.

200-VALIDATE.
    EVALUATE LS1-JOB-CODE
        WHEN '01'    SET BEN01 TO TRUE
        WHEN '02'    SET BEN02 TO TRUE
        WHEN '03'    SET BEN03 TO TRUE
        WHEN OTHER   MOVE '0000' TO LS1-SICK-VAC-DAYS
                     MOVE 'Y' TO LS1-ERROR-SW
    END-EVALUATE.
END PROGRAM DKA101BN.
```

8.4. SAMPLE SUBPROGRAM THAT IS COMPATIBLE WITH BOTH COMPILERS

This program is the DOS/VS COBOL compatible version of the previous program (DKA101BN). EVALUATE and SET were replaced by IF and MOVE statements. The END PROGRAM statement was removed. Other than that, even with no ENVIRONMENT DIVISION, it compiles with no fatal errors under both COBOL II and DOS/VS COBOL.

```
IDENTIFICATION DIVISION.

PROGRAM-ID.
    DKA101B2.

*AUTHOR.
*    David S. Kirk.

*DATE-WRITTEN.
*    April, 1991.


* -------------------------------------------
* Validates job code and returns appropriate sick and
* vacation days allowed.
* -------------------------------------------

DATA DIVISION.
LINKAGE SECTION.

01   LS1-RECORD.
     05   LS1-JOB-CODE              PIC XX.
     05   LS1-SICK-VAC-DAYS         PIC XXXX.
     05   LS1-ERROR-SW              PIC X.

PROCEDURE DIVISION USING LS1-RECORD.

100-MAIN-MODULE.
    MOVE 'N' TO LS1-ERROR-SW
    PERFORM 200-VALIDATE
    GOBACK.

200-VALIDATE.
    IF LS1-JOB-CODE = '01'
        MOVE '1421' TO LS1-SICK-VAC-DAYS
    ELSE
        IF LS1-JOB-CODE = '02'
            MOVE '1014' TO LS1-SICK-VAC-DAYS
        ELSE
            IF LS1-JOB-CODE = '03'
                MOVE '2128' TO LS1-SICK-VAC-DAYS
            ELSE
                MOVE '0000' TO LS1-SICK-VAC-DAYS
                MOVE 'Y' TO LS1-ERROR-SW.
* This is the end of source.
```

8.5. SAMPLE SORT WITH A NESTED STRUCTURE

This program is the SORT program (example 8.1) and its CALLed subprogram (example 8.3), combined into a nested program structure. Many parts of the SORT program have been removed to focus on the nested structure. Notice that the CALL statement passes no data, the CALLed subprogram has no PROCEDURE DIVISION USING statement, nor does it have a DATA DIVISION. Because both programs now reference the same data names, debugging and documentation are improved.

```
TITLE 'SORT Program with nested CALL'
IDENTIFICATION DIVISION.
PROGRAM-ID. DKA10200.
ENVIRONMENT DIVISION.
INPUT-OUTPUT SECTION.
FILE-CONTROL.
    .
    .
DATA DIVISION.
FILE SECTION.
    .
    .
WORKING-STORAGE SECTION.
    .
    .
01  WS5-DATA-PASSED          GLOBAL.
    05  WS5-JOB-CODE             PIC XX.
    05  WS5-SICK-VAC-DAYS.
        10  WS5-SICK-DAYS        PIC 9(2).
        10  WS5-VACA-DAYS        PIC 9(2).
    05  WS5-SUB-DATA REDEFINES WS5-SICK-VAC-DAYS  PIC X(4).
        88  BEN01                VALUE '1421'.
        88  BEN02                VALUE '1014'.
        88  BEN03                VALUE '2128'.
    05  WS5-ERROR-SWITCH         PIC X     VALUE 'N'.

PROCEDURE DIVISION.
000-SORT.
    SORT SD3-SORT-FILE
    .
    .
100-MAIN-MODULE.
    PERFORM 1000-INITIALIZE
    PERFORM 2000-PROCESS-ROUTINE UNTIL ALL-DONE
    PERFORM 3000-WRAPUP.
```

```
1000-INITIALIZE.
    OPEN OUTPUT FD2-PRINT-FILE
    MOVE ZEROS TO WS1-DATE
     .
     .


2000-PROCESS-ROUTINE.
    PERFORM 2100-RETURN-PAYROLL
    IF NOT ALL-DONE
     .
     .


2100-RETURN-PAYROLL.
    RETURN SD3-SORT-FILE
        AT END
            MOVE 'Y' TO WS1-EOF-SW
        NOT AT END
            ADD 1 TO WS1-INCOUNT
    END-RETURN.
2200-ASSEMBLE-DETAIL.
    MOVE WS5-JOB-CODE TO WS4-JOB-CODE-OUT
     .
     .


2300-PRINT-HEADING.
    ADD 1 TO WS1-PAGENUM
     .
     .


2400-WRITE-DETAIL.
    WRITE FD2-PRINT-REC AFTER ADVANCING WS1-LINE-SPACE
    MOVE 1 TO WS1-LINE-SPACE
    ADD 1 TO WS1-LINECOUNT.

2500-VALIDATE-JOB-CODE.
    MOVE SD3-JOB-CODE-IN TO WS5-JOB-CODE
    CALL 'DKA101BN'
    IF WS5-ERROR-SWITCH EQUAL 'Y'
        SET WS4-JOBCODE-ERROR TO TRUE
    ELSE
        SET WS4-GOOD-JOBCODE TO TRUE
    END-IF.
3000-WRAPUP.
    CLOSE FD2-PRINT-FILE.
```

```
TITLE 'This is the shortened subprogram'
IDENTIFICATION DIVISION.
PROGRAM-ID. DKA101BN.
PROCEDURE DIVISION.
1.  MOVE 'N' TO WS5-ERROR-SWITCH
    PERFORM 200-VALIDATE
    GOBACK.

200-VALIDATE.
    EVALUATE WS5-JOB-CODE
        WHEN '01'    SET BEN01 TO TRUE
        WHEN '02'    SET BEN02 TO TRUE
        WHEN '03'    SET BEN03 TO TRUE
        WHEN OTHER   MOVE '0000' TO WS5-SUB-DATA
                     MOVE 'Y' TO WS5-ERROR-SWITCH
    END-EVALUATE.
END PROGRAM DKA101BN.
END PROGRAM DKA10200.
```

8.6. DL/1 SAMPLE PROGRAM THAT WORKS WITH BOTH COMPILERS

This program contains minor violations as did the earlier programs. This is to be expected sometimes. Notice the balance of control and action and that status from PERFORMs is checked immediately. Keeping control at the higher level produces cleaner code. Note also that each paragraph contains only one period.

If you are familiar with DL/1 programs, you will notice that it does not contain the usual ENTRY 'DLITCBL' statement. That requirement still appears in many DL/1 reference manuals, but it hasn't been needed since the PROCEDURE DIVISION USING statement became available.

The structure contains a DO WHILE within another DO WHILE. This lets the program use its own structure to access structured data.

This program compiles under

- DOS/VS COBOL with LANGLVL(1) for ANSI 68
- DOS/VS COBOL with LANGLVL(2) for ANSI 74
- COBOL II for ANSI 85

yet follows all guidelines in this book. Compatibility was preserved by including FILLER entries and by not using the END PROGRAM statement.

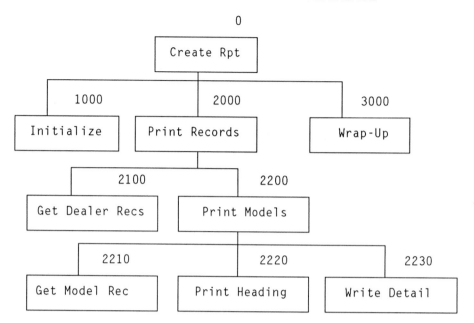

```
IDENTIFICATION DIVISION.

PROGRAM-ID.
   DKA10300.
*AUTHOR.
*    David S. Kirk.

*DATE-WRITTEN.
*    April 1991.
*****************************************************
*                                                 *
* PROGRAM: Reads a training database and prepares *
* a simple report. The database structure is      *
*                                                 *
*                                                 *
*                                                 *
*                                                 *
*                                                 *
*                                                 *
*                                                 *
*                                                 *
*                                                 *
*                                                 *
*                                                 *
*****************************************************
```

```
ENVIRONMENT DIVISION.

INPUT-OUTPUT SECTION.

FILE-CONTROL.
    SELECT FD1-PRINT-FILE
        ASSIGN TO REPT103.

DATA DIVISION.

FILE SECTION.

FD  FD1-PRINT-FILE
    RECORD CONTAINS 132 CHARACTERS
    BLOCK CONTAINS 0 RECORDS
    RECORDING MODE IS F.

01  FD1-PRINT-REC                    PIC X(132).

WORKING-STORAGE SECTION.

01  WS1-WORK-FIELDS-REC.
    05  WS1-EOF-SW              PIC X.
        88 ALL-DONE                    VALUE 'Y'.
        88 NOT-EOF                     VALUE 'N'.
    05  WS1-PAGENUM             PIC S999  COMP-3.
    05  WS1-SPACE               PIC S999  COMP-3 VALUE 1.
    05  WS1-LINES               PIC S999  COMP-3 VALUE 55.

01  WS2-HEADING-LINE1-REC.
    05  FILLER                       PIC X(40)  VALUE SPACES.
    05  FILLER                       PIC X(17)
                            VALUE 'DL/1 DL/1 WORKSHOP'.
    05  FILLER                       PIC X(3)   VALUE SPACES.
    05  FILLER                       PIC X(5)   VALUE SPACES.
    05  FILLER                       PIC X(5)   VALUE 'PAGE '.
    05  WS2-PAGENUM                  PIC ZZ9.
    05  FILLER                       PIC X(51)  VALUE SPACES.

01  WS3-DETAIL-REC.
    05  FILLER                       PIC X(2)   VALUE SPACES.
    05  WS3-VENDOR                   PIC X(30)  VALUE SPACES.
    05  FILLER                       PIC X(1)   VALUE SPACES.
    05  WS3-PART-DESC                PIC X(20)  VALUE SPACES.
    05  FILLER                       PIC X(5)   VALUE SPACES.
    05  WS3-PART-PRICE               PIC $$$$,$99.
    05 FILLER                        PIC X(20)  VALUE SPACES.
```

```
* ——DL/1 WORK AREAS BEGIN HERE ——————————

 01  WS4-UNQUAL-VENDOR-SSA.
     05  FILLER              PIC X(9)      VALUE 'VENDOR   '.

 01  WS5-QUAL-PART-SSA.
     05  FILLER              PIC X(9)      VALUE 'PART    ('.
     05  FILLER              PIC X(8)      VALUE 'PARTYPE '.
     05  FILLER              PIC X(2)      VALUE ' ='.
     05  FILLER              PIC X         VALUE 'B'.
     05  FILLER              PIC X         VALUE '&'.
     05  FILLER              PIC X(10)     VALUE 'PARTPRIC >'.
     05  FILLER              PIC S9(6)     VALUE 000100.
     05  FILLER              PIC X         VALUE ')'.

* #### VENDOR SEGMENT FOLLOWS
        COPY VENDSEG.

* #### PART SEGMENT FOLLOWS
        COPY PARTSEG.

        COPY IMSFUNC.

 LINKAGE SECTION.

        COPY VENDPCB.

 PROCEDURE DIVISION USING DL1-DB-PCB.

 000-CREATE-REPORT.
     PERFORM 1000-INITIALIZE
     PERFORM 2000-PRINT-RECORDS
             UNTIL DL1-DB-STAT-CODE = 'GB'
     PERFORM 3000-WRAP-UP
     MOVE 0 TO RETURN-CODE
     GOBACK.

 1000-INITIALIZE.
     OPEN OUTPUT FD1-PRINT-FILE
     MOVE SPACES TO DL1-DB-STAT-CODE
     MOVE ZEROS TO WS1-PAGENUM.

 2000-PRINT-RECORDS.
     PERFORM 2100-GET-VENDOR
     IF DL1-DB-STAT-CODE NOT EQUAL 'GB'
         MOVE 3 TO WS1-SPACE
```

```
            MOVE VEND-NAME TO WS3-VENDOR
            PERFORM 2200-PRINT-PARTS
                    UNTIL DL1-DB-STAT-CODE = 'GE'.

 2100-GET-VENDOR.
    CALL 'CBLTDLI' USING
         GN
         DL1-DB-PCB
         VEND-SEG
         WS4-UNQUAL-VENDOR-SSA.

 2200-PRINT-PARTS.
     PERFORM 2210-GET-PARTS
     IF DL1-DB-STAT-CODE = ' '
         MOVE PART-DESC TO WS3-PART-DESC
         MOVE PART-PRICE TO WS3-PART-PRICE
         PERFORM 2220-PRINT-HEADING
         PERFORM 2230-WRITE-DETAIL.

 2210-GET-PARTS.
     CALL 'CBLTDLI' USING
          GNP
          DL1-DB-PCB
          PART-SEG
          WS5-QUAL-PART-SSA.

 2220-PRINT-HEADING.
     IF WS1-LINES > 50
         ADD 1 TO WS1-PAGENUM
         MOVE WS1-PAGENUM TO WS2-PAGENUM
         MOVE 1 TO WS1-LINES
         MOVE 2 TO WS1-SPACE
         WRITE FD1-PRINT-REC FROM WS2-HEADING-LINE1-REC
                   AFTER ADVANCING PAGE.

 2230-WRITE-DETAIL.
     WRITE FD1-PRINT-REC FROM WS3-DETAIL-REC
                   AFTER ADVANCING WS1-SPACE LINES
     ADD WS1-SPACE TO WS1-LINES
     MOVE 1 TO WS1-SPACE.

 3000-WRAP-UP.
     CLOSE FD1-PRINT-FILE.

 * THIS IS THE END OF SOURCE
```

8.7. SAMPLE STUB PROGRAM

One of the strengths of structured, top-down development is the use of stub programs. A stub program is one that does nothing, but must be CALLed from a program higher in the structure during early development stages. This allows subordinate programs to be executed, even though nothing is being done. Here is a simple stub program that works well. This example takes maximum advantage of the optional entries in COBOL II and the presence of the implicit EXIT PROGRAM code that is generated. CALLs to this subprogram will execute successfully and set a RETURN-CODE of zero. The END PROGRAM statement is optional.

```
ID DIVISION.
PROGRAM-ID.  programname.
END PROGRAM programname.
```

SUMMARY

Other than the second example, none of these programs made extensive use of COBOL II. In fact, many of the examples demonstrated coexistence techniques instead. If possible, I encourage a migration from DOS/VS COBOL to COBOL II with deliberate speed. Continuing to code at the ANSI 74 level when you have access to ANSI 85 features is frustrating. These sample programs are not recommendations. Instead, they are examples of what you can code in a COBOL subset.

Large shops with a variety of CICS, DL/1, and other environments may need to adopt a subset of COBOL, especially if many of the programs are reusable. Once you have your programs migrated to COBOL II, start using the new features. The use will refuel your momentum. Otherwise, you will find yourself continuing to code using older techniques. Until you feel comfortable with COBOL II's features, the pressure of the moment will constrain your growth. Don't let it happen.

Related Publications

One of the goals of all professional programmers is to have an adequate reference library, not full of concept books or other books for novices, but full of books that contribute to building applications. It was with this in mind that I developed this list.

9.1. FROM QED

These books from QED were referenced within this book because they share in the goal of helping the professional programmer develop better mainframe systems. Each book complements the material in this book by providing in-depth information about the various IBM platforms in which COBOL applications run. These books should not be referenced for COBOL-specific information or for examples of COBOL techniques. Their value is in their specialization in the topics specified.

These books may be ordered directly from QED. The first price shown is the U.S. price; the second is in Canadian dollars. Prices are subject to change. Phone 800-343-4848, in MA 617-237-5656, or fax 617-235-0826.

VSAM: The Complete Guide to Optimization & Design,
  Order No. 3144, $39.95 / $47.95.
How to Use CICS to Create On-Line Applications: Methods and
  Solutions, Order No. 1826, $39.95 / $47.95.
IMS Design and Implementation Techniques, Second Edition,
  Order No. 2822, $39.95 / $47.95.
SQL for DB2 and SQL /DS Application Developers, Order No. 3039,
  $34.95 / $41.95.

9.2. FROM IBM

Your shop may already have a library of IBM manuals, but all too often they are out-of-date. This listing may help you confirm whether appropriate IBM reference material is available to you. Most of these books contain information you may need only occasionally, if at all. These books were selected by me because they either provide more in-depth information about COBOL II or they provide information on the VSE operating environment. You should check with your technical staff to confirm what IBM publications are appropriate for your environment; this list may be incomplete or list the incorrect IBM manual for your shop.

Whenever you use IBM manuals, you should check that the release level of the book corresponds with the level of software you are using. For example, if your shop is using a release level higher than version 3.2 of COBOL II, and your COBOL II manuals reflect support for Release 3.2, there will be features in the manual that won't function. Likewise, if your library's manuals specify VSE/AF and you are using VSE/ESA, there will be features available that you will be unaware of. When in doubt, check with your technical staff.

9.2.1   For Programming with COBOL II

GC26-4047, *VS COBOL II Language Reference*. This is a complete definition of the COBOL II language, including all syntax.

SC26-4697, *VS COBOL II Application Programming Guide*. This provides a variety of tips and instructions for coding, compiling, and executing applications.

SC26-4049, *VS COBOL II Debugging*. This is a complete guide to debugging, including instructions on the debug language and mechanics of using COBTEST in batch and on-line. A complete presentation on dump reading mechanics is also included.

SX26-3721, *VS COBOL II Reference Summary*. This is a small book (not a reference card) that contains all COBOL II statements. It contains no material not found in other texts here.

SC26-4301, *Report Writer Programmer Guide*. This book provides syntax and other instructions for using the Report Writer Preprocessor with COBOL II. (This is a separate software product that may not be installed at your company.)

SC28-6478, *DOS/VS COBOL Compiler and Library Programmer's Guide*. This book is needed if your run unit includes DOS/VS COBOL modules; you will need this book to diagnose any run-time error messages that have the prefix IKF.

9.2.2. FOR SAA

SC26-4354, *SAA Common Programming Interface, COBOL Reference.* This defines SAA considerations for COBOL II. If your shop is committed to SAA across several platforms, this will help you.
GC26-4341, *SAA Overview.*
GC26-4675, *SAA Common Programming Interface, Summary.*

9.2.3. For CICS

SC33-0713, *CICS/VSE Application Programmer's Reference.*
SC33-0712, *CICS/VSE Application Programming Guide.*

9.2.4. For DL/1

SH24-5009, *DL/1 DOS/VS Application Programming: High Level Programming Interfaces.*
SH24-5029, *DL/1 DOS/VS Interactive Resource Definition and Utilities.*

9.2.5. For SQL/DS

SH09-8025, *SQL/DS Application Programming for VSE.*

9.2.6. For VSE System Services

SC33-6513, *VSE/ESA System Control Statements.*
SC33-6511, *VSE/ESA Guide to System Functions.*
SC33-6514, *VSE/ESA Diagnostic Tools.*
SC33-6507, *VSE/ESA Messages and Codes.*
SC33-6517, *VSE/ESA System Utilities.*
SC33-4044, *DOS/VS SORT/MERGE II Application Programming Guide.*
SC33-6535, *VSE/VSAM Programmer's Reference.*
SC33-6532, *VSE/VSAM Commands and Macros.* This is the manual that explains VSAM status codes.

Index

RESPONSE FORM

COBOL II VSE Power Programmmer's Desk Reference

I want to hear from you. You may have questions, you may find errors, or you may have comments that will help me develop the next edition of the book. The purpose of this book is to help you, the professional programmer. Thank you.

David Shelby Kirk

_____

Dear Dave,

_____

_____

_____

_____

_____

_____

_____

_____

_____

_____

If a reply is desired, please fill in your address.

_____

_____

_____

Please mail to David S. Kirk, c/o QED Information Sciences, Inc. POB 82-181, Wellesley, MA 02181.